REASON OVER PRECEDENTS

Recent Titles in
Contributions in Legal Studies

A History of the Anglo-American Common Law of Contract
Kevin M. Teeven

"We Have a Duty":
The Supreme Court and the Watergate Tapes Litigation
Howard Ball

The Shaping of Nineteenth-Century Law:
John Appleton and Responsible Individualism
David M. Gold

Comparative Constitutional Federalism:
Europe and America
Mark Tushnet, editor

Church–State Constitutional Issues:
Making Sense of the Establishment Clause
Donald L. Drakeman

The Politics of Obscenity:
Group Litigation in a Time of Legal Change
Joseph F. Kobylka

An Essential Safeguard:
Essays on the United States Supreme Court and Its Justices
D. Grier Stephenson, Jr., editor

A "Representative" Supreme Court?
The Impact of Race, Religion, and Gender on Appointment
Barbara A. Perry

State Constitutions and Criminal Justice
Barry Latzer

The Sixth Amendment in Modern American Jurisprudence:
A Critical Perspective
Alfredo Garcia

Positive Neutrality:
Letting Religious Freedom Ring
Stephen V. Monsma

Questioning the Law in Corporate America:
Agenda for Reform
Gerald L. Houseman

REASON OVER PRECEDENTS

Origins of American Legal Thought

Craig Evan Klafter

Contributions in Legal Studies, Number 73
Paul L. Murphy, Series Editor

Greenwood Press
Westport, Connecticut • London

Library of Congress Cataloging-in-Publication Data

Klafter, Craig Evan.
Reason over precedents: origins of American legal thought / Craig Evan Klafter.
p. cm. — (Contributions in legal studies, ISSN 0147–1074; no. 73)
Includes bibliographical references and index.
ISBN 0–313–28675–2 (alk. paper)
1. Stare decisis—United States. 2. Judicial process—United States. I. Title. II. Series.
KF429.K56 1993
347.73′001—dc20
[347.30701] 92–45071

British Library Cataloguing in Publication Data is available.

Library of Congress Catalog Card Number: 92–45071
ISBN: 0–313–28675–2
ISSN: 0147–1074

First published in 1993

Greenwood Press, 88 Post Road West, Westport, CT 06881
An imprint of Greenwood Publishing Group, Inc.

Printed in the United States of America

The paper used in this book complies with the Permanent Paper Standard issued by the National Information Standards Organization (Z39.48–1984).

10 9 8 7 6 5 4 3 2 1

To the memory of Edmund Chatten Ballantyne

Contents

Preface

The study of intellectual history has often been problematic. This is largely due to the difficulties in determining what ideas have had the greatest influences on a given society or individual and in proving that a society or individual has been influenced by those ideas. As a focus of intellectual history, law resolves these problems. Law represents some of the highest ideals in a society and governs how that society functions. Lawyers, rather conveniently, cite the sources of their ideas. Thus, through the law, perhaps more than any other subject of intellectual history, it is relatively easy to trace the ideological influences on a society. Nevertheless, the study of law as a source of intellectual history has been too often ignored.

Over the years that I have been working on this book, I owe debts to many people and institutions. While I cannot mention them all here, I would like to note the special assistance of a few. The late Anthony Paul Grech, Curator, of the Library of the Bar Association of the City of New York often helped me locate rare materials not available in any other location. Mark H. Jones, State Archivist, devoted many days guiding me through the collections of the Connecticut State Library. Maeva Marcus of the United States Supreme Court secured access for me to materials in the Supreme Court Library. Oceana Publications, Inc. allowed me to review the law library of Transylvania University which it had recently purchased. The staffs of the Bodleian Law Library and the Rhodes House Library have always delighted me with their professionalism and courtesy. This study, which originated at Oxford University, was supervised by Professor J. R. Pole who was the perfect advisor, knowing when to provide assistance and when to leave me to my own devices. I have most appreciated the fact that he treated me as a colleague from the moment I met him. Dr. Duncan MacLeod was a helpful sounding-board and source of encouragement. Professor Peter Stein, Professor Harold Hyman and Mark J. Mahoney read the entire manuscript and offered valuable suggestions. At an early stage of my research, Professor Stanley Katz provided me with an hour of advice, which saved me time and provided me with direction throughout my research.

I am grateful for the financial support that I have received. The British Government provided me with an Overseas Research Student Award, which in conjunction with a University of Oxford Bursary paid my tuition. I have also been fortunate to receive grants from the Bryce and Read Fund and from the St. Catherine's College Academic Expenditure Fund, which have helped me defray the costs of my research.

In spite of all the assistance provided by all these people and institutions, this book would never have been completed if it were not for the support of my wife and families on both sides of the Atlantic.

Introduction

The fundamental question addressed herein is what were the origins of American legal thought. While the origins of an American legal science can be traced back into America's colonial past, it was not until the post-Revolutionary and early National periods that these threads came together to form a unique system of American legal thought. No doubt the study of what Roscoe Pound called "the formative era of American law" and James Willard Hurst called "the profession's golden age of public leadership" is not a novel subject. In the past twenty years, a host of legal historians have put forward arguments about the origins of the American legal system and its influence in shaping American society. Their research, however, has almost exclusively focused upon court opinions. It is my contention that this body of work has overemphasized the role of judges at the expense of the true functionaries in the development of the American legal system—lawyers.

Alexis de Tocqueville, in *Democracy in America,* confirms the importance of looking more to lawyers than to judges in order to understand the true legal spirit of America. He wrote:

> It must not, however, be supposed that the legal spirit of which I am speaking has been confined, in the United States, to the courts of justice; it extends far beyond them. As the lawyers constitute the only enlightened class which the people does not mistrust, they are naturally called upon to occupy most of the public stations. They fill the legislative assemblies, and they conduct the administration; they consequently exercise a powerful influence upon the formation of the law, and upon its execution.[1]

From their position in American society, lawyers, more than any other group, were best suited to put into practice a uniquely American system of legal thought.

The natural starting point for determining the role of American lawyers in the development of an American legal science is the legal education that they received. Indeed, while numerous historians have written about legal developments between 1779 and 1830, none has adequately explained the vital role legal education played in developing an American legal science. It is the contention herein that the true origins of American legal thought can be found in America's post-Revolutionary and early National period law schools, for these were the first American institutions to develop and teach an entire system of legal thought. This system, based on ideas imported from European natural law writings, was disseminated throughout the legal community through the publication of analytical law treatises and instilled into legal practice by the redaction of a modified doctrine of *stare decisis*. Finally, this new method of legal thought had a significant impact on the Americanization of the English common and statutory law, fostered a continuing conflict between judicial activists and judicial conservatives, encouraged the litigiousness of the American people and contributed to the dominant role law has played in American politics and society.

American legal education underwent significant changes between 1779 and 1830 as compared to the colonial period. It instilled in the United States's first generation of lawyers a dynamic conception of law, constantly improving as it was encouraged to adapt to the needs of a changing society.

One result of American legal education during this period which was more significant than has been recognized was the publication by St. George Tucker, one of America's foremost legal educators, of an Americanized edition of Blackstone's *Commentaries,*[2] which limited Blackstone's influence on the American legal community and helped introduce into American legal thought the propriety of questioning laws against the standards of human reason. Tucker's greatest influence was to bring the law down from the high altar on which it had been placed by Blackstone. He used Montesquieu's relativism to establish the appropriateness of questioning the law and to show that reason should be the law's ultimate test. He described constitutions as the people's primary means of redacting reason into a defense against unreasonable laws and the unreasonable application of laws. Thus Tucker introduced a method of viewing the law which, presented in a work that became the standard text for a generation of lawyers, separated American legal thought from Blackstone and the English legal system.

St. George Tucker was not alone in his work. There were numerous legal educators who also assumed the role of analytical treatise author who emphasized the use of a scientific legal method, developed from ideas that originated in the works of European natural law writers and transported to America initially through Blackstone's *Commentaries*, to explain the law. This generation of legal educators carried these ideas further, to develop a unique American legal methodology that incorporated the use of reason to question the soundness of common law precedents. By recognizing man's reason as being superior to the common law, these men instilled into American legal thought a system whereby legal precedents could be judged prior to their acceptance as controlling law and judicially replaced if they were determined to be unsound.

During America's post-Revolutionary and early National periods, these educators—aided by thousands of their students who quickly assumed most prominent positions in the Bar successfully—encouraged jurists to redact into American legal practice a modified doctrine of *stare decisis* which provided that precedents established by American courts should be strictly adhered to while permitting English precedents to be questioned against the standards of utility, logic, morality and such conflicting American law and policy as already existed either because they had not yet been adopted or sanctioned by American courts or because they were determined to be in conflict with each other. As attorneys and judges became more familiar with the use of this method, they even developed a willingness to question domestic precedents against the powerful comparative standards of morality and constitutional law. While this willingness to judge domestic precedents removed some predictability from the American legal system, it instilled a dynamic whereby laws could be more rapidly adapted to new and changing circumstances.

The influence of American legal education continued as the methodology taught was employed to Americanize English statutory and common law. Post-Revolutionary and early National period legal educators and their former students persuaded judges to mould principles of law, particularly in the areas of property law, commercial law and family law, to the economic needs and republican values of the new nation. Civil law gained entrance into American jurisprudence as jurists sought models for replacing laws they had judged unsound or inapplicable. Judicial activists extended this power to statutes, executive orders and civil practices through the advent of judicial review. Finally, those former students who were committed to extensive reformation of the law changed their forum to state legislatures, where through the passage of statutes, the law continued to be actively modified. This legislative activity came to head in the form of the American codification movement. Although this movement was unsuccessful in accomplishing its goal of replacing the entire common law with a comprehensive code, complete areas of the law, most notably concerning property and crime, were replaced with subject-specific codes.

The implications of these activities were far-reaching. The tension that developed between those who advocated the expansive use of courts to modify the law and an aggressive use of judicial review and those who sought to limit this power was the origin of the modern conflict of judicial activism versus judicial conservatism. Armed with the ability to question the law, American lawyers encouraged the litigiousness of the American people and were instrumental in creating a legal system that would settle political, as well as legal, disputes.

Examination of this progression and development of ideas reveals that the influence of American post-Revolutionary and early National period legal education on America was much greater than has previously been supposed, not only in the field of the law proper, but in the extent of its influence on American society and politics.

NOTES

1. Alexis de Tocqueville, *Democracy in America,* trans. by Henry Reeve, 2 vols. (London: Longman, Green, Longman and Roberts, 1862), pp. 329–330.

2. St. George Tucker, *Blackstone's Commentaries: with Notes Of Reference, to the Constitution and Laws, of the Federal Government of the United States; and of the Commonwealth of Virginia*, 5 vols. (Philadelphia: William Young Birch and Abraham Small, 1803).

1

American Institutional Legal Education and the Instillment of a Dynamic Conception of Law, 1779–1829

The years between 1779 and 1860 have been regarded as the most important in American legal history. Roscoe Pound referred to them as "The Formative Era of American Law."[1] Daniel J. Boorstin explained the events of this period as "one of the unheralded creative outbursts of modern legal history."[2] William E. Nelson described how, during this period, the common law was Americanized by judges and legislators reacting to strong economic, social and political changes that resulted from the birth of the American nation.[3] Morton J. Horwitz argued that judges developed a perception of law that allowed them to play a role, along with legislators, in governing society, promoting socially desirable conduct and bringing about social change.[4] Yet in all these works, the role of legal education in encouraging these developments has been almost wholly overlooked.

Even scholars of legal education have paid little attention to changes that occurred during this period. Alfred Z. Reed and Albert J. Harno devoted only a few pages to such changes in their early studies.[5] While Gerald W. Gawalt discusses the role of legal education in fostering the growth of the Massachusetts bar from a weak corporate guild into a powerful profession, he does not concern himself with the substance of that education.[6] Robert Stevens, in his work on the history of American legal education, saw little prior to 1850 to write about.[7] And, Alfred S. Konesfsky and Andrew J. King concluded, in the process of editing the papers of Daniel Webster, that despite the establishment of a couple of private law schools, legal education in the post-Revolutionary and early National periods remained unchanged as compared to legal education during the colonial period.[8] The consensus of historians appears to be that nothing of great significance happened to American legal education from the American Revolution until, at the earliest, 1829 when Joseph Story was appointed Professor of Law at Harvard University.

Indeed, Konesfsky and King go even further, contending that not only did legal education not have any positive impact on the law during this period, but it served to impede legal progress. They wrote:

> the process of reading law induced a rigid, unquestioning attitude toward legal studies. The process of legal education seemed determined to treat law as an autonomous order. Emphasis on law as a self-contained body of principles impeded the legal system's capacity to respond to changes occurring in society in general. This limitation on the growth and expansion of the law also resulted from the lack of a self-conscious attitude among lawyers about the concept and process of change in the legal system. Despite all the complaints about the boredom, prolongation, and limited value of legal education, lawyers talked about or instituted relatively little reform. . . . Whatever innovations took place were accomplished without the benefit of the "teaching" bar.[9]

In this chapter, it is shown that, in fact, American legal education between 1779 and 1829 underwent significant changes as compared to the colonial period, changes that played an important role in allowing American law to adapt dynamically to the needs of a new nation.

The American Revolution had a significant impact on the education of the first generation of American lawyers. The Revolution caused the exodus of a large number of lawyers, particularly the most able of the profession, who remained loyal to the Crown. In addition, a sizable number of attorneys entered public service as these positions were created by the new government. This depletion of practitioners was soon followed by an increase in legal activity, initially in the areas of debt collection and recovery of property and, as the economy improved, in more general areas of practice. With a limited number of attorneys to handle a steadily increasing work load, the profession became wealthy and developed a need for additional members.

The most important impact of the American Revolution on the legal profession came through the imposition of loyalty oaths, which were designed to preclude Tory attorneys from practicing law in America. For example, on 9 October 1779, the New York legislature suspended from practice all attorneys, solicitors and counsellors at law who had been licensed prior to April 1777. This suspension could only be revoked by a jury of inquiry establishing upon oath that the applicant had supported the American cause.[10] So many New York lawyers were unable to pass the loyalty test that the bar of the state Supreme Court almost ceased to exist, with only nine attorneys still admitted to practice before it.[11]

This created such a great problem for the Court that within a year a rule of court was issued to make it easier for practitioners before the inferior Court of Common Pleas to gain admittance to practice before the Supreme Court.[12] Although New York offers the clearest example of the attempt to preclude loyalist lawyers from practicing law, it was by no means unique. Similar laws were passed in New Jersey, Pennsylvania, Maryland, New Hampshire and Massachusetts. The remaining states instituted laws that , although they did not expressly prohibit loyalists from the practice of law, made their lives difficult. In addition, all the states passed laws preventing loyalists from holding public office.[13]

The impact of these laws did not affect the majority of colonial lawyers, who were Whigs. Rather, the giants of the legal profession, who were generally Tory, were the most significantly affected.[14] For example, New York lost the services of Peter Van Schaack, who had revised the statutes of colonial New York; Maryland's Daniel Dulany, a graduate of Eton College and Clare Hall, Cambridge and a Middle Templar who was considered by Charles Carroll to be "indisputably the best lawyer on this continent,"[15] was forced to give up his practice; and John Randolph of Virginia, Attorney-General and Judge of the Vice-Admiralty Court from 1766 to 1775, was compelled to seek refuge in England.[16]

Many colonial Whig attorneys gave up their practices in order to hold political office in the new nation. There was a great need to replace loyalist colonial judges with Whig jurists. In addition, Lawrence Friedman has noted that lawyers dominated the legislatures and executive branches of the states and the Congress.[17] Although many continued to practice, the demands of public office forced these lawyers to limit the time they could devote to their private legal work. However, due to the exposure of politics, their legal skills were in great demand, so many lawyer-politicians sought partners or younger attorneys to work with them.[18]

The Revolution was soon followed by a period during which the amount of available legal work increased significantly. The country had been left with great public and private debt, compounded by the Treaty of Paris which permitted the collection of pre-war British debts.[19] As a result, there was a great need for lawyers to assist with debt collection and recovery of property held pursuant to confiscatory laws. The abundance of this legal work proved most profitable to the post-Revolutionary legal profession. Jackson Turner Main noted that "the educated lawyer probably made more money than anyone else in the thirteen states except for the luckiest of merchants or those great landowners who avoided debts."[20]

Thus, the initial impact of the American Revolution on the bar was a depletion of the number of practicing attorneys. At the same time, the amount of available legal work and fees increased. As a result, a vacuum was created within the ranks of the profession, which attracted many to the study of law. The principal problem was that the colonial systems of legal education were viewed by many as inadequate to fulfil the increased need for qualified lawyers.

The earliest means of entering the legal profession available to colonial Americans involved returning to the mother country, where one could seek to become a barrister by attending one of the Inns of Court.[21] The Inns had an illustrious history, well known to the leaders of the post-Revolutionary bar, of offering a systematic course of legal training including lectures, tutorials, moots and access to prestigious libraries. During the American colonial period, however, the Inns had deteriorated into clubhouses for the profession, which no longer offered formalized legal education.[22] In 1772, Henry Tucker advised his son, St. George Tucker, to study under George Wythe in Virginia instead of attending the Inns, "for if I am rightly informed no care is taken of you in the Inns of Court of London, every student to do as he pleases."[23] The Inns still conferred the qualification of barrister, however, and the few wealthy colonists who could afford attendance were able to acquire social prestige, business contacts and such basic knowledge of the law as could be learned from being around lawyers and the law courts.[24] Nevertheless, the anti-English sentiment after the Revolution discouraged this option, and the number of Americans attending the Inns decreased significantly.[25]

The first form of American legal education was self-education. It had been the dominant form of training in the early eighteenth century, but the scant availability of law books in America contributed to poor educational standards.[26] Even those students who were fortunate enough to borrow a few books or to have access to a law library found that the requirements for admission to practice were lax. Patrick Henry was typical. He devoted only six weeks to the study of Coke and the Virginia Statutes before he sought permission to practice. The majority of his examiners concluded that he knew little of the law, but they nevertheless approved him because they thought he would learn quickly.[27] The obvious problems with this method of education led to a period after the Revolution when all of the states except Virginia passed laws requiring at least some specified period of clerkship before admittance to practice, thus precluding self-education as a sole means of legal training.[28]

Clerkships were the most prominent form of legal education during the colonial period. A pupil would learn the law from an established practitioner for a fee of one hundred to two hundred pounds by serving as his assistant for several years. The clerk devoted much of his time to copying forms and pleadings. He also had the opportunity to accompany his master to court and thus could witness legal proceedings, strategy and style. As the clerk gained experience, he was given responsibility for legal research and trial preparation. Although some lawyers acquired several clerks, most would work only with one at a time. At its best, the clerkship system offered the prospective lawyer personal guidance in his study of law, first-hand experience with legal practice and invaluable access to a law library.[29]

Unfortunately, clerkships seldom worked this well, because the clerkship system was plagued with numerous problems. Thomas Jefferson complained about masters who busied their pupils with repetitious and menial work which kept them from their studies.[30] William Livingston added that masters would seldom supervise their clerks in the reading of law.[31] Peter Van Schaack argued that much of the clerk's time was wasted hunting through texts when a few minutes of a lawyer's time would have been sufficient.[32] Josiah Quincy, President of Harvard College, succinctly stated the problems with the clerkship system:

"Regular instruction there was none; examination as to progress in acquaintance with the law, —none; occasional lectures, —none; oversight as to general attention and conduct, —none. The student was left to find his way by the light of his own mind. . . ."[33] Although some attorneys received excellent educations through this system, they were the exceptions. A substantial majority of lawyers who trained as clerks were inadequately prepared to practice law.

Of the nine American colleges that had been established during the colonial period, only three had offered courses concerned with law. These courses were typical of a scholarly approach to law and were not intended to provide practical preparation for legal practice. Harvard College taught law as part of a course on "Ethicks [*sic*] and Politics"; Kings College titled its course "The Chief Principles of Law and Government"; and the College of Philadelphia taught civil law as part of the study of politics.[34]

There were numerous reasons why colonial colleges had not taken up vocational legal instruction. Most had agreed with the English tradition of separating scholarly from professional legal training.[35] Others had lacked the financial resources necessary to expand into professional education.[36] In Massachusetts, college legal education had been prevented from developing due to opposition from the Bar, which, motivated by monopolistic reasons, sought to restrict the number of lawyers admitted to practice.[37] There was also the question of economic demand, for there had been little need for lawyers and thus little need for formal legal education during much of the colonial period.[38] Lastly, even if colonial colleges had offered vocational legal instruction, it is doubtful whether they could have competed successfully with widely available legal apprenticeships or the prestige and opportunities provided by attendance at the Inns of Court.

After the American Revolution, new forms of vocational legal instruction were needed that were capable of meeting the suddenly increased demand for lawyers. In some colleges, professors of law were appointed, but most of them sought to provide undergraduate students with a general knowledge of law rather than to offer vocational legal instruction. A few law professors did seek to offer a comprehensive system of professional legal education, but prior to 1828, only the College of William and Mary and Transylvania College had succeeded in graduating significant numbers of students directly into the practice of law. The first experiments in American legal education after the Revolution followed the model of the establishment of the Vinerian Professorship of Law at Oxford. Law professorships of this kind were established at the College of William and Mary (1779), the College of Philadelphia (1790), Brown College (1790), Columbia College (1794), Transylvania College (1798), Yale College (1801), Middlebury College (1806), Harvard University (1815) and the University of Maryland (1814).[39] Yet with the exceptions of the College of William and Mary and Transylvania College, none had any immediate success in offering a program of legal education designed to prepare law students for the practice of law.

The dilemma faced by most early professors was that although they were hired to educate undergraduates principally in the theory of law and politics, they could only attract students if they offered vocational legal instruction. James Wilson of the College of Philadelphia, James Kent of Columbia, David Howell of Brown, Daniel Chapman of Middlebury, Elizur Goodrich of Yale and Isaac Parker of Harvard were all prey to this difficulty. For example, James Wilson, who focused his lectures on developing a complete philosophy of American law, discontinued them within two years of their start because of lack of interest.[40] Attendance at James Kent's course of lectures, which concentrated on the theory, history and duties of civil government, declined from forty-three lawyers and law students, most of whom were not affiliated with the College, during his first year to two students during his second year.[41] He wrote to his brother, "The small encouragement with which my lectures have been received by the public this year has cooled and dulled my ardor for finishing and perfecting them."[42] Kent submitted his resignation the following year.[43] These early professorships failed because law students wanted practical, not academic, legal education.[44]

Historians, however, should not be too quick to fault these professors for the nature of their instruction, for few educational institutions were willing to support practical legal instruction, which was perceived as being incompatible with their classical liberal arts curricula. An early attempt at legal education within the University of Maryland is revealing. In 1814, David Hoffman was appointed Professor of Law at the university.[45] In 1817, he published a work that advertised his intention to offer a course of legal education designed to prepare students for direct entry into the practice of law.[46] The *North American Review* commented on it saying, "we have not the slightest hesitation to declare that it contains by far the most perfect system for the study of the law that has ever been offered to the public."[47] Nevertheless, during Hoffman's tenure at Maryland, he was plagued by a lack of institutional support for his instruction. In a series of letters between Hoffman and the Trustees of the University of Maryland, Hoffman complained about the university's failure to provide him with "a *suitable building, furniture* and *library*" necessary for the instruction of law. The Trustees denied any problem and asserted that the law department was adequately supported. As was typical of most educational institutions during this period, the Trustees of the University of Maryland were unwilling to devote resources to support vocational legal instruction. This inadequate support delayed the opening of the law school until 1822 by which time Hoffman had contributed over $20,000 of his own money to the law department.[48] Ultimately, it was not until 1831 that Maryland first awarded a law degree.[49]

The only colleges that successfully offered practical legal education prior to 1828 were those which strongly supported a comprehensive program of vocational legal education. The first to succeed was the College of William and Mary, which, with the strong encouragement of both Thomas Jefferson (Governor of Virginia and a member of the Board of Visitors of the College at that time) and the Reverend James Madison (President of the College), appointed George Wythe (a justice of Virginia's High Court of Chancery) to fill the position of Professor of Law and Police.[50]

The focus of Wythe's instruction, encouraged by the College, was vocational law and politics. Wythe and Jefferson considered these aspects of training to be inseparable and expected William and Mary law students to eventually become statesmen.[51] In order to prepare his graduates for a career in law and politics, Wythe instituted a moot court and a mock legislature. The moot court was designed to offer an understanding of legal procedure and court practice. The mock legislature was intended to offer an understanding of the creation and interpretation of statutes and to prepare students for the role of politician. The remainder of the course was devoted to a series of lectures in which Wythe discussed substantive law by adapting William Blackstone's *Commentaries on the Laws of England*[52] and Matthew Bacon's *A New Abridgement of the Law*,[53] the key textbooks for the course, to the American legal experience. The success of this program in offering practical legal instruction is confirmed by the fact that Wythe's graduates were usually immediately admitted to practice without a subsequent clerkship.[54]

Transylvania College in Lexington, Kentucky, was also successful in offering vocational legal instruction during this early period. As had occurred at the College of William and Mary, the Board of Trustees of Transylvania, composed of a number of William and Mary law graduates, gave strong support to the establishment of a practically oriented law department, including allocating funds for the purchase of faculty offices, a lecture hall and an extensive law library.[55] Between 1799 and 1816, Transylvania had five successive professors of law and politics: George Nicholas (1798), James Brown (1799), Henry Clay (1806), John Monroe (1807) and John Pope (1814)—Nicholas, Brown and Clay had previously been students of Wythe at the College of William and Mary and all emphasized vocational legal instruction.[56] Transylvania's most important contribution was to offer legal instruction on the postgraduate level, making it unnecessary for it to provide a liberal arts education and giving the law faculty the opportunity to focus on practical legal instruction.[57]

The College of William and Mary and Transylvania College, as the first two colleges to offer vocational legal instruction, had an important impact on early American legal education. The most significant contributions of the two institutions were: a belief in understanding the role of classical history and law as the foundation for modern law; an emphasis on the use of European natural law writings to understand legal issues; the creation of expositions of constitutional interpretation; and a perception of the law as malleable through the use of reason in the face of a society's changing values and needs.

George Wythe was the first American law professor to use history and political philosophy to determine those ideas which were the basis for the common law. His method had been developed while serving with Edmund Pendleton and Thomas Jefferson on a legislative committee designed to make the laws of Virginia consistent with the new State Constitution. Wythe had been required to evaluate and propose alterations to the common law derived from the time of the Glorious Revolution up to American independence. It appears from the available sources that his technique had been to take a principle of law, trace its original intent back to antiquity, consider its political implications and then judge its suitability to be included in American law.[58]

Wythe based his substantive legal instruction primarily on Blackstone's *Commentaries* and Matthew Bacon's *A New Abridgement of the Law*. Much of the law presented in these works was inapplicable to the new American nation, and Wythe devoted considerable time in his law lectures to explaining where and why the authors' exposition of the common law had been revised in America. Governor John Tyler of Virginia wrote in reference to Wythe's lectures:

> Judge [Spencer] Roane [of the Virginia Supreme Court of Appeals] has read them, or most of them, and is highly pleased with them, thinks they will be very valuable, there being so much of his own sound reasoning upon great principles, and not a mere servile copy of Blackstone, and other British commentators,—a good many of his own thoughts on our constitutions and the necessary changes they have begotten, with that spirit of freedom which always marked his opinions.[59]

The process of inquiry Wythe employed, however, conflicted with one of Blackstone's principal goals in writing his *Commentaries*.[60]

William Blackstone in his *Commentaries* had taken great pains to place the common law upon a pedestal so as to protect it from what he perceived to be the destructiveness of reason. In his analysis of the Revolution of 1688, he cautioned:

> care must be taken not to carry this enquiry farther, than merely for instruction or amusement . . . I therefore rather chuse [*sic*] to consider this great political measure, upon the solid footing of authority, than to reason in it's [*sic*] favour from its justice, moderation, and experience: because that might imply a right of dissenting or revolting from it, in case we should think it unjust, oppressive, or inexpedient. Whereas, our ancestors having most indisputably a competent jurisdiction to decide this great and important question, and having in fact decided it, it has now become our duty at this distance of time to acquiesce in their determination; being born under that establishment which was built upon this foundation, and obliged by every tie, religious as well as civil, to maintain it.[61]

In his discussion of devises, gifts of real property by the last will and testament of the donor, Blackstone warned "experience soon shewed [*sic*] how difficult and hazardous a thing it is, even in matters of public utility, to depart from the rules of the common law; which are so nicely constructed and so artificially connected together, that the least breach in any one of them disorders for a time the texture of the whole."[62] Daniel Boorstin summarized Blackstone's fear of destroying the common law, noting, "Naturally, Blackstone, who saw the law as the bulwark of existing society, could not be satisfied with a theory which pointed the way to dangerous inquiry. The Science of Law was not enough. There must also be a

Mystery of Law, a decent veil to protect ultimate values from the devouring gaze of Reason."[63]

Wythe, on the other hand, instructed his students about the laws of a new society with different values than the mother country. His technique of legal inquiry was designed to impart to his students an understanding of how the common law developed and how and why it had been revised in the United States. Wythe had no fear of the dangers that Blackstone perceived in applying reason to the law.

Indeed, George Wythe went so far as to instruct his students, through the use of a mock legislature, in how to revise the common law through statutes. One of his students described the mock legislature as follows:

> He has form'd us into a Legislative Body, consisting of about 40 members. Mr. Wythe is speaker to the House, & takes all possible pains to instruct us in the Rules of Parliament. We meet every Saturday & take under our consideration those Bills drawn up by the Committee appointed to revise the laws, then we debate & alter (I will not say amend) with the greatest freedom. . . . [64]

Through his adaptation of Blackstone's *Commentaries* to American circumstances and his use of a mock legislature to modify the common law by statutes, Wythe imparted to his students an understanding of how English common law had been changed and could be changed by American legislatures to make it more compatible with American circumstances.

In 1799, George Wythe resigned his professorship to devote himself full time to the High Court of Chancery which was then regularly meeting in Richmond. St. George Tucker, a former student of Wythe's, was elected to replace him the following year. Tucker's contribution was to impose a structured course of legal instruction on the College of William and Mary, to emphasize the role of the new Federal Constitution on American law and to encourage his students to advocate judicial activism, as well as legislative reform, as a means of keeping the law consistent with American values.

Tucker began his tenure by modifying the legal education system at the College of William and Mary. In a "Plan for Conferring Degrees on the Students of Law in the University of William and Mary," Tucker required law students to attend law lectures for two years; perform assigned exercises; take private examinations covering ancient and modern history, ancient and modern constitutions (particularly of the United States and of Virginia), ethics, the law of nations and principles of government and British acts incorporated into American law; and study the books presented in a reading list which included the leading works of law, political philosophy and economics—many of which were by European natural law writers.[65]

St. George Tucker also relied on Blackstone's *Commentaries* to serve as the basis for his lectures. However, whereas Wythe had merely noted what aspects were changed by American law, Tucker perceived the work as a continuous threat to American law and values. In one of his earliest lectures, Tucker noted that while the *Commentaries* was a brilliant and indispensable work, its apparent perfection made it dangerous:

> The transcendental merit of the Commentaries on the Laws of England precludes every idea of improvement, on the method observed in them; and where the law remains unaltered, it would be presumption to deviate from the authority, or even the language of their Author, the precision of the one being equal to the weight of the other. The consequence of such a deviation, were it adopted, would infallibly be the loss of some portion of that perspicuity, and basic purity of diction, which are more conspicuous in that work than in any other, I remember to have read. Yet as the genius of our government differs materially from that of Great Britain, and as our laws have undergone a variety of changes since the revolution, insomuch, as in many instances to have lost all resemblance to former laws on the same subject, it will not infrequently happen, that we must reject or controvert the doctrines of the learned commentator, as they apply to our Government, how firmly soever they may stand the test of scrutiny, or opposition in their native soil.[66]

Thus, while Tucker used the *Commentaries* as the basis for his lectures, he found frequent occasion to comment at considerable length on those aspects of Blackstone's work deemed inapplicable to or contradicted by the nature, principles, or policy of the United States.[67]

St. George Tucker had, as had Wythe, gained experience analyzing Blackstone's exposition of the law as a member of a Virginia legislative committee initially charged with revising the statute laws of Virginia. Tucker became frustrated, however, when the General Assembly restricted the revisors to merely compiling the old statutes. He would discover a better forum for advocating his reform when in 1788 he was elected a judge of the Virginia General Court. There, in a case which predated *Marbury v. Madison*[68] by ten years, he held that the Virginia Constitution of 1776 was a sovereign act of the people and therefore the supreme law, and that any prior or future statute in conflict with it was null and void.[69] This decision would not only open the way for Tucker to play an active role in reviewing and reforming, when necessary, laws that would come before him on the bench, but was representative of his belief in the active role of the legal profession and the judiciary to constantly scrutinise laws.[70]

As a result of these experiences, St. George Tucker, in comparison to George Wythe, developed a more pragmatic and less scholarly technique for studying law. Tucker believed that the foremost means for determining the applicability of English law to the United States was to judge its consistency with the various constitutions of the United States. When these documents were moot on or unclear about an issue, Tucker, no longer relying on the classical scholarship of his former teacher, would rely on the writings of the European natural law writers, as interpreters of the lessons of antiquity, in addition to the historical pronouncements of colonial predecessors, to consider the soundness of the application of foreign law to America.

Tucker's methodology is revealed in a lecture titled "Of the Cognizance of Crimes and Misdemeanours," which explored what criminal laws were in effect and what branch of government had the authority to enforce them. He began by explaining that the complicated system of the federal government required a return to fundamental principles, which was achieved by considering the theories of the European natural law writers that had served as the foundation for the Constitution. His analysis, which was aided by the writings of Montesquieu and Grotius, concluded that while the federal government was given jurisdiction over certain expressed crimes such as those which occurred on the high seas, counterfeiting, and offenses against the law of nations, it had no common law of its own. This was left to the states, individually, which had exclusive jurisdiction over criminal laws derived from the common law.[71]

To determine which common laws were adopted by individual states, it would be necessary to determine which laws were brought over from England by those who originally settled the colonies and then if those laws were altered since by the colonies or states. Tucker believed:

> When the American colonies were first settled by our ancestors, it was held, as well by the settlers, as by the Judges and Conveyors of England, that they brought hither, as a birth-right and inheritance, so much of the common law, as was applicable to their local situation, and change of circumstances. But each colony judged for itself, what parts of the common law were applicable to its new condition; and in various modes, by legislative acts, by judicial decisions, or by constant usage, adopted some parts, and rejected others.[72]

For example, Tucker discussed the revision of the English common law by Virginia. He noted that the procedural law concerning trial by jury was altered to allow anyone, regardless of their character or qualification, to serve on juries; that statutes were enacted first to authorize and then to limit the institution of slavery; and that judicial decisions had established a right of expatriation.[73] Wythe's inquiry would typically have ceased at this point. Tucker, however, advocated further analysis and, if necessary, activism.[74]

The final step in Tucker's approach to the study of law was described in a lecture titled, "A Short Inquiry into the Principles, Constitutions & mutual relations of the Government of the Commonwealth of Virginia, and the federal government of the United States of America; with a brief examination of the powers entrusted to them severally, by their respective Constitutions." Here, Tucker argued for the necessity of determining whether a law or its application was consistent with state and federal constitutions. Reflecting his Anti-Federalism, he devoted considerable time in his lecture to explaining how the Virginia and United States constitutions limited governmental power. But Tucker went beyond scholarly analysis by instilling in his students a sense of their role in advocating judicial activism by encouraging them to argue the constitutionality of laws and legislation.[75]

Legal education at the College of William and Mary under the direction of St. George Tucker had become less scholarly and more pragmatic than it had been under Wythe. Wythe's ultimate goal had been to mould his students into statesmen possessing the scholarly abilities of European natural law writers and leading the country through legislative activities. In contrast, Tucker sought to educate his students to become judicial activists, seeking to limit the expansion of government through a pragmatic understanding of constitutional restraints and the theories from which they were derived. Both approaches to the study of law would serve as important models for the future of American legal education.

In 1804, after some administrative difficulties with the College's Board of Visitors, St. George Tucker resigned his professorship to become a judge on the Virginia Court of Appeals. During the next thirty years, the chair in Law and Police would have three occupants—William Nelson (1804–13), Robert Nelson (1813–18) and James Semple (1819–34). Unfortunately, no evidence as to the substance of their instruction has yet come to light.

St. George Tucker was not the only student of Wythe's to play a significant role in American legal education during this period. In 1798, the Board of Trustees of Transylvania College in Lexington, Kentucky, appointed George Nicholas, a 1772 graduate of the College of William and Mary and a former law student under Wythe, Professor of Law and Politics. Nicholas had an active political career as a staunch Anti-Federalist serving in the Virginia House of Delegates, the Virginia Convention which ratified the United States Constitution and the first Kentucky Constitutional Convention. He was also the first Attorney General of Kentucky. Of the scarce materials that survive concerning the substance of legal instruction at Transylvania, the influence of Nicholas's Anti-Federalist views is pervasive.[76]

When Nicholas became the head of the department of law, he established America's first course on constitutional law, which he presented as the cornerstone of legal instruction at Transylvania. In his first outline for this course, he established two fundamental principles upon which constitutional law was based—(1) "no Constitution affords any real security to liberty, unless it is considered as sacred and inviolate" and (2) "every violation of such a Constitution must be made in one of two ways; either by an assumption by the government at large of greater powers than are given to it by the Constitution or by one branch of the government assuming to itself, or having transferred to it by the other branches, powers which the Constitution declares shall be exercised only by the other branches or by the whole government." With this foundation established, Nicholas concentrated on imparting to his students the following principles: the judiciary had the authority to rule acts of Congress unconstitutional; the general welfare clause had not bestowed broad powers of legislation on Congress; all powers not expressly delegated were reserved; and, a strictly delegated power cannot be re-delegated.[77]

George Nicholas died less than ten months after his appointment. Nevertheless, his doctrinaire exposition of constitutional interpretation continued to influence legal education at Transylvania. James Brown, Nicholas's successor, combined the teaching of law and the teaching of Republican philosophy "with such fidelity that Thomas Jefferson advised young Virginians to study at Transylvania."[78] It is difficult to imagine that Henry Clay, Brown's successor, kept his political passions from dominating his law lectures. Through this emphasis on legal instruction, Nicholas, Brown and Clay, while probably encouraging a form of legal analysis similar to that taught at William and Mary (all three had studied under George Wythe), stressed that legal education was inseparable from constitutional orientation.[79]

The role of the College of William and Mary and Transylvania College in American legal education was no doubt important. However, their direct impact on instructing the first generation of American lawyers was limited. Although forty individuals attended George Wythe's law course in 1779, only nineteen law students are known to have graduated from the College during Wythe's ten-year tenure.[80] St. George Tucker did not fare any better, attracting fifty students altogether and graduating twelve or thirteen law students.[81] As for Transylvania, there is no record of the number of law students prior to 1821. However, John Wright, Jr. has noted that the school "was doubtless small."[82] During this early period, college legal instruction was overshadowed by proprietary law schools.

Proprietary law schools were the most successful institutions offering legal instruction during this period in that not only did they have far more graduates than college law departments, but, unlike college law graduates who typically went on to clerkships, almost all of the graduates of proprietary law schools directly entered practice. Proprietary law schools were privately owned, usually profit-making, institutions which offered vocational legal instruction independent of colleges or universities. Most of the schools were owned and operated by state court judges who had plenty of spare time and a desire to supplement their often inadequate salaries without facing charges of conflict of interest if they practiced law.[83] In a few of the larger institutions, partners were brought in and instructors and examiners were hired. The centerpieces of the schools were their law libraries, which were among the best in America.[84] The favored mode of instruction was a combination of lectures, tutorials and moot courts. All the proprietary law schools were dedicated to providing groups of students with regular instruction in the law.

There were thirteen proprietary law schools started between 1784 and 1828 which conform to this model. They were distributed among seven states (Connecticut, New York, Massachusetts, Vermont, Maryland, Virginia and Tennessee) and attracted students from every state and territory in the country. Their years of greatest popularity were between 1810 and 1823. In total, they were directly responsible for educating over sixteen hundred lawyers.[85]

The lifeblood of these schools was their ability to attract students away from clerkships through the speed and ease of their courses of study and the strong reputations of their proprietors. Bates Turner's law school in Fairfield, Vermont, for example, attracted 175 students between 1806 and 1812, an extraordinary number, largely because it was known for preparing law students for admission to practice in much less time than would otherwise be required.[86] The Litchfield law school, as did others, appealed to students by informing them that its lectures were so simple and organized that no prior preparation was required. James Gould, one of Litchfield's proprietors, informed a prospective student:

> As to your inquiry respecting studies preparatory to my lectures, I can only say that my lectures are intended to systematize and simplify the science of the Law, in order that the student, on entering upon his studies, may begin with ease and advantage to himself—any preparatory study is of course unnecessary.[87]

All of the schools attracted students because of the reputations of their proprietors; out of seventeen, eight were judges of their respective state's highest courts, one was a United States Senator, one a United States Congressman, one the chief judge of a state's trial court and one was one of the nation's most noted patent attorneys.[88] Attendance at a proprietary law school was an attractive alternative to apprenticeship in a law office.

Nevertheless, the cost of attendance at a proprietary law school, which often exceeded that of a clerkship, must have deterred many who would otherwise wish to enrol. Expenses at law schools ranged from $200 per year ($50 for tuition and $150 for board and expenses) at the Needham law school to $350 per year ($100 for tuition and $250 for board and expenses) at Litchfield.[89] In addition, many proprietary law students had to bear the cost of extensive travel to attend these institutions. For example, of Litchfield's 1016 students, 525 traveled from out of state and 224 traveled more than 200 miles. In comparison, fees for clerkships were usually between $100 and $225 per annum, and most individuals completed their clerkships within their home towns.[90] The high cost of going to a proprietary law school meant that, in spite of their advantages over legal clerkships, only the sons of the wealthier members of society could afford to attend. This should not be taken to indicate that law schools fostered elitism with the intent of stratifying the profession. On the contrary, the majority of law school proprietors published their lectures so as to impart the educations offered at these institutions to law students who could not afford to attend. Tapping Reeve wrote that he published his lectures on domestic relations with the "expectations . . . that . . . it should be found beneficial to the learner . . . [and] . . . equally valuable to all parts of our country."[91] Zephaniah Swift published his lectures, writing that it was "the best method to diffuse this knowledge through all ranks."[92] If the cost of attending proprietary law schools can be characterized as elitist, the publication of the lectures offered at these institutions must be characterized as egalitarian.

Although a college degree was not considered a prerequisite for attendance at proprietary law schools, having attained a liberal arts education was considered essential to the intelligent study of law. The majority of law school students about whom information survives had graduated from college. Those law school students who had not acquired a college education were provided with a brief course of general instruction which was to be completed before they could begin their legal studies. Peter Van Schaack wrote out a plan for such a course which suggested six categories of learning that law students would have frequent occasion to use in their study and practice of law:

1. The English, Latin and French Tongues.
2. Writing, Arithmetick [*sic*], Geometry, Surveying, Merchants Accounts or Book Keeping.
3. Geography, Chronology, History.
4. Logick [*sic*] and Rhetorick [*sic*].
5. Divinity [including ethics].
6. Economicks [*sic*] and Politics.[93]

Never before in the English-speaking world had a liberal arts education been a prerequisite for the study of law. The reason for this change was that legal instruction, as presented in proprietary law schools, would no longer be based on mere memorization of rules and procedures. Instead, the law would be taught as a science emphasizing the diverse reasons for its development which could be best understood by inquiry from a liberally educated mind.

The method of legal instruction at proprietary law schools was developed in response to the confused state of American law after the Revolution. The suitability of applying aspects of English common and statutory law to America was questioned, and some even suggested replacing the common law with codes.[94] Disagreements about constitutional interpretation and the role of the courts ruled the day.[95] American statutes adopted after the Revolution were poorly publicized, and reports of court opinions were largely unavailable.[96] Zephaniah Swift, proprietor of the Windham law school, summed up the problem as it applied to his own state's laws: "No country is favored with a more perspicuous code than the state of Connecticut; yet in no country is it more arduous and difficult to obtain a systematic understanding of the law."[97]

The faculty of proprietary law schools realized the difficulty of the task before them, realizing they would have to present an organized system of American law where none had previously existed. Henry St. George Tucker, son of St. George Tucker and proprietor of the Winchester law school, explained:

> [a law teacher] must, moreover, be blessed with an analytical mind, which can draw order out of chaos, and arrange his numerous materials so that they will illustrate each other, instead of producing embarrassment and confusion; for it is his province to unravel a tangled skein, to conduct his pupil through labyrinths which can only be threaded by those who have studied their complicated plan.[98]

Proprietary law school teachers needed help in tackling this task. Their search for assistance took them to Blackstone's *Commentaries*; the only comprehensive series of lectures on the common law published prior to 1826. Its genius, according to Henry St. George Tucker, was the way in which, by classifying the various aspects of law, the law was brought into the rank of the sciences:

> The student . . . instead of being ushered into a disordered magazine, where the treasures of knowledge are thrown together like heaps of lumber, now finds himself introduced as it were into a beautifully arranged museum, where he commands at first a general view of the various compartments and of different classes. He then descends to particular families, and readily acquires an acquaintance with each by attention to the peculiarities of the species; while in each is still to be traced the common principles of their genius.[99]

Categorization, however, was only the first step in developing a science of law. It would have to be combined with a technique for studying law.

Blackstone's methodology was designed to show that the common law was a science of human experience. He began by reducing the law to its "primary rules and fundamental principles" and, through a comparison with the precepts of the law of nature and the practices of other countries, depicted the common law as having developed from reasonable solutions to human disputes. Lastly, he showed how the law had been gradually improved by the courts through careful application to new circumstances and harmed by legislators rushing to correct perceived inconsistencies.[100] Through all of this, however, Blackstone discouraged his readers from questioning the validity of the law. As Daniel Boorstin has noted: "Man was discouraged from any attempt to improve the law because the English system contained latent, undiscoverable perfections which he might unwittingly destroy."[101]

Superficially, the method adopted in proprietary law schools was a replica of that developed by Blackstone. The Litchfield law school, for example, organized its law lectures in the same manner in which Blackstone categorized the *Commentaries*. Of the twenty-seven lectures given at Litchfield in 1808, thirteen shared titles exactly with Blackstone's chapter headings and subclassifications.[102] In addition, James Gould stated that the primary object of his lectures was "to show the reason of the law by tracing its rules so far as I am able to their proper principles."[103] Nevertheless, there was an important difference—proprietary law school teachers were unwilling to accept Blackstone's unquestioning reverence for the common law.

The method for the study of law adopted in the proprietary law schools, although based on Blackstone, emphasized that the law could be fallible. Sylvester Gilbert, proprietor of the Hebron law school taught his students that tracing a law back to its roots did not necessarily mean that it was valid. According to Gilbert, laws must have been originally peaceable and acquiesced in, reasonable and certain and compulsory and consistent. If a law failed to meet these criteria, it was to be given no weight.[104] Zephaniah Swift, of the Windham law school, noted that although it was "an established doctrine that decisions of courts are to be held in the highest regard . . . if the determination has been found on mistaken principles or a rule adopted has become inconvenient a subsequent court may vary from it."[105] These pronouncements about the imperfection of the law were not confined to discussions about legal methodology. Rather, a perception of the law as a series of concepts constantly needing revision was prevalent throughout many of the more substantive law lectures.

In lectures at various schools, instructors consistently noted where and why the English common law was incorrect and if it had or needed to be changed in America. For example, in a lecture on mercantile law given at Litchfield, James Gould explained that, according to English common law, fraud in the consideration of a contract did not necessarily and not in all circumstances render the contract void (although the injured party could sue for damages). Gould emphasized, however, that Connecticut courts had decided this to be unfair and considered all such contracts void because a party to a contract would often have to perform contractual obligations without any hope of recovering damages.[106] In addition, in a lecture on "title by forfeiture" delivered at the Winchester law school, Henry St. George Tucker stated that the common law requirement that lands, tenements and hereditaments be forfeited by those convicted of crimes was "modified and in part abolished by the following provision of our law."[107] These examples of a continuous annotation of the common law during most law lectures show how law students were taught to regard the law as not only fallible but improvable. It was not enough, however, to suggest merely that the law could be changed as circumstances required. Proprietary law school teachers imparted to their students the belief that as lawyers it would be their job to constantly encourage the improvement of the law. Nowhere was this point made clearer than in the schools' moot courts.

Moot courts were developed at proprietary law schools as a means of instructing students in the practical application of what they had learned from their studies. A hypothetical case would be presented to students who would be required to research the law and present written and oral arguments according to proper court procedures. The Charles James Faulkner Papers, housed in the Virginia Historical Society, contain the most extensive record of a proprietary law school's moot court proceedings. Faulkner became president of the Moot Court Club at the Winchester Law School in 1829.

A review of the records of the Winchester moot court reveals clear patterns of how students were to shape their legal arguments. Hypothetical cases were constructed to emphasize how unjust results could come from the application of legal principles to everyday disputes. Students were taught to approach a case by first determining, based on their own sense of right and wrong, what the proper result should be. Then they were to search through the law noting legal authorities that both supported and countered the result they sought. There were no limitations placed on what authorities could be used. The briefs indicate a wide breadth of sources from law reports throughout the region to the works of European natural law writers including works by Blackstone, Montesquieu, Beccaria, Vattel, Burlamaqui and Matthew Bacon. Finally, the relevant authorities were compared and contrasted emphasizing the faults in those against the position being taken. The theme underlying all of the arguments was that it was the advocate's responsibility to seek modification of legal principles as new situations required.[108]

A representative case which came before the moot court concerned a defectively executed will. In this case, Mr. Bell devised his personal property to his daughter (Sarah) and his real estate to his son. The will, however, was improperly executed in that there was only one witness when the law required two. Sarah Bell was the plaintiff in the action claiming that her father died intestate and therefore she was entitled to a statutory allocation of all the property. There were two legal questions suggested by Henry St. George Tucker. (1) How far should equity interfere to counter the express provisions of a statute? (2) Does the present case present any problems for interference? The nature of this case and of the legal questions raised depict how the moot court was used to impart to students a practical appreciation of their future role in encouraging the development of law.[109]

The most important feature of the legal education provided by proprietary law schools was the fact that it imparted to students an understanding of the law as a dynamic institution filled with errors needing to be constantly corrected. First, students were provided with the methods necessary to understand the science of law. Second, they were taught that the law was fallible. Third, they were shown, through corrections and modifications made by American courts and legislatures, that the law was improvable. Lastly, they were convinced that it was to be their role through their legal practices to advocate the continual improvement of the law. The impact of this legal education played a key role in the development of American law and legal thought.

Maxwell Bloomfield has suggested that the leaders of the bar sought to promote a national legal uniformity through this education. He wrote: "Concerned at the threat of further social disorganization, bar leaders called for the establishment of national law schools to promote uniformity of thought on legal issues. . . ." In support of this claim Bloomfield quotes Peter DuPonceau, one of the founders of the Law Academy of Philadelphia, who stated, "With a succession of able professors the genuine spirit of our law may be preserved through a series of ages; legislative innovations, if not prevented, may be directed into a proper channel, and uniformity in judicial decisions may be in great degree, if not entirely, secured" and David Hoffman, Professor of Law in the University of Maryland, who wrote, "And as it is from those who have been *students* of this profession, if not from its *practitioners*, that the nation draws the largest portion of its legislators and statesman, there is an obvious reason for somewhat enlarging the circuit of the law student's acquirements, arising from the probable combination of the counsellor with the politician."[110]

While this desire for legal uniformity is representative of views held by some leaders of the Bar, it is not attributable to all, or even the majority, of legal educators.

By suggesting that all legal educators promoted legal uniformity, Bloomfield ignores the political nature of early American legal education. While staunch federalists such as DuPonceau and Hoffman tended to favor legal uniformity among the states, Republicans were in opposition to this goal. Professor George Nicholas of Transylvania College opposed "with uncompromising tenacity, the federalistic conception of the concentration of power" that legal uniformity would have brought about.[111] St. George Tucker of the College of William and Mary also argued that "the authority and obligation of the common law . . . must depend solely on the constitutional or legislative authority of each state, respectively; as contained in their several bill of rights, constitutions, and legislative declarations . . . which, being different in different states, and wholly independent of each other, cannot establish any uniform law. . . ."[112] Even Zephaniah Swift and Sylvester Gilbert, both moderate federalists, chose to teach the laws of the state of Connecticut rather than argue the existence of a federal common law.[113] Although some legal educators actively promoted legal uniformity, the majority either opposed the idea or did little to promote it. Thus, the similarity of legal developments among the individual United States cannot be attributed to the nature of legal education during this period. Better explanations can be found in the existence of numerous pre-Kent and Story legal treatise which encouraged the uniformity of state legal developments.[114]

The influence of proprietary law schools on American law and legal thought was principally achieved through the accomplishments of their graduates, a disproportionate number of whom (as compared to other lawyers) became the leaders of the American bar and held prominent political positions.[115] Data necessary for compiling statistics about the role of proprietary law school graduates and faculty in the legal profession during this period are almost impossible to come by. However, materials concerning the legal profession in the state of Connecticut are reasonably complete. They show that, although proprietary law school graduates and faculty only comprised on average 10% of the population of lawyers in Connecticut between 1820 and 1830, they made up 70% of the state's delegation to the 21st through 25th Congresses, 50% of the state's federal legal appointments and 34.5% of the state's judicial appointments. While the representativeness of Connecticut may be questioned, these figures provide a sense of the impact that proprietary law schools had on the accomplishments of the legal profession.[116]

The preeminence of proprietary law schools in American institutional legal education rapidly declined after 1829. Although this type of school would continue to be established as late as 1883, particularly in the areas of America's frontier where competition from colleges and universities was limited, newly established college law schools began to dominate the vocational education of lawyers around 1829. Colleges had begun to perceive the advantages to society, and to their own finances, of offering practical legal instruction, and they had the advantage over proprietary law schools that they could offer a degree on completion of a course of study. Many early proprietary law schools ceased to exist because of the death of their owners. Others lost faculty to college law schools seeking to build on their reputations. Two colleges, Yale and Washington and Lee, even incorporated proprietary law schools into their own law departments. Proprietary law schools had great difficulty competing with colleges offering vocational legal instruction.[117]

In summary, American legal education between 1779 and 1829 underwent significant changes as compared to the colonial period. Contrary to the views espoused by Konesfsky and King, the process of reading law did not induce "a rigid, unquestioning attitude toward legal studies" nor did it "impede the legal system's capacity to respond to changes occurring in society."[118] Rather, vocational law schools, an important means of legal instruction during the post-Revolutionary and early National periods, instilled in their graduates a conception of the law as a dynamic institution constantly improving as it is encouraged to adapt to the needs of a changing society.

NOTES

1. Roscoe Pound, *The Formative Era of American Law* (Boston, MA: Little, Brown and Company, 1938).

2. Daniel J. Boorstin, *The Americans: The National Experience* (New York: Vintage Books, 1965), p. 35.

3. William E. Nelson, *Americanization of the Common Law* (Cambridge: Harvard University Press, 1975), p. 8. Nelson might have better described this process as the "Massachusettsation" of the common law, for the workings of the Massachusetts bench were not often representative of what went on in the rest of the country.

4. Morton J. Horwitz, *The Transformation of American Law 1780–1860* (Cambridge: Harvard University Press, 1977), p. 30.

5. Alfred Z. Reed, *Training for the Public Profession of the Law* (New York: The Carnegie Foundation, 1921), pp. 116–135; Albert J. Harno, *Legal Education in the United States* (San Francisco: Bancroft-Whitney Co., 1953), pp. 23–34.

6. Gerald W. Gawalt, *The Promise of Power: The Emergence of the Legal Profession in Massachusetts 1760–1840* (Westport, CT: Greenwood Press, 1979).

7. Robert Stevens, *Law School: Legal Education in America from the 1850's to the 1980's* (Chapel Hill: The University of North Carolina Press, 1983), pp. 3–5.

8. Alfred S. Konesfsky and Andrew J. King, eds., *The Papers of Daniel Webster*, 2 vols. (Hanover, NH: University Press of New England, 1982), 1:4.

9. Ibid., 1:4–5.

10. Claude Halstead Van Tyne, *The Loyalists in the American Revolution* (Gloucester, MA: Peter Smith, 1959), p. 195.

11. Anton-Hermann Chroust, *The Rise of the Legal Profession in America*, 2 vols. (Norman: University of Oklahoma Press, 1965), 1:10. The New York Supreme Court is New York's trial court. The highest court in the state is the Court of Appeals.

12. *Minutes of the Supreme Court of Judicature of the Province of New York, 1775–1781*, p. 177, cited in Paul M. Hamlin, *Legal Education in Colonial New York* (New York: New York University Law Quarterly Review, 1939), p. 127 n. 3.

13. Van Tyne, *Loyalists*, pp. 318–326.

14. Roscoe Pound, *The Lawyer from Antiquity to Modern Times* (St. Paul, MN: West Publishing, 1953), p. 178; Wallace Brown, *The King's Friends* (Providence, RI: Brown University Press, 1965), p. 265.

15. E. Alfred Jones, *American Members of the Inns of Court* (London: The Saint Catherine Press, 1924), pp. 68–72.

16. Ibid., pp. 178–179.

17. Lawrence M. Friedman, *A History of American Law* (New York: Simon and Schuster, 1973), p. 560.

18. Hamlin, *Legal Education*, p. 95.

19. Merrill Jensen, *The New Nation* (New York: Vintage Books, 1950), pp. 278–281.

20. Jackson Turner Main, *The Sovereign States, 1775–1783* (New York: Franklin Watts, 1973), pp. 56, 57, 84–85.

21. England offered two additional methods to gain entrance into the legal profession: (1) to become a solicitor, a practitioner before the Chancery Courts, through membership at one of the Inns of Chancery; or (2), to become an attorney, a practitioner before the law courts, through an articled clerkship. However, both systems were considered inadequate means of legal education during this period, and there is no evidence to indicate that any American colonialists took advantage of them. See: Robert Robson, *The Attorney in Eighteenth-Century England* (Cambridge: Cambridge University Press, 1959), p. 52; Harry Kirk, *Portrait of a Profession* (London: Oyez Publishing, 1976), p. 48.

22. W. S. Holdsworth, *The Disappearance of the Educational System of the Inns of Court*, 69 U. PA. L. REV. 201 (1921); William Blackstone, *Commentaries on the Laws of England*, 4 vols. (1765; reprinted Chicago: The University of Chicago Press, 1979), 1:25, 31.

23. Henry Tucker to St. George Tucker, 1 August 1772, Tucker-Coleman Collection, Swem Library, College of William and Mary, Williamsburg, Virginia.

24. Hamlin, *Legal Education*, p. 22.

25. Jones, *American Members*.

26. Daniel J. Boorstin, *The Americans: The Colonial Experience* (New York: Vintage Books, 1958), p. 200.

27. Charles R. McManis, *The History of First Century American Legal Education: A Revisionist Perspective*, 59 (part 2) WASH. U. L. Q. 597, 603 (1981).

28. Reed, *Training*, pp. 83–84.

29. Charles E. Consalus, *Legal Education During the Colonial Period, 1663–1776*, 29 J. LEGAL ED. 295, 308 (1978); W. Hamilton Bryson, *Legal Education in Virginia, 1779–1979* (Charlottesville, VA: University Press of Virginia, 1982), p. 3.

30. Dumas Malone, *Jefferson the Virginian* (Boston, MA: Little, Brown and Company, 1948), p. 67.

31. William Livingston, "Sic vos, non vobis, Mellificatis opis," *The New-York Weekly Post-Boy*, 19 August 1745, reproduced in Hamlin, *Legal Education*, Appendix VI.

32. Letter from Peter Van Schaack to Henry Van Schaack, 2 January 1769, in Henry C. Van Schaack, *The Life of Peter Van Schaack, LL.D.* (New York: D. Appelton & Co., 1842), p. 9.

33. Josiah Quincy, "An Address Delivered at the Dedication of the Dane Law College in Harvard University, October 23, 1832," reproduced in Perry Miller, ed., *The Legal Mind in America* (Ithaca, NY: Cornell University Press, 1969), pp. 210–211.

34. Reed, *Training*, p. 114.

35. Consalus, *Legal Education*, at 306.

36. Charles R. McKirdy, *The Lawyer as Apprentice: Legal Education in Eighteenth Century Massachusetts*, 28 J. LEGAL ED. 124, 125–126 (1976).

37. Gerald W. Gawalt, *Massachusetts Legal Education in Transition, 1766–1840*, 17 AM. J. LEGAL HIST. 27 at 28 (1973).

38. McManis, *First Century American Legal Education*, at 600.

39. Reed, *Training*, p. 423; Stevens, *Law School*, p. 12 (n. 15); Frederick C. Hicks, *Yale Law School: The Founders and the Founders' Collection* (New Haven, CT: Yale University Press, 1935), p. 39.

40. Harno, *Legal Education*, p. 24.

41. William Kent, *Memoirs and Letters of James Kent, LL.D.* (Boston, MA: Little, Brown & Co., 1898), p. 77.

42. James Kent to Moss Kent, 4 January 1796, Kent Papers, Library of Congress, Washington, DC.

43. William Kent, *Memoirs*, p. 77.

44. See also: Reed, *Training*, pp. 137–142.

45. Thomas L. Shaffer, *David Hoffman's Law School Lectures, 1822–33*, 32 J. Legal Educ. 127, 127 (1982).

46. David Hoffman, *A Course of Legal Study* (Baltimore, MD: Coale and Maxwell, 1817).

47. Quoted in an advertisement bound in David Hoffman, *Introductory Lectures* (United States Library of Congress Law Library, KF272.H6, Washington, DC).

48. David Hoffman, *To the Trustees of the University of Maryland in Relation to the Law Chair* (Baltimore, MD: J.D. Toy, 1826), pp. 2–6.

49. Shaffer, *Hoffman's Lectures*, at 129.

50. Police was used in the sense of civil organization.

51. Thomas Jefferson to James Madison, 26 July 1780, in Thomas Jefferson, *The Papers of Thomas Jefferson*, ed. Julian P. Boyd et al., 23 vols. to date (Princeton, NJ: Princeton University Press, 1950–), 3:507.

52. William Blackstone, *Commentaries on the Laws of England*, 4 vols. (Oxford: The Clarendon Press, 1765).

53. Matthew Bacon, *A New Abridgement of the Law*, 8 vols. (London: E. and R. Nutt, 1736).

54. Bryson, *Legal Education*, p. 23; W. Edwin Hemphill, "George Wythe, America's First Law Professor and the Teacher of Jefferson, Marshall and Clay" (M.A. thesis, Emory University, 1933), p. 50 and Appendix C; Charles T. Cullen, "St. George Tucker and Law in Virginia, 1772–1804" (Ph.D. dissertation, University of Virginia, 1971), p. 166.

55. An Act for the Union of the Transylvania Seminary and Kentucky Academy, 1798 Ky. Acts 234, ch. 166; Board of Trustees Minutes, 16 April 1799 to 22 March

1816, Department of Special Collections, Transylvania University, Lexington, Kentucky.

56. Board of Trustees Minutes, 16 April 1799 to 22 March 1816, Department of Special Collections, Transylvania University, Lexington, Kentucky; "An Address by Charles Kerr On the Occasion of the Sesqui-Centennial of the Signing of the Constitution," Under the Auspices of Transylvania College, 6 October 1937, Transylvania University Library, Lexington, Kentucky, pp. 10–12; *Dictionary of American Biography*, s.v.

57. *A Catalogue of the Officers and Students of Transylvania University* (Lexington, KY: T. Smith, 1821), p. 1; Hemphill, "George Wythe," p. 49.

58. E. Lee Shepard, "George Wythe," in Bryson, *Legal Education*, pp. 751–754; *The Works of Henry Clay*, ed. Calvin Colton (New York: Henry Clay Publications, 1896), 1:43; William Swindler, *John Marshall's Preparation for the Bar—Some observations on his law notes*, 2 Am. J. Legal Hist. 207–213 (1967).

59. John Tyler to Thomas Jefferson, 12 November 1810, reprinted in Lyon Gardiner Tyler, *The Letters and Times of the Tylers* (Richmond, VA: Whittet & Shepperson, c1884–1896), 1:249–250.

60. Hemphill, "George Wythe," p. 50.

61. Blackstone, *Commentaries*, 1:205.

62. Ibid., 2:376.

63. Daniel Boorstin, *The Mysterious Science of Law* (Cambridge: Harvard University Press, 1941), p. 25.

64. John Brown to William Preston, 6 July 1780, reprinted in *William & Mary Quarterly*, Series 1, (1900–1901), 9:80.

65. St. George Tucker, "Plan for Conferring Degrees on the Students of Law in the University of William and Mary," St. George Tucker Uncatalogued Writings, Tucker-Coleman Collection, Earl Gregg Swem Library, College of William and Mary, Williamsburg, Virginia. Tucker's reading list is reprinted in Appendix I.

66. St. George Tucker's Lecture Notebooks, Tucker-Coleman Collection, Earl Gregg Swem Library, College of William and Mary, Williamsburg, Virginia, Box 62, 2:5.

67. Ibid., p. 6.

68. 5 U.S. (1 Cranch) 137 (1803).

69. Kamper v. Hawkins, 1 Va. 20 (1793).

70. Cullen, "St. George Tucker," pp. 110–111.

71. Tucker's Lecture Notebooks, Box 62, 2:55–59.

72. Ibid., p. 59.

73. Ibid., Box 63, vol. 7.

74. Ibid., Box 62, 2:59–61.

75. Ibid., Box 63, 1:1–41.

76. *Who Was Who in America, Historical Volume 1607–1896* (Chicago: A.N. Marquis Co., 1967), s.v.

77. "An Address by Charles Kerr," pp. 10–12.

78. Niels Sonne, *Liberal Kentucky*, 1780–1828 (New York: Columbia University Press, 1939), p. 68.

79. John D. Wright, Jr., *Transylvania: Tutor to the West* (Lexington, KY: The University Press of Kentucky, 1975), pp. 44–92.

80. Imogene E. Brown, *American Aristides: A Biography of George Wythe* (Rutherford, NJ: Fairleigh Dickinson University Press, 1981), pp. 201–214.

81. William T. Barry to his brother, 30 January 1804, reprinted in *William & Mary Quarterly*, Series 1 (1904), 13:109.

82. Wright, Jr., *Transylvania*, p. 43.

83. Friedman, *A History*, p. 121.

84. Hicks, *Yale*, p. 4; "List of texts in Law School Library," 15 June 1843, Woodruff Collection, Litchfield Historical Society, Litchfield, Connecticut.

85. See Appendixes II and III.

86. Abby Hemenway, "Bates Turner," *Vermont Historical Magazine* 2 (1871): 312.

87. James Gould to Augustus Hand, 9 August 1827, Reeve Collection, Litchfield Historical Society, Litchfield, Connecticut.

88. See Appendix II.

89. Creed Taylor, *Journal of the Law School, and of the Moot-Court attached to it; at Needham, in Virginia* . . . (Richmond, VA: J. & G. Cochran, 1822), pp. iii–iv; Sidney Morse to Jedediah and Elizabeth Morse, 7 December 1814, Reeve Collection, Litchfield Historical Society, Litchfield, Connecticut.

90. Gawalt, *Massachusetts Legal Education*, at 34; Robert H. Wettach, ed., *A Century of Legal Education* (Chapel Hill: University of North Carolina Press, 1947), p. 15.

91. Tapping Reeve, *The Law of Baron And Femme* . . . (New Haven, CT: Oliver Steele, 1816), preface.

92. Zephaniah Swift, *A System of the Laws of the State of Connecticut*, 2 vols. (Windham, CT: John Byrne, 1795) 1:1.

93. Peter Van Schaack, "The sciences necessary for a lawyer are . . . ," undated, Van Schaack Family Papers, Columbia University Library, New York, NY.

94. Friedman, *A History*, pp. 93–100; Peter Stein, *The Attraction of the Civil Law in Post-Revolutionary America*, 52 Va. L. Rev. 403–434 (1966).

95. Richard E. Ellis, *The Jeffersonian Crisis: Courts and Politics in the Young Republic* (New York: W.W. Norton & Co., 1974).

96. St. George Tucker, *Blackstone's Commentaries: with Notes of Reference, to the Constitution and Laws, of the Federal Government of the United States; and of the Commonwealth of Virginia*, 5 vols. (Philadelphia: William Young Birch and Abraham Small, 1803), 1:iv.

97. Swift, *A System of the Laws*, 1:1.

98. Henry St. George Tucker, "Introductory Lecture," in his *Commentaries on the Laws of Virginia, comprising the substance of a course of lectures delivered to the Winchester law school* (Winchester, VA: Tucker, 1831), p. 2.

99. Ibid., p. ii.

100. Blackstone, *Commentaries*, 1:36.

101. Boorstin, *The Mysterious Science*, p. 105.

102. "Litchfield Law School Lecture Notes," 1808, Connecticut State Library, Hartford, CT, 974.62 L719Ln Vault 3.

103. Charles Warren, *History of the Harvard Law School and of Early Legal Conditions in America*, 3 vols. (Cambridge, MA: Harvard University Press, 1908), 1:183–184.

104. Abiel A. Loomis, "Hebron Law Lectures" (1814), Connecticut State Library, Hartford, Connecticut, p. 17.

105. Swift, *A System of the Laws*, p. 17.

106. "Law Lectures of Reeve & Gould," Robert Troup Papers, New York Public Library, New York, New York, pp. 3–4.

107. Henry St. George Tucker, *Commentaries*, Vol. 1, Book 2, Ch. 15.

108. Winchester Law School Materials, Charles James Faulkner Papers, Virginia Historical Society, Richmond, Virginia, Box 47.

109. Ibid., No. 3.

110. Maxwell Bloomfield, *David Hoffman and the Shaping of a Republican Legal Culture*, 38 MD. L. REV. 673 at 679–680 (1979).

111. "An Address by Charles Kerr," p. 8.

112. Tucker, *Blackstone's Commentaries*, I: 432.

113. Swift, *A System of the Laws*; "Journal or Chronical of Sylvester Gilbert," Connecticut State Library, Hartford CT, 920.G375 Vault.

114. See: Daniel Chipman, *An Essay on the Law of Contracts, for the Payment of Specifick Articles* (Middlebury, VT: J. W. Copeland, 1822); Tapping Reeve, *A Treatise on the Law of Descents in the Several United States of America* (New York: Collins & Hannay, 1825); Gulian C. Verplanck, *An Essay on the Doctrine of Contracts: being An Inquiry how contracts are affected In Law And Morals by Concealment, Error, Or Inadequate Price.* (New York: G. & C. Carvill, 1825); Samuel Livermore, *A Treatise on the Law of Principal and Agent; and of Sales by Auction*, 2 vols. (Baltimore, MD: Joseph Robinson, 1818).

115. The educational influence of these institutions was also extended to law students who chose clerkships or self-education through the publications of their faculty and students. This is discussed in Chapter 3.

116. The Secretary of State of Connecticut, *The Connecticut Register* (New London, CT: Samuel Green, 1820); The Secretary of the State of Connecticut, *The Connecticut Annual Register* (New London, CT: Samuel Green, 1830).

117. Reed, *Training*, Appendix 1.

118. Konesfky and King, *Daniel Webster*, 1:4–5.

2

St. George Tucker and the Influence of Blackstone's *Commentaries* on American Legal Education

It has become an established notion of American history that William Blackstone's *Commentaries on the Laws of England* had a significant influence on American law and legal education.[1] Daniel J. Boorstin has noted that:

> in the first century of American independence, the *Commentaries* were not merely an approach to the study of law; for most lawyers they constituted all there was of the law. The influence of Blackstone's ideas on the framers of the Federal Constitution is well known. And many an early American lawyer might have said, with Chancellor Kent, that "he owed his reputation to the fact that, when studying law . . . he had but one book, Blackstone's *Commentaries*, but that one book he mastered."[2]

Dennis R. Nolan concurred with Boorstin, claiming that Blackstone's influence on the American Bar through legal education was unfettered and significant.[3] This position, however, is in need of revision.

The leaders of the post-Revolutionary American Bar turned to the *Commentaries*, not so much as a treatise on law, but as a model for developing American systems of legal education. Along with methods to make the diffusion of legal knowledge easier, however, the *Commentaries* included an aristocratically biased exposition of the law and descriptions of laws neither valid in nor suited to the United States. Americans perceived Blackstone's presentation of the common law as a tool for use by the landed gentry as aristocratic, for they did not distinguish between the aristocracy and the landed gentry. Henry Wheaton, a member of the commission that rewrote New York's property law between 1826 and 1828 and a Reporter for the United States Supreme Court, explained: "In England, the continuance of the landed property in the hands of the aristocracy is the basis upon which the monarchy itself may be said to rest, but, with us, it should never be forgotten that it is the partibility, the frequent division and unchecked alienation of property, that are essential to the health and vigour of our republican institutions."[4] As a result, a debate ensued among leading American lawyers concerning the influence Blackstone was to be allowed in the American legal community.

The single most important product of this debate was the publication of a highly successful Americanized edition of the *Commentaries* edited by St. George Tucker.[5] Tucker used the works of European natural law writers to question Blackstone's presentation of the law and to judge its suitability for America. As a result, St. George Tucker's edition of the *Commentaries* limited Blackstone's influence on American legal education more than has been recognized, and it introduced into American legal thought the propriety of questioning laws against the standards of human reason.

After the American Revolution, leading American lawyers referred to Blackstone's *Commentaries* in response to a need to repopulate rapidly the ranks of the profession. The Revolution had caused a vacuum in the number of practicing attorneys: loyalist lawyers had been forced to emigrate, and many of the remaining practitioners were attracted to Government posts; at the same time, legal work, particularly that concerned with debt collection and property disputes, was steadily increasing. Of the colonial systems of legal education, clerkships and self-instruction were viewed as being inadequate and attendance at the Inns of Court was no longer acceptable. Thus, the leaders of the American Bar addressed themselves to developing systems of legal education better suited to fulfil post-Revolutionary American needs.

They began their inquiry by referring to William Blackstone's *Commentaries on the Laws of England*. There were nearly twenty-five hundred copies of the *Commentaries* available in the American colonies prior to the Declaration of Independence, including over fifteen hundred sets of the first American edition, published in 1771. This edition was available only by subscription: eight hundred and forty-nine people, including a substantial majority of the leadership of the American Bar, subscribed.[6]

The *Commentaries* were unique among literature available to Americans in that they were concerned largely with issues of legal education—issues similar to the ones being faced by the leaders of the post-Revolutionary American Bar. Legal education in England was also in great need of improvement. Blackstone devised his program at a time when the Inns of Court and Chancery were in decline,[7] when universities offered instruction only in civil law[8] and when the English clerkship system received many of the same complaints leveled at its American counterpart.[9] Whereas the Americans were looking to design an educational system suited to their image of the future needs of America, Blackstone desired to create an educational system suited to his image of the future needs of England. Living in a time of economic and political upheaval, Blackstone, as a member of the landed gentry, sought to use his talents to ensure that political power remained in the hands of the ruling classes.

The period in which the *Commentaries* were composed was a time of increasing hostility against England's ruling elite. A previously less significant commercial and bourgeois segment of society was growing into a powerful economic force as a result of the prosperity of the eighteenth century. As a result of their new economic status, members of this segment of society sought to increase their political power. They distrusted the patrician leadership of Parliament and sought to challenge it by opening up the political system.[10] This threat, noted John Brewer, "was an alarming development for all members of the Parliamentary classes."[11]

Blackstone's reaction to this threat was characteristic of his position as a member of one of the Parliamentary classes. Although his father had been a merchant, his mother's family, the Biggs of Wiltshire, were members of the landed gentry. His education—Charterhouse and Pembroke College, Oxford—was typical of his status. Any further doubt about his position in society is dismissed by his election to Parliament in 1761 as a defender of country interests.[12] These interests feared the possibility that the middle classes might acquire political power. It was their belief that only "men of calm, deliberate reason—the aristocracy of talent, which happened to coincide with the owners of landed property—should govern."[13] Blackstone shared the idea that political power should remain in the hands of those who possessed property.

An early opportunity to express his view came in response to the Oxfordshire election of 1754. Whereas only freeholders had previously held the right to vote, in this election the franchise was extended to copyholders. Blackstone was retained by Sir Charles Mordaunt, M.P., a prominent supporter of country interests, to contest the legality of this extension of suffrage in the courts. Sir Charles grew impatient with the civil suit and, as an alternative, decided to seek the passage of a bill in Parliament to prevent future extensions of the right to vote. At his request, Blackstone published a treatise on the subject, intended to persuade members of Parliament to support the bill.[14] Blackstone stated the basis for his argument:

> every member of the community . . . is entitled to a vote in electing those delegates, to whose charge is committed the disposal of his property, his liberty and his life. And this ought to be allowed him . . . provided it be probable that such a one will give his voice freely, and without influence of any kind. But since that can hardly be expected in persons of indigent fortunes, or such as are under the immediate dominion of others, . . . all popular states have therefore been obliged to establish certain qualifications; whereby some, who are suspected to have no will of their own, are excluded from voting. . . .[15]

The rationale expressed here was so in tune with the views of the country interests and other members of the Parliamentary classes that the House passed the bill within a month.[16] This was, however, only a narrow victory. Blackstone could not ignore the increasing political power of a more radical segment of society which was threatening the ruling elite in more diverse ways.[17]

The future of England would be a time of increasing political and economic tension between the ruling classes and the increasingly powerful middle class. As a member of the elite, Blackstone feared this development, but unlike other members of the Parliamentary classes, he foresaw the need to develop a tool, in addition to Parliamentary action, that could be used to maintain the status quo.

The ultimate tool for Blackstone was the law, and the *Commentaries* became his principal forum for teaching the elite of England how they should use the law to safeguard their positions. The *Commentaries* were intended for the use of the elite of English society—" our gentlemen of independent estates and fortune, the most useful as well as considerable body of men in the nation."[18] It was not his aim to make all these people practicing lawyers. Rather, by educating these men in at least "a few leading principles" of law, he sought to protect them from "inferior agents" and "gross and notorious imposition."[19] Blackstone's aim was to give the non-lawyer ruling classes of England sufficient legal training to protect their economic and political power base—their possession of property.

The legal cornerstone of the *Commentaries* is the supremacy of the right to property. Blackstone stated: "So great moreover is the regard of the law for private property, that it will not authorise the least violation of it; no, not even for the general good of the whole community."[20] By establishing the right to property as the supreme right protected by the law, he developed a means by which powers based upon property could not be infringed. Among these powers were all major political rights—the right to vote, to stand for Parliament and to serve on juries. Blackstone's rationale for this, which relied on traditional seventeenth-century doctrine, was that people who lack property can too easily be bought and thus "have no will of their own."[21] Hence Blackstone employed a near perfect means by which the elite could fend off political encroachment from the middle class. The elite faced two challenges—to limit the franchise to freehold property holders and to maintain their freehold property interests. So long as they succeeded, their political survival was ensured. Blackstone's gift to his elite brethren was to show them how the law could be used to accomplish this end.

His problem was how to transform the law, which had always been a difficult discipline to study, into a subject that educated non-lawyers could easily learn. Blackstone's interest in addressing this problem is explained in his preface to *An Analysis of the Laws of England*,[22] which according to Professor John M. Finnis was intended to be "an exact outline or abstract" of the *Commentaries*."[23] Blackstone wrote that his goal in the *Commentaries* was:

> to mark out a plan of the laws of England, so comprehensive as that every title might be reduced under some or other of its general heads, which the student might afterwards pursue to any degree of minuteness; and at the same time so contracted, that the gentleman might with tolerable application contemplate and understand the whole.[24]

Blackstone sought to make the *Commentaries* into a textbook for instruction and into a treatise for reference.

Blackstone's method on undertaking this task was modeled on that of Jean Jacques Burlamaqui in his *The Principles of Natural and Political Law*.[25] Burlamaqui emphasized the importance of uncovering the fundamental principles that lay beneath the legal system and then categorizing the law in accordance with those principles.

Blackstone modified this approach by presenting the law as deserving unquestioning aesthetic reverence. He was concerned that people would come to feel that anyone might understand all the criteria of law and would conclude that law could be tested by the standards of human reason. Daniel Boorstin explained:

> A sublime and incomprehensible natural grandeur was found in the disorder, complexity, and even in the obscurity of the law. Man was discouraged from any attempt to improve the law because the English system contained latent, undiscoverable perfections which he might unwittingly destroy. The aesthetic appeal of the laws of England, although to some extent rationally explained in the *Commentaries*, itself seemed a cause for limiting the scope of man's destructive reason.[26]

For example, in Blackstone's explanation of fundamental principles, he always emphasized the close relationship of English laws to the laws of nature, suggesting that English law had the aesthetic virtues of nature.[27]

Blackstone utilized this approach in his description of property law. He began by stating that man's right to possess property originated in *Genesis*, where God gave to man "dominion over all the earth."[28] Pursuant to this, an individual in the state of nature acquired a right to property as long as he used it (e.g., a man resting in the shade of a tree had the right not to be ejected from that spot). "But when mankind increased in number, craft, and ambition," wrote Blackstone, "it became necessary to entertain conceptions of more permanent dominion. . . ."[29] After explaining the development of this need by rendering a detailed legal history of the feudal system, he then proceeded to present eighteenth-century property law categorized according to the various forms of ownership of property (e.g., freehold, joint-tenancy) and according to how an individual obtained legal title to property (e.g., purchase, occupancy). The end result was to transform English property law, which had been long presented as a hodge-podge of details and procedures, into an elegant science through systematization based on principles.

Blackstone applied this technique to all aspects of the English legal system and through his *Commentaries* used it to present the law in a manner that could be easily understood and referred to, while placing laws out of the reach of destructive reasoning. Although the *Commentaries* had been designed to benefit the landed interests, their easily accessible presentation of the law was well suited to the American situation. But just as this intellectual invasion was gaining momentum, the American legal profession was faced with a dilemma.

The American Revolution was viewed by the colonists, in part, as a struggle to regain lost English legal rights. Yet years of war against perceived unreasonable Parliamentary action caused people to question the desirability of adopting the English legal system. The focal point for this dilemma among legal educators was Blackstone's *Commentaries*, which threatened to entrench the English legal tradition, without qualification, into the new United States. Some lauded Blackstone's simplified method of presentation and clear organization. Others welcomed the scholarly contribution of the *Commentaries* while expressing concern about its aristocratically biased legal philosophy. And yet others were so fearful of the unchecked adoption of Blackstone's anti-republican presentation of the English legal system that they sought to prevent the *Commentaries* from influencing American law. Battle lines in this debate were drawn along political party lines.

Staunch Federalists, most notably Tapping Reeve and Peter Van Schaack, embraced Blackstone's work.[30] No doubt they found a need technically to modify points of law that were out of step with American decisions. They did not regard Blackstone's bias particularly bothersome, however, nor did they find a need to object to American law students' ferocious appetites for the *Commentaries*.

Moderate Federalists, such as James Wilson and Zephaniah Swift, however, exhibited reservations about the text. Wilson cautioned readers:

> As I have mentioned Sir William Blackstone, let me speak of him explicitly as it becomes me. I cannot consider him a zealous friend of republicanism. One of his survivors or successors in office, has characterized him by the appellation of an anti-republican lawyer. On the subject of government, I think I can plainly discover his jealousies and attachments. . . . As author of the *Commentaries* he possesses uncommon merit. . . . In public law, however, he should be consulted with a cautious prudence. . . . On every account, therefore, he should be read and studied. He deserves to be much admired; but he ought not to be implicitly followed.[31]

Although Wilson was troubled by Blackstone's anti-republican leanings, he still found much about it to admire and recommend—in particular, its exposition of the law as it applied to English conditions, much of which was still applicable to American conditions.

Swift's hesitation about the *Commentaries* was evident in his *A System of the Laws of the State of Connecticut*,[32] which flattered Blackstone by applying his method and organization to American law while purposefully excluding his anti-republican bias. Indeed, unlike Blackstone, who geared his writings to the elite of English society, Swift dedicated his work to "a more general diffusion of knowledge among all classes of people."[33] He intended this work to replace the *Commentaries* within Connecticut.

These moderate Federalists were sufficiently concerned about the *Commentaries* to take modest actions to prevent its unquestioned influence on American law. A group of Republican lawyers, however, believed that much more drastic action was required. Republican lawyers, such as St. George Tucker and Thomas Jefferson, spearheaded a campaign to drastically limit Blackstone's influence in America. They advocated the exclusion of the text from American legal education because they thought the presentation too superficial and the substantive bias too pervasive. Tucker complained:

> the student who had read the *Commentaries* . . . was lead [sic] to believe that he was a thorough proficient in the law. . . . This sudden revolution in the course of study may be considered as having produced effects almost as pernicious as the want of a regular and systematic guide, since it cannot be doubted that it has contributed to usher into the profession a great number, whose superficial knowledge of the law has been almost as soon forgotten, as acquired.[34]

Jefferson wrote to Horatio G. Spafford, "I join in your reprobation of our . . . lawyers for their adherence to England and monarchy, in preference to their own country and its constitution. . . . I ascribe much of this to the substitution of Blackstone for my Lord Coke, as an elementary work."[35] As the Republicans read it, the *Commentaries* were not suited to the education of the first generation of American lawyers.

The task of preventing the use of Blackstone proved most difficult. Tucker's concern could be dealt with by supplementing the *Commentaries* with additional reading or forms of instruction. Jefferson's concern could be too easily dismissed by Federalists as being based upon partisan politics. In their search for alternative means of discounting Blackstonian influence, Republicans found a champion in Charles-Louis de Secondat, Baron de la Brède et de Montesquieu.

Montesquieu's *De L'Esprit des Lois* [*The Spirit of Laws*][36] was implanted into the American legal tradition during the period between 1760 and 1802. Paul Merrill Spurlin has noted that in colonial newspapers between 1760 and 1776, "in actual inches quoted, when sources were named, Montesquieu surpassed Locke and compared favourably with Blackstone."[37] Between 1762 and 1797, a steady flow of foreign editions of *The Spirit of Laws* entered America, as is indicated by numerous American newspaper advertisements offering their sale.[38] Many of the educational leaders of the post-Revolutionary American Bar obtained copies of the text during this period.[39] More importantly, the work had so great an impact on these leaders that they recommended it as required reading to law students.[40] By the time the first American edition of *The Spirit of Laws* was published in 1802, Montesquieu had become a leading authority for American jurisprudence.[41]

Although *The Spirit of Laws* was most widely read for its pronouncements on the structure of government, lawyers also found in it much insight into the issues of legal education. Montesquieu's particular contribution concerned how much of the English legal tradition should be relied upon in creating the American legal system. By setting out to discover the fundamental principles on which the law was based, Montesquieu argued that the law is inherently tied to the physical environments from which it arises. Since the physical environment of America was different from that of England, Montesquieu was employed to argue that English law must first be Americanized, where necessary, before it could be adopted into American law.

Montesquieu began his inquiry, as did Blackstone, by showing that laws are based upon fundamental principles: "I have laid down the first principles, and have found that the particular cases follow naturally from them; that the histories of all nations are only consequences of them; and that every particular law is connected with another law, or depends on some other of a more general extent."[42] But whereas Blackstone delved into legal principles in order to argue the supremacy of property rights and in order to systematize the law so that it could be more easily taught, Montesquieu resorted to first principles as a means for discovering the character of society.

Montesquieu called this the "general spirit of mankind." He described it as being a societal soul which is formed by the influences of climate, religion, laws, government, precedents, morals and customs. The variation of these influences from society to society results in each having a unique soul. The unique soul in turn permeates a society's institutions and affects their interactions. An understanding of this, according to Montesquieu, is essential to any societal leader since the introduction of a change in one institution must be consistent with the societal soul and may affect other institutions.[43]

The importance of this philosophy to the question of the acceptance of foreign laws into a society was explained by Montesquieu as he described the role of positive laws:

> They should be adapted in such a manner to the people for whom they are made, as to render it very unlikely for those of one nation to be proper for another.
>
> They should be relative to the nature and principle of the actual, or intended government; whether they form this principle, as in the case of political laws, or whether they support it, as may be said of civil institutions.
>
> They should be relative to the climate, whether hot or cold, of each country, to the quality of the soil, to its situation and bigness, to the manner of living of the natives, whether husbandmen, huntsmen, or shepherds; they should have a relation to the degree of liberty which the constitution will bear; to the religion of the inhabitants, to their inclinations, riches, number, commerce, manners, and customs. In fine they have relations amongst themselves, as also with their origin, with the object of the legislator, and with the order of things on which they are established, in all with different lights they ought to be considered.[44]

Montesquieu argued here that the requirements of nature are different in every society. Since laws must be made in conformity to the requirements of nature, laws can only be made to apply to a given society. While there is an obvious tension between Montesquieu's relativism and the notion of inalienable rights, they were not mutually exclusive. Inalienable rights were universal rights that political institutions were designed to secure, while laws were the instruments these institutions used to accomplish this end. Laws could vary from country to country, depending on local circumstances, and still maintain the goal of securing the same unalienable right. For example, two countries could recognize the right not to be discriminated against on the basis of race. One country, with a multiracial population and a history of discrimination, may consider it necessary to establish affirmative action laws, whereas another country, with a racially homogeneous population and no history of discrimination, faced with an immigration of members of another race, might consider it sufficient to establish a law that prohibits racial discrimination without establishing a system of quotas. Both the concepts of relativism and inalienable rights exist without conflict.

By introducing Montesquieu's philosophy into the debate over the unqualified acceptance of the *Commentaries* into American law, opponents of Blackstone found an ally to help temper the influence of English law. According to Gilbert Chinard, Thomas Jefferson was one of the first American lawyers to espouse Montesquieu's views:

> Everywhere in the Spirit of Laws, he found illustrations of the theory which he maintained all his life that laws and constitutions are variable and changing and must be altered in accordance with climate, local conditions, and new circumstances. He even went one step further than Montesquieu in his relativism, when he proclaimed that a generation had no right to bind by laws the following generation.[45]

Jefferson relied on this philosophy in revising the laws of the state of Virginia.

Between 1776 and 1780, Jefferson played a key role in introducing a series of legal reforms to the Virginia legislature designed to prevent English law as presented by Blackstone from establishing itself in Virginian jurisprudence. As the leading member of the Committee of Revisors Appointed by the General Assembly of Virginia, he was largely responsible for introducing one hundred and twenty-six bills which served to revise the common law, criminal law, the law of descents, laws concerning religious freedom, laws concerning public education, the statute laws of Virginia and English statutes. Within ten years, due to the additional efforts of James Madison, almost all these bills were enacted into law. Jefferson had succeeded in politically limiting the influence of the *Commentaries* on Virginia law.[46]

St. George Tucker, however, was still apprehensive about Blackstone's influence. Tucker's concerns were threefold: (1) in spite of the revision of the laws of Virginia, most lawyers and judges would still rely on the *Commentaries* because they lacked access to the revised laws;[47] (2) the anti-republican influence of Blackstone still threatened other states and the federal government; and (3) law students would be seduced by the *Commentaries* before having an opportunity to learn of its faults[48]. By 1790, Tucker realized that Blackstone was too firmly established in America to be effectively banned.[49] He still believed, however, that Blackstone's influence could be curtailed.[50]

Tucker set out via American legal education to limit the *Commentaries* influence on lawyers and the judiciary. He began as Professor of Law and Police at the College of William and Mary in 1790. He assigned *The Spirit of Laws* and quoted extensively from it in his lectures with the aim of using Montesquieu's relativism to justify questioning the applicability of English law, as described by Blackstone, to America.[51] Tucker then utilized the works of European natural law writers (including, in order of the degree of use, Montesquieu, John Locke, Emmerich von Vattel, Jean-Jacques Rousseau, Matthew Bacon, Thomas Paine, Francis Hutcheson, Jean-Jacques Burlamaqui, James Burgh, Baron Samuel von Pufendorf and Hugo Grotius) to show that reason should be the ultimate test in determining the soundness of the law and its application. As the decade progressed, Tucker sought to reach a wider audience through the publication of his own edition of the *Commentaries*, which offered a step-by-step guide to Blackstone's limitations.

St. George Tucker's edition of the *Commentaries* was designed primarily to show where and why Blackstone's presentation of English law was not properly suited to American society. He wrote: "as the common law is a collection of general customs, it may not be amiss to inquire whether particular customs have any, or what force, among us."[52] He achieved this by adding footnotes to the text where laws and legal concepts did not apply to America, directing the reader to an editor's appendix which included a series of essays. These essays can be grouped into three parts: those which concern dispelling Blackstone's anti-republican bias, those which concern the reception of the common law into America and those which concern how English law had been revised by American law or question the soundness and applicability to the United States of English law yet to be revised. In all, Tucker showed, contrary to the teachings of Blackstone, that the law could and should be questioned.

St. George Tucker began his inquiry by disputing Blackstone's anti-republican bias. This bias, according to Tucker, was rooted in the proposition that sovereign power resides wherever laws are made.[53] In England, this meant that sovereignty lay with Parliament and that the only people who should have access to that power were members of the Parliamentary classes.[54] Against this view, Tucker argued that sovereignty should lie with the people. Relying on Rousseau and James Burgh, he wrote that the right of making laws can be acquired only by the consent of the people.[55] This consent is given when people enter into written compacts designed, citing Thomas Paine, to authorize government to enact and enforce only specific types of laws.[56]

In the United States, these written compacts initially took the form of state constitutions. Later the states agreed to relinquish some of their authority to a federal government. The federal constitution which ensued was a written compact between the states and the federal government authorized by the people. Hence, the people granted limited powers to the states, which the states in turn, with the consent of the people, divided with the federal government. The people were the ultimate power granting authority. But according to Tucker, the power to grant authority to govern is only part of sovereign power.[57]

Sovereign power also requires the ability to make sure that government does not overstep its authority. In the United States, this power was retained by the people and by the states as representatives of the people. Tucker declared:

> But to guard against encroachments on the powers of the several states, in their politic character, and of the people, both in their individual and sovereign capacity, an amendatory article was added, immediately after the government was organised, declaring; that the powers not delegated to the United States, by the constitution, nor prohibited by it to the states, are reserved to the states, respectively, or to the people. And, still further, to guard the people against constructive usurpations and encroachments on their rights, another article declares; that the enumeration of certain rights in the constitution, shall not be construed to deny, or disparage, others retained by the people. The sum of all which appears to be, that the powers delegated to the federal government, are, in all cases, to receive the most strict construction that the instrument will bear, where the rights of a state or of the people, either collectively, or individually, may be drawn in question.[58]

These amendments were not, in Tucker's view, the only means for ensuring that powers retained by the people and the states were not usurped by the federal government. Tucker wrote:

> If it be asked, what would be the consequence in case the federal government should exercise powers not warranted by the constitution, the answer seems to be, that where the act of usurpation may immediately affect an individual, the remedy is to be sought by recourse to that judiciary, to which the cognisance of the case properly belongs. Where it may affect a state, the state legislature, whose rights will be invaded by every such act, will be ready to mark the innovation and sound the alarm to the people: and thereby either effect a change in the federal representation, or procure in the mode prescribed by the constitution, further "declaratory and restrictive clauses," by way of amendment thereto.[59]

If the government should ever grossly abuse its power, Tucker argued, referring to Francis Hutcheson and quoting from the Declaration of Independence, the people would be freed from the obligations of their compact and could insist upon a new form of government.[60] In this way, governments depend "upon the nature and extent of those powers which the people have reserved to themselves, as the Sovereign; or rather, upon the extent of those, which they have delegated to the government; or, which the government in the course of its administration may have usurped."[61] Thus, sovereignty does not rest with those who make laws; it rests with those who authorize government to make laws and who can limit and even retract governmental power—the people.

Having both highlighted and dispelled Blackstone's anti-republican bias, Tucker turned his attention to the reception of English law in America. Blackstone wrote of this issue noting that colonies are of two types: those deserted and uncultivated claimed by right of occupancy, and those peopled and cultivated claimed by conquest or ceded by treaty. English people who colonized by right of occupancy took with them aspects of the English law which were suited to their new situations. In conquered or ceded territories with prior laws of their own, the law at the time of acquisition remained in effect until changed by the king. Blackstone ascribed America to this latter group stating that it was obtained either by conquest or by treaties. Thus, he argued that Americans had no right to claim the common law and were instead subject to the laws previously in existence and to the control of Parliament.[62]

Tucker contested this, claiming that the British who colonized America brought with them the rights and privileges of Englishmen. He noted, citing Pufendorf and Grotius, that a justly conquered or ceded nation must submit to the government of the conquerors or of those to whom they have been ceded.[63] Moreover, he wrote, quoting Grotius, that "when a people, by one consent, go to form colonies, it is the original of a new and independent people; for they are not sent out to be slaves, but to enjoy equal privileges and freedom."[64] The British who settled America conquered it, with the exception of New York and New Jersey which were ceded to England by the Treaty of Breda in 1667, and brought with them that portion of English law which they considered necessary to maintain their rights.

The colonists, finding themselves in a new country, remote from England, needed municipal laws and the right to adapt them to their circumstances. "The municipal laws of the parent state," wrote Tucker, "being better known to them, than those of any other nation, a recurrence to them would naturally be had, for the decisions of all questions of right and wrong, which should arise among them, until leisure and experience should enable them to make laws better adapted to their own peculiar situation."[65] He argued that only the colonists could have judged the applicability of English law to local circumstances and cited the Crown's granting to the colonies of legislatures of their own as proof.

Colonial legislatures took immediate action, according to Tucker, to modify the common law to fit their own domestic concerns. Massachusetts changed inheritance laws that had favored the eldest son so that they distributed the estate to all the immediate family. Rhode Island and Pennsylvania adopted laws that fostered religious freedom. In Virginia, laws were passed for relief of creditors against fraudulent devises. By the eve of the American Revolution, Tucker argued, each colony had developed its own body of laws.[66]

Tucker thus turned his attention to the effect of the Revolution on the reception of English law. He argued that the common and statutory laws of England, founded on monarchical government and inconsistent with democratic principles, were annulled in each state by the establishment of democratic governments. In addition, all other parts of English law that had not been brought into use by colonial governments were made obsolete and incapable of revival except by constitutional or legislative authority. On the other hand, all laws in use prior to the Revolution, not falling into the above categories, even if they were repugnant to the common law, were unquestionably established. State constitutions, noted Tucker, confirmed the existence and authority of the common law and statutes in use at the time of their ratification and also authorized future changes by state legislatures.[67]

In describing the impact of the Revolution on English law, Tucker pointed out that the impact was manifested differently from state to state. He noted that when the American states declared themselves independent of the crown, each state from that moment became sovereign and independent of Great Britain and all other powers. Each state had its own constitution and laws; there was no common law amongst them, only the law of nations. He wrote:

> From hence it follows, that the adoption of the common law, or statutes of England, in one state, or in several, or even in all, although it might produce a general conformity, in their municipal codes, yet as such adoption was the separate act of each state, it could not operate so as to give to those laws a sanction superior to any other laws of the states, respectively; inasmuch as each state would still have retained the power of changing, or rejecting them, whenever it should think proper.[68]

Thus Tucker argued that as a result of the Revolution, there was no such thing as a national common or municipal law.

The remaining issue Tucker addressed was the effect the United States Constitution had on the reception of English law in America. Tucker began by pointing out that in establishing the federal government, the intention was, as confirmed by the Tenth Amendment, to give it only limited powers. He explained, referring to Vattel, that the Tenth Amendment is nothing more than "an express recognition of the law of nations" which permits independent states to unite in a confederacy. Although the states may voluntarily permit the federal republic to exercise some of their sovereign powers, they will still retain their independent sovereignty.[69] In addition, he argued, quoting Matthew Bacon, that the powers given to the federal government, in order to be consistent with maintaining independent state sovereignty, must be strictly interpreted.[70]

Tucker then examined all the "enumerated" powers in the Constitution and concluded that there was no grant of general jurisdiction to either federal or state courts in cases at common law. Nevertheless, he discussed the claim that this jurisdiction might have been granted by implication. He presented five arguments in opposition to this view. First, the Tenth Amendment bars such a construction. Second, it would be absurd to grant to the federal government power to revive parts of English law that state constitutions had rejected. Third, such a construction abridging the rights of sovereign states by implication could be used as precedent to virtually annihilate the states. Fourth, numerous provisions of state constitutions which mandated changes in the common law and which authorized legislatures to modify the law would be nullified. Fifth, references to the common law, to common law rights, or to common law courts in the United

States Constitution refer to the laws of the several states rather than the laws of the federal government. Tucker argued that federal courts could assume jurisdiction only over cases where jurisdiction was expressly granted by the Constitution.[71]

In all, Tucker concluded that the only English laws validly received into America originated from the period before the Revolution—a period during which Blackstone's *Commentaries* had had little impact. As Tucker portrayed events, the only influence Blackstone's work was entitled to in post-Revolutionary America was to explain that portion of the common law in use prior to the American Revolution which had not been modified or nullified by the Revolution, by state constitutions or by state legislative action. Tucker was, in effect, cautioning his readers not to view the *Commentaries* as a statement of American common law, for this would have given to Blackstone the power of modifying American common law—a power reserved to state legislatures and courts by state constitutions. What remained for Tucker to explain was which aspects of English law, as portrayed by Blackstone, had been changed in America or required revision because of their questionable soundness and applicability to the United States.

Tucker discussed many examples of laws that had undergone, or would undergo, such revisions. For example, he examined the law of expatriation, which was in need of new interpretation in order to allow Americans to free themselves from allegiance to the Crown. Pursuing his political objections to Blackstone's elitism based on property ownership, he also devoted a substantial portion of his discussion to American property law.

The right of expatriation was central to Americans' claims of independence. If it did not exist, the majority of the population of America could not claim United States citizenship. Blackstone opposed the right of expatriation, noting that "it is a principle of universal law, that the natural born subject of one prince cannot by any act of his own, no, not by swearing allegiance to another, put off, or discharge his natural allegiance to the former."[72]

Tucker countered this position on the grounds that there was nothing in divine law, natural law, or the law of nations to support Blackstone's statement. He showed that expatriation was not prohibited by divine law, noting that the Old Testament records that the Israelites were expatriated from Egypt by the hand of Jehovah himself. He argued that the law of nature did not prohibit expatriation, since in nature all men were equal and thus not subject to the control of princes. And he deferred to the conclusions of Vattel, Grotius, Burlamaqui and Pufendorf, noting that the law of nations prescribed that "every man hath a natural right to migrate from one state to another."[73] In spite of all this, however, Tucker still found the need to refer to the philosophical writings of John Locke in order to show that reason alone could disprove Blackstone's claim.[74]

Locke argued, according to Tucker, that those who believed expatriation to be illegal based it on the notion that a father who swore allegiance to a prince bound his posterity as well through the inheritance of his property. This notion was considered unsound "for his son, when a man, being altogether as free as the father, any act of the father can no more give away the liberty of the son, than it can of any body else."[75] The son, upon coming of age, would be free to give up his father's property and thus free to emigrate. Tucker implied that all the arguments above were the basis for a Virginia act, and for Pennsylvania and Vermont constitutional declarations, that confirmed an individual's right to emigrate.[76]

Tucker reserved his greatest attention for property law. "The almost total change in the system of laws relative to property, both real and personal, in Virginia," wrote Tucker, "appeared more particularly to demand a strict scrutiny, and investigation."[77] His treatment of the law of descents and the modes of acquiring unoccupied or waste and unappropriated lands are representative. Of all the areas of property law, Blackstone said that "the doctrine of descents, or law of inheritances in fee-simple [*sic*], is a point of the highest importance; and is indeed the principal object of the laws of real property in England."[78] It was deserving of this position because it virtually ensured the elite's right to property and to the political power linked to property ownership.

After the Revolution, however, the law was changed in America to make it more compatible with democratic ideals. One of the first steps taken in Virginia was the passage of an act declaring that the tenants of real property by estate in tail would thereafter hold the same in fee simple, thus giving them the right and freedom to sell or transfer their land. In 1785, the Virginia legislature rewrote the whole body of the law of descents.[79]

Tucker described these changes, showing step-by-step how the new rules were directly contrary to the common law as expressed by Blackstone. Under the new law, land could only be inherited in fee simple, whereas the common law had allowed land to be offered for inheritance with numerous restrictions. The estate of a person who died intestate, which had been guaranteed to the eldest son (not including bastards) according to the common law, would go to all his children equally—including bastards. Where two equal claimants to an estate existed, the common law would give any real property to both in joint-tenancy, thus preserving the whole of the land for future generations. Virginia statute mandated that such property be transferred as tenancy in common, thus permitting either recipient to sell or transfer his share. Where the common law had permitted property to be held until a beneficiary was born, Virginia required that the beneficiary should already be alive. In all, Tucker showed that the new statute had made Blackstone's essay on descents useless in Virginia.[80]

The mode of acquiring unoccupied or waste and unappropriated lands was of little importance to Blackstone. England had no waste and unappropriated lands, and, according to the *Commentaries*, title by occupancy was "confined by the laws of England within a very narrow compass; and was extended only to a single instance."[81] In a country as vast and undeveloped as the United States, laws favoring occupancy and development of waste and unappropriated lands were desirable.

Tucker explained that, prior to the Revolution, waste and undeveloped lands could only be acquired by royal grant, by vote of the General Assembly or by grant of the Governor. But, in 1779, the Virginia legislature passed an Act that completely revamped the mode of acquiring these lands. This Act did more than just modify English law; it introduced into Virginia entirely new laws exclusively suited to the needs of a frontier society. It instituted the notion of adverse possession—a method of acquisition of title to real property by mere possession for a statutory period under certain conditions. It permitted any person to acquire title to any amount of waste and unappropriated lands desired (excluding certain areas), by paying two dollars to the commonwealth. It also authorized any person to acquire title to land forfeited or escheated to the state, by paying 25 pounds per hundred acres. Pursuant to this Act, any citizen of Virginia could obtain fee simple title to land, which would not have been possible in Blackstone's England.[82]

Tucker had demonstrated that considerable caution was required in the use of Blackstone's *Commentaries* as a reference by American lawyers. His treatise served to highlight and clarify the anti-republican bias of the *Commentaries*. He also demonstrated that, although Blackstone might be of use as a reference for the application of the common law as it existed prior to the Revolution, the *Commentaries* not only did not cover aspects of the new and developing American laws, but indeed often opposed the very foundations of such laws.

As American politics shifted at the beginning of the nineteenth century, the American Bar grew to appreciate Tucker's concerns about Blackstone. Tucker had sought the publication of his work as early as 1794, but until 1801 the Philadelphia publishing community did not perceive sufficient demand to merit publication. During this six-year period, James Wilson and Zephaniah Swift had been sent copies of Tucker's manuscript. They were won over by the work, and strongly encouraged its publication. When St. George Tucker's *Blackstone's Commentaries: with Notes of Reference, to the Constitution and Laws, of the Federal Government of the United States; and of the Commonwealth of Virginia* was finally published in Philadelphia by William Young Birch and Abraham Small in 1803, it was an instant success.[83]

While detailed sales records for Tucker's *Blackstone* have not survived, communications between Tucker and his publisher provide some insight into the number of books sold. On 7 April 1802, Abraham Small wrote to Tucker, stating that his firm planned three printings of the work in the amounts of 2,500, 1,500 and 1,000 copies, respectively.[84] According to the terms of the publication agreement, Birch and Small would pay royalties at the rate of $2.50 per copy up to 1,000 copies or $4,000 for the entire copyright.[85] By 22 February 1803, two and a half months prior to publication, the number of subscribers was so great that Birch and Small decided to pay Tucker $4,000 for the right to publish all 5,000 copies of the work.[86] It appears that all copies of the first edition were sold, for on 13 February 1818, Small wrote to tell Tucker of his intention to publish a second edition.[87] To put these numbers in perspective, the first American printing of

Blackstone's *Commentaries* in 1771 had sales of 849 copies and it has been estimated that there were 2500 copies of the *Commentaries* in use in the colonies by 1776.[88]

St. George Tucker's work became the definitive edition of Blackstone available in America until 1852, when John L. Wendell published his edition. Charles T. Cullen noted:

> Until the introduction of the case method of teaching law in the late nineteenth century commentaries and treatises were actually the only texts or references students and lawyers had for studying American law, and St. George Tucker's Blackstone was the only summary of similar dimensions available until Chancellor James Kent of New York began publishing his *Commentaries on American Law* in 1826.[89]

Elizabeth Bauer found that Tucker's *Blackstone's Commentaries* acquired popularity with the United States Supreme Court.[90] In addition, Alfred Z. Reed claimed that Tucker's work "fixed the Blackstone Tradition in this country."[91] Unfortunately, Reed had not realized that Tucker had fixed a severely limited and altered Blackstone tradition in America.

Tucker's greatest influence on this tradition was to bring the law down from the high altar on which it had been placed by Blackstone. He used Montesquieu's relativism to establish the appropriateness of questioning the law, and the works of European natural law writers to show that reason should be the law's ultimate test. He described the state and federal constitutions as the people's primary means of redacting reason into a defence against unreasonable laws and the unreasonable application of laws. In all, Tucker introduced a method of viewing the law which, presented in a work that became the standard text for a generation of lawyers, separated American legal thought from Blackstone and the English legal system.

NOTES

1. William Blackstone, *Commentaries on the Laws of England* (Oxford: The Clarendon Press, 1765).
2. Daniel J. Boorstin, *The Mysterious Science of the Law* (Cambridge: Harvard University Press, 1941), p. 3. See also: Daniel J. Boorstin, *The Americans: The Colonial Experience* (New York: Vintage Books, 1958), p. 202.
3. Dennis R. Nolan, *Sir William Blackstone and the New American Republic: A Study of Intellectual Impact*, 51 N.Y.U. L. REV. 731 (1976).
4. Quoted in Peggy A. Rabkin, *Fathers to Daughters: The Legal Foundations of Female Emancipation* (Westport, CT: Greenwood Press, 1980), p. 66.
5. St. George Tucker, *Blackstone's Commentaries: with Notes of Reference, to the Constitution and Laws, of the Federal Government of the United States; and of the Commonwealth of Virginia*, 5 vols. (Philadelphia: William Young Birch and Abraham Small, 1803).

6. James Bradley Thayer, *The Teaching of English Law at Universities*, 9 HARV. L. REV. 169, 170 (1895); Sir William Blackstone, *Commentaries on the Laws of England*, 4 vols. (Philadelphia: Robert Bell, 1771–1772), 4: "Names of the Subscribers."

7. William Blackstone, *Commentaries on the Laws of England*, 4 vols. (1765; reprinted Chicago: The University of Chicago Press, 1979), 1:25.

8. Ibid., p. 3.

9. Ibid., p. 31; Harry Kirk, *Portrait of a Profession* (London: Oyez Publishing, 1976), p. 48.

10. H.T. Dickinson, *Liberty and Property: Political Ideology in Eighteenth-Century Britain* (London: Methuen & Co., 1977), p. 195.

11. John Brewer, *Party Ideology and Popular Politics at the Accession of George III* (Cambridge: Cambridge University Press, 1981), p. 267.

12. Stanley N. Katz, "Introduction," Blackstone, *Commentaries* (1765; reprinted Chicago: The University of Chicago Press, 1979), 1:iii–iv.

13. Dickinson, *Liberty and Property*, p. 165.

14. R.J. Robson, *The Oxfordshire Election of 1754: a study in the interplay of city, county and university politics* (Oxford: Oxford University Press, 1949), pp. 144–146; Lewis C. Warden, *The Life of Blackstone* (Charlottesville, VA: The Michie Co., 1938), pp. 132–133; William Blackstone, *Considerations on the question, whether tenants . . . are freeholders qualified to vote in elections for knights of the shire* (London: Printed for R. Baldwin, 1763).

15. William Blackstone, *Law Tracts*, 2 vols. (Oxford: The Clarendon Press, 1762), 1:106.

16. Warden, *Life of Blackstone*, pp. 132–133.

17. Dickinson, *Liberty and Property*, p. 195.

18. Blackstone, *Commentaries*, 1:7.

19. Ibid.

20. Ibid., p. 135.

21. Ibid., p. 165.

22. William Blackstone, *An Analysis of the Laws of England*, 6th ed. (Oxford: The Clarendon Press, 1771).

23. John M. Finnis, *Blackstone's Theoretical Intentions*, 12 NAT. L. F. 163, 164 (1967).

24. Blackstone, *An Analysi*, p. iv.

25. Jean Jacques Burlamaqui, *The Principles of Natural and Political Law* (Geneva: Chez Barrillot & Fils, 1747); Paul Lucas, *Ex parte Sir William Blackstone, "Plagiarist": A Note on Blackstone and the Natural Law*, 7 AM. J. LEGAL HIST. 142 (1963).

26. Boorstin, *Mysterious Science*, p. 105.

27. Ibid., pp. 85–105.

28. Blackstone, *Commentaries*, 2:2.

29. Ibid., p. 4.

30. Nolan, "Sir William Blackstone," p. 762.

31. James Wilson, *The Works of the Honourable James Wilson, L.L.D.*, ed. Bird Wilson, 2 vols. (Philadelphia: Lorenzo Press, 1804), 1:21–22.

32. Zephaniah Swift, *A System of the Laws of the State of Connecticut* (Windham, CT: John Byrne, 1795).

33. Swift, *A System of the Law*, 1:4.

34. Tucker, *Blackstone's Commentaries*, 1:iv.

35. Thomas Jefferson, *The Writings of Thomas Jefferson*, ed. H.A. Washington, 9 vols. (Washington, DC: Taylor and Maury, 1853–1854), 6:334, quoted in Julian S. Waterman, *Thomas Jefferson and Blackstone's Commentaries*, 27 ILL. L. REV. 629, at 637 n.49 (1932–1933).

36. Charles-Louis de Secondat, Baron de la Brède et de Montesquieu, *De L'Esprit des Lois* [The Spirit of Laws] (Geneva: Barillot, 1748).

37. Paul Merrill Spurlin, *Montesquieu in America, 1760–1801* (New York: Octagon Books, 1969), p. 157.

38. *Maryland Gazette*, 26 August 1762; *Boston Gazette*, 23 September–7 October 1771 & 29 March–9 August 1784; *General Advertiser* (Philadelphia), 28 June–1 September 1791 & 8 May–18 May 1793; *Aurora General Advertiser* (Philadelphia), 14 August–6 November 1797.

39. Paul Merrill Spurlin, *The French Enlightenment in America* (Athens: The University of Georgia Press, 1984), pp. 88–89; Albert J. Harno, *Legal Education in the United States* (1953; reprinted Westport, CT: Greenwood Press, 1980), p. 22. Specific references to key individuals are as follows: James Wilson—Francois Jean de Chastellux, *Voyages de M. le Marquis de Chastellux dans l'Amerique septentrionale dans les annees 1780, 1781, & 1782*, 2 vols. (Paris: Prault, 1786), I:185–186; Peter Van Schaack—Peter Van Schaack to Henry Walton, 3 June 1788, in Henry C. Van Schaack, *The Life of Peter Van Schaack, LL.D.* (New York: D. Appleton & Co., 1842), p. 54; James Kent—James Kent, *Commentaries on American Law*, 4 vols. (1826; reprinted New York: Da Capo Press, 1971), 1:1; Thomas Jefferson—Gilbert Chinard, *The Commonplace Book of Thomas Jefferson* (Baltimore, MD: The Johns Hopkins Press, 1926); St. George Tucker—Tucker, *Blackstone's Commentaries*, 1: Editor's Appendix, p. 43.

40. Spurlin, *Montesquieu*, p. 259; Simon E. Baldwin, *The Study of Elementary Law, The Proper Beginning of a Legal Education*, 13 YALE L. J. No. 1 (1903).

41. Montesquieu, *The Spirit of Laws*, trans. by Thomas Nugent, 5th ed. (1773; reprinted Worcester, MA: Isaiah Thomas, Jr., 1802).

42. Montesquieu, *The Spirit of Laws*, trans. by Thomas Nugent, ed. by David Wallace Carrithers (1750; reprinted Berkeley: University of California Press, 1977), p. 91.

43. Ibid., pp. 289–297.

44. Ibid., pp. 104–105.

45. Chinard, *Commonplace Book*, p. 38.

46. Dumas Malone, *Jefferson the Virginian* (Boston, MA: Little, Brown and Company, 1948), pp. 261–263.

47. Tucker, *Blackstone's Commentaries*, 1:xii.

48. Ibid., p. iv.

49. Ibid., p. v.

50. Ibid., p. xviii.

51. Charles T. Cullen, *St. George Tucker and Law in Virginia 1772–1804* (New York: Garland Publishing, 1987), pp. 145, 205.

52. Tucker, *Blackstone's Commentaries*, 1:ix.

53. Ibid., p. 48.

54. Dickinson, *Liberty and Property*, p. 165; Blackstone, *Law Tracts*, 1:106.

55. Tucker, *Blackstone's Commentaries*, 1: Editor's Appendix, pp. 8, 9.
56. Ibid., 1: Editor's Appendix, p. 9.
57. Ibid., 1: Editor's Appendix, pp. 142–146.
58. Ibid., 1: Editor's Appendix, p. 154.
59. Ibid., 1: Editor's Appendix, p. 153.
60. Ibid., 1: Editor's Appendix, pp. 12, 13.
61. Ibid., 1: Editor's Appendix, p. 14.
62. Ibid., 1: Editor's Appendix, pp. 107–108.
63. Ibid., p. 382.
64. Ibid., p. 383.
65. Ibid., p. 384.
66. Ibid., pp. 384–405.
67. Ibid., pp. 405–411.
68. Ibid., pp. 406–407.
69. Ibid., p. 412.
70. Ibid., p. 413.
71. Ibid., pp. 412–433.
72. Tucker, *Blackstone's Commentaries*, 2:369.
73. Ibid., 2: Editor's Appendix, p. 93.
74. Ibid., pp. 90–93.
75. Ibid., p. 94.
76. Ibid., pp. 94, 96.
77. Tucker, *Blackstone's Commentaries*, 1:x.
78. Tucker, *Blackstone's Commentaries*, 3:201.
79. Ibid., 3: Editor's Appendix, pp. 11, 12; "An Act directing the Course of Descents," 1785 Va. Acts c. 60.
80. Tucker, *Blackstone's Commentaries*, 3: Editor's Appendix, pp. 12–52.
81. Ibid., 3:258.
82. Ibid., 3: Editor's Appendix, pp. 3–10.
83. William Tatham to St. George Tucker, 17 January 1795 & 30 January 1795, Zephaniah Swift to St. George Tucker, 1 June 1796. Tucker-Coleman Collection, Earl Gregg Swem Library, College of William and Mary, Williamsburg, VA.
84. Abraham Small to St. George Tucker, 7 April 1802. Ibid.
85. St. George Tucker to Birch and Small, 21 August 1802. Ibid.
86. Receipt and Note from Birch and Small to St. George Tucker, 22 February 1803, Ibid.
87. Abraham Small to St. George Tucker, 13 February 1818. Ibid.
88. "Names of the Subscribers," in Sir William Blackstone, *Commentaries on the Laws of England*, 4 vols. (Philadelphia: Robert Bell, 1771–1772); Waterman, *Jefferson and Blackstone*, 27 Ill. L. Rev. 629, 630 (1933).
89. Cullen, *St. George Tucker*, p. 162.
90. Elizabeth Bauer, *Commentaries on the Constitution, 1790–1860*, Studies in History, Economics and Public Law, No. 575 (New York: Columbia University Press, 1952), p. 346.
91. Alfred Z. Reed, *Training for the Public Profession of the Law* (1921; reprinted New York: Arno Press, 1976), p. 117.

3

Analytical Law Treatises and the Advent of American Legal Methodology

Between 1794 and 1826, the American Bar produced a number of legal treatises that played an essential role in the development of the American legal system and, in particular, American legal thought. Yet this first generation of legal treatises has been largely ignored by historians. Morton J. Horwitz, for example, contended that the American treatise tradition was "inaugurated" with James Kent's *Commentaries* in 1826. Although he noted "earlier efforts," he dismissed them claiming that they were "designed for the nonpracticing gentleman lawyer."[1] Lawrence M. Friedman acknowledged the existence of these early law books and claimed, contrary to the opinion of Horwitz, that "they were written for the practicing lawyer." Nevertheless, he deemphasized their importance because he believed that the "rigorously practical" focus of these books meant that "systematic legal theory was studiously ignored."[2] Although these early works often lacked the sophistication of later scholarship, they offered the only published analyses of the American legal system, with the exception of a few journal articles, available to the bar during the first fifty years of American independence. Consequently, they deserve greater attention than they have heretofore received.

The contribution made by the first generation of American law treatises was central to the development of a uniquely American legal system. These works were written to educate law students who could not obtain institutional legal instruction, to encourage jurists to define and unify the American legal system and to provide Americans with the general legal knowledge deemed necessary for them to be active citizens of a democracy. The most far-reaching impact achieved by these texts, however, was to introduce to a mass audience a new legal methodology that deemphasized the English and Colonial American practice of strictly adhering to legal precedents in favor of a belief in the greater use of man's reason by questioning legal precedents against the standards of utility, logic, morality and comparative American law and public policy. It was in this manner that American legal treatises contributed to the establishment of a distinctly American legal thought.

American legal treatises published during the post-Revolutionary and early National periods took different forms. The most popular works were practical manuals which explained the duties of Justices of the Peace. Other texts were compilations of the law combining reprints of statutes and court opinions. Some publications organized and restated the law and today would be described as legal digests. The most revealing works, however, were analytical law treatises, which combined an orderly presentation and restatement of the law with detailed analysis. These later books, which are most akin to the modern definition of a legal treatise, are the focus here.

American analytical law treatises had an enormous impact on the legal community. They appealed to almost every legal specialist in that they covered a wide variety of legal subjects, including contracts, bankruptcy, patent law, medical jurisprudence, domestic law, equity, property law, civil procedure, expatriation and military law. They were widely available, having been published throughout the United States from Maine to Washington, DC and from Massachusetts to Ohio. Two works were even republished in London. The popularity of analytical legal treatises was so strong that, although specific sales figures are not available, most enjoyed numerous editions and several were simultaneously published in multiple cities.[3]

These treatises were written by the elite of the American bar. Biographical information survives for twenty of the twenty-four authors. Of the twenty, sixteen held prominent legal positions, including United States Supreme Court Justice, Connecticut Supreme Court Chief Justice, Vermont Supreme Court Chief Justice, Ohio Supreme Court Justice, Pennsylvania Supreme Court Justice, Connecticut Supreme Court Justice, Massachusetts Supreme Court Justice, United States District Court (Virginia) Judge, United States District Attorney (Virginia), Pennsylvania Attorney-General, Massachusetts Attorney-General, New York Supreme Court Reporter, United States Supreme Court bar member, College of William and Mary Professor of Law and Police, University of Maryland Professor of Law, Middlebury College Professor of Law, Litchfield Law School Proprietor, Windham Law School Proprietor, New York Law Institute Founder and Law Academy of Philadelphia Founder, with many authors having held several positions. From their posts at the top of the legal profession, they saw the legal treatise as a means of guiding the American judicial system through its troubled adolescent phase.[4]

In the years immediately following the American Revolution, the American legal system faced numerous problems. Tory lawyers, who comprised much of the leadership of the colonial bar, were prevented from practicing because of loyalty oaths, and the best rebel lawyers left their legal practices for positions in the new government. As a result, the American bar was left understaffed and plagued by mediocrity. Differing laws from state-to-state inhibited economic growth. The creation of a new government raised questions about the application of English common law to American circumstances. The authors of analytical legal treatises responded to these problems and, in the process, helped to shape a new, distinctly American legal system.

Most treatise authors saw publication as a means of enticing a large number of students into legal practice and of raising the quality of the profession. Tapping Reeve realized the need to educate the many law students who were unable to attend his proprietary law school and thus dedicated his first treatise to the learner rather than to the jurist.[5] Nathaniel Chipman believed that his treatise would be "useful to students, by exciting them to the due use of their reasoning powers, as well as the power of memory; and by furnishing them with some hints for a proper estimate of precedents, their principles and application."[6] William Wyche, fearful that legal apprentices, having been exposed only to English law books, would be unable to discriminate between English and American legal practice, hoped that his first treatise would be of "considerable utility to students in the Profession."[7] Given that only a small percentage of prospective lawyers were able to obtain institutional legal instruction and that clerkships usually provided inadequate training, analytical legal treatises such as these were the foremost source of legal knowledge available to most American law students between 1794 and 1826.

A second focus of these treatises was to convince practicing attorneys, jurists and legislators of the desirability of defining and uniting the American legal system. Daniel Chipman advocated the adoption of a "settled, uniform, and known system" of the law of contracts for the payment of specific articles as a means of encouraging interstate economic development.[8] Although his idea of a universal law governing commercial transactions was not realized until the Uniform Commercial Code was finally adopted in 1967, his arguments contributed to keeping the state-by-state development of commercial laws within common bounds.[9] Tapping Reeve wrote of the difficulty in dealing with the differing laws of real property in the several states and encouraged the establishment of a general law of descents.[10] John Milton Goodenow argued that the doctrines of English common law pertaining to crimes and punishment should be replaced by statutes because they were too inconsistent to be adopted in America.[11] In response to this and other concerns, all the States enacted legislation to modify common law crimes and punishments along similar lines. The legal systems of the individual states could have developed in widely different ways for, in spite of some limitations placed on state law by the federal constitution, it was within the power of the individual states to develop their laws as they saw fit. By emphasizing the importance of settling and unifying the American legal system, analytical legal treatises helped to keep the development of individual state laws, for the most part, within similar confines.

A third goal of treatise writers was to educate the non-lawyer. Zephaniah Swift believed that general knowledge of the law was necessary to the success of a democracy. He observed that "every citizen in the state, ought to acquire a knowledge of those laws, that govern his daily conduct, and secure the invaluable blessings of life, liberty and property."[12] Samuel Livermore wrote for merchants in the hope that a knowledge of the law of principal and agent would allow them to "avoid litigation and expense."[13] And, Gulian C. Verplanck hoped that his work would "succeed in awakening the public mind to the conviction of the necessity of making our law of Sales and Contracts perfectly rational and consistent. . . ."[14] It was the opinion of these authors that wide-spread legal knowledge was essential to the political and economic success of the country.

As important as these three goals were, readers were particularly attracted to the treatise authors' various explanations of the methodology of law. David Hoffman explained:

> The value of method is, we acknowledge, a trite topic of dissertation; but in the inquiries of the American law student this method becomes indispensable: where the ideas and language are remote from those of common life; where the terms are, in an especial degree, peculiar to the science, and of various and singular derivation; and where the body of forms, as well as principles, depends to a very great extent, on institutions and systems which have long since passed away.[15]

While legal method was emphasized in order to facilitate a better understanding of a legal system based on ancient and foreign circumstances, its more important implication was that it revolutionized the way Americans perceived the law by emphasizing the importance of man's reason over precedents.

The cornerstone of American legal methodology was the scientific manner in which the law was presented. This approach constituted an extension of an idea deeply rooted in the European Enlightenment. Peter Gay has noted: "The Philosophes celebrated the scientific revolution, accepting its findings, and imitating its methods. They pushed its philosophical implications far beyond what the scientists themselves would have thought warranted. They tried to apply the scientific style of thinking to the regions of aesthetic, social, and political theory."[16] American analytical treatise authors carried this scientific approach further by successfully applying it to legal theory.

The basis for this scientific approach to legal theory was the categorization and simplification of the law. The works of Zephaniah Swift and Tapping Reeve are the best representatives of this class of treatises in their use of this technique. Swift categorized American law into six broad topics: the powers of government; the rights of persons; the rights of things; private wrongs and the mode of redress; crimes and punishment; and the principles of equity. Within these topics, Swift established subcategories. For example, the topic "private wrongs and the mode of redress" included subcategories such as replevin, trespass, trover and assumpsit. He explained that this approach was "intended to afford the student the satisfaction and delight of arranging his studies in proper method, or extending his mind at one view thro [*sic*] all the various branches of jurisprudence, of beholding the connection and mutual dependence of all the parts, and of comprehending the beautiful order, and symetry [*sic*] of the whole."[17]

Tapping Reeve categorized the law of domestic relations into four broad topics: "baron and femme," "parent and child," "guardian and ward" and "master and servant." For each of these topics, he established a series of subcategories. Thus, "master and servant" was reduced to discussions of slavery, apprenticeship, menial servants, day laborers, principals and agents, factors, brokers, auctioneers, attorneys, a master's liability for the acts of his servant and a master's right to punish his servant. The object of this categorization, as described by Reeve, was "to bring into one connected view, the law on the various subjects respecting which they treat" so that "the principles which govern each subject" will be discovered and "a desirable uniformity in the law will be observed; and its symmetry will be preserved from being marred."[18]

Simplification was the next order of business, and both authors accomplished this by heading each subcategory with a simple definition noteworthy for its lack of technical jargon. Swift wrote of trespass: "it may be laid down as a general rule, that all unlawful acts that injure things personal, either by the taking them away from the owner, by destroying them, or by damaging them, are deemed trespasses."[19] Reeve defined a guardian as "one, that legally has the care and management of the person, or estate, or both, of a child, during his minority, whose father has deceased."[20] The reason for including simplified definitions such as these was explained by Swift as follows: "all that technical intricacy which has so long disfigured the science of jurisprudence, will be avoided, and our laws simplified and systematized, will be presented in a form intelligible to every capacity."[21]

The next methodological step was to explain the legal precedents which served as the rationale for these categories and simplified definitions of law. Reeve and Swift began by reducing a common area of precedents to general rules of law and the fundamental principles upon which they were based. In considering precedents arising from a series of cases on matrimonial law, Tapping Reeve extracted the rule of law "that a wife cannot so contract, as to bind herself." He then explained how this rule was based upon two fundamental principles. The first, "the right of the husband to the person of his wife," indicated that, "if she could bind herself by her contracts, she would be liable to be arrested, taken in execution, and confined in a prison; and then the husband would be deprived of the company of his wife, which the law will not suffer." The second, "the law considers the wife to be in the power of the husband," dictated that "it would not be . . . reasonable that she should be bound by any contract which she makes during the coverture, as it might be the effect of coercion."[22] In his discussion of case law on the topic of the age and capacity to commit crimes, Swift uncovered the rule of law that an infant under the age of seven years cannot be convicted of a crime. He explained that this was founded on the following two principles: (1) that there can be no criminality without a vicious will, and (2) "the exertion of the will is wanting" in an infant "on account of a defect of understanding." Thus, since no vicious will could be said to exist in an infant under the age of seven, he could not be convicted of committing a crime.[23] With precedents thus reduced to rules and principles, the rationale behind the law could be more easily presented and understood.

Analytical treatise authors applied the scientific methods of categorization and simplification to the law so as to portray it as a system made easily comprehensible by its internal order and logic. In this manner, American legal treatise writers presented the law as a subject that could readily be understood.

This means of using scientific methodology to uncover the rationale behind the common law was not a creation of American legal treatise writers. William Blackstone in his *Commentaries on the Laws of England* had previously suggested a similar approach. Blackstone viewed the application of scientific methodology to the common law as a valuable means of instruction, but he warned against using this approach to question legal precedents. As quoted earlier, Daniel Boorstin has noted that "through the vocabulary of a rationalist aesthetic, the eighteenth-century student of law was being led to an unquestioning reverence. . . . Man was discouraged from any attempt to improve the law because the English system contained latent, undiscoverable perfections which he might unwittingly destroy."[24] Blackstone had built upon the English common law tradition of strictly adhering to legal precedents by encouraging a perception of the law as hallowed or sacred.[25] Indeed, he even went so far as to discourage any attempt at betterment of the law. By applying scientific method to the study of the common law, Blackstone became an Enlightenment figure. Yet, by advocating that this approach should be limited, he must also be considered as anti-Enlightenment.

The American Revolution caused American jurists to reconsider Blackstone's view. With the success of the Revolution, Americans sought to define their newfound nationhood. This task necessitated reflection on a number of English institutions that had shaped colonial life.[26] The common law system was one such institution, and many found much in it at variance with American values.[27] James Wilson wrote:

> But further; many parts of the laws of England can, in their own nature, have neither force or [*sic*] application here. Such are all those parts, which are connected with ecclesiastical jurisdiction and an ecclesiastical establishment. Such are all those parts, too, which relate to the monarchical and aristocratick [*sic*] branches of the English constitution. Every one, who has perused the ponderous volumes of the law, knows how great a proportion of them is filled with the numerous and extensive titles relating to those different subjects. Surely they need not enter into the elements of a law education in the United States.[28]

St. George Tucker concurred, writing:

> by the rejection of the sovereignty of the Crown of England, not only all the laws of that country by which the dependence of the colonies was secured, but the whole *lex prerogativa* (or *Jura Corona* before mentioned) so far as respected the person of the sovereign and his prerogatives as an individual, was utterly abolished: and, that so far as respected the kingly office, and government, it was either modified, abridged, annulled, according to the several constitutions and laws of the states, respectively: consequently, that every rule of the common law, and every statute of England, founded on the nature of regal government, in derogation of the natural and unalienable rights of mankind; or, inconsistent with the nature and principles of democratic governments, were absolutely abrogated, repealed, and annulled, by the establishment of such a form of government in the states, respectively.[29]

As American treatise writers examined these cases, they realized that other areas of the law were affected by the same unacceptable precedents. They therefore began to question the reverence accorded to legal precedents by Blackstone and the English legal tradition. Nathaniel Chipman explained:

> The common law of England is a system of rules, supported by precedents, handed down from remote antiquity. These precedents have . . . been held in too great veneration. A number of precedents, in point, however obscure, or uncertain the principles, upon which they were founded, have been held, fully decisive of a similar question; and yet many of these precedents were made at a time, when the state of society, and of property, were very different, from what they are at present; in an age when the minds of men were fettered in forms; when forms were held to be substances, and abstractions, real entities.[30]

Peter S. Du Ponceau agreed as he complained about the judges of Westminster Hall. "The law which they administer," he wrote, "with the exception of a few statutes, the construction of which still rests with themselves, consists entirely of a series of their own and their predecessors' decisions on particular cases. There is no appeal to the power of logic, or the supremacy of principles. Judicial opinions solemnly delivered, must not be impugned, for they are the law of the land, as much if they had been enacted by the parliament with all the solemn forms of legislation." By contrast, Du Ponceau described the United States as a place where "the common law has not and can never have, so long as our constitution subsists, such a sanctuary as is provided for it there, nor such a body of high priests entrusted with its exclusive guardianship."[31]

The criticism leveled at English common law by these authors created a dilemma. If the doctrine of *stare decisis* was to be completely abandoned, the legal system would resort to being based on the whims of the judiciary—a practice unacceptable in a democratic society where legal rights and obligations could not exist without judicial predictability. American analytical treatise authors responded to this problem by advocating a system in which the soundness of a legal precedent could be judged prior to its acceptance as valid and controlling law. This necessitated the application of known comparative standards. American treatise authors suggested a variety of approaches including utility, logic, morality, and compatibility with other law and public policy.

This concept constituted such a revolutionary departure from English and colonial American legal thought that James Wilson, the father of American jurisprudence, found the need to justify it philosophically. In doing so, he relied on David Hume's belief that the justification for laws is in their utility to society.[32] He postulated that as society's needs changed, its common law had to change. Wilson explained it as follows:

> It is the characteristick [*sic*] of a system of common law, that it be accommodated to the circumstances, the exigencies, and the conveniences of the people, by whom it is appointed. Now as these circumstances, and exigencies, and conveniences insensibly change, a proportioned change, in time and degree, must take place in the accommodated system. But though the system suffer these partial and successive alterations, yet it continues materially and substantially the same.[33]

The problem with the English system of common law, according to Wilson, was that its practice of revering and strictly adhering to legal precedents prevented it from adapting, in a timely fashion, to the substantially different needs of the American nation. He complained: "By the revolution in the United States, a very great alteration—a very great improvement as we have already seen, has taken place in our system of government: ought not a proportioned alteration—ought not a proportioned improvement to be introduced into our system of law."[34] Wilson's justification for America's changed perception of legal precedents was that the English common law system was too slow in adapting to America's sense of utility. Wilson was, of course, speaking as a Scotsman who was instrumental in transplanting Scottish utilitarian jurisprudence into America.[35] His emphasis on the utility law provides to society was, in effect, the beginning of an American legal tradition of reliance on utilitarian philosophy to justify a change in the law.

C. Paul Rogers III has recently described the role of Scots law in post-Revolutionary and nineteenth-century America as "the neglected jurisprudence." While he accepts that Scottish law influenced aspects of American law, he claims that the substantive impact was severely limited. No doubt, direct substantive links between Scottish and American law are difficult to find. But the impact of eighteenth-century Scottish utilitarian jurisprudence on American legal thought and ultimately on American substantive law were great.[36]

Indeed, the role of utility was so prominent in changing America's conception of the law that it served not only as a justification for questioning precedents but also as the premier standard against which precedents were judged. Anthony Laussat, Jr., employed utility to argue against a principle of English common law which allowed a recklessly wasteful man to manage his own estate at the expense of his family. Laussat wrote:

> Every one who is not a minor, a lunatic, or an ideot [*sic*], is allowed at common law to manage his own estate without restriction, and with perfect freedom from the prohibition of the civilians in relation to prodigality. "Sic utere tuo, ut alienum non laedas," is said to be the only regulation of domestic economy, prescribed by the law of England: yet this is scarcely a reason for the permission of wastefulness, as the acts of a prodigal are an immediate injury to his family, who have a powerful right by the law of nature, to a proper maintenance and support."[37]

Zephaniah Swift described the use in Connecticut of the standard of utility to modify English procedural law concerning the collection of debt. Connecticut courts, said Swift, were concerned about a multiplicity of suits caused by an English rule that provided that "whenever a person has recovered a judgement, an action of debt will at any time lie on that judgement, while it is subsisting." Practically speaking, since a judgement expired after a year and a day, creditors would periodically file new actions of debt to keep their claims alive. This was considered to be an inefficient use of court time, so Connecticut courts deviated from this practice by adopting a rule whereby executions could "be prayed out on a judgement at any time during the life of all the parties." Thus, an action of debt was sustained until a judgement could be satisfied without having to renew suit.[38] Peter Du Ponceau relied on the standard of utility to encourage the abolishment of English precedent that required imprisonment for debt. He believed that it was more useful for a creditor to obtain compensation than revenge through punishment. He wrote that if imprisonment for debt "should be abolished, it is to be hoped that a greater hold will be given to the creditor on the property of his debtor than he has by the existing laws: that for instance, the doctrine of liens will be further extended, and outstanding debts made liable to attachment or execution, under suitable regulations."[39] The use of utility to question precedents was favored in America because it allowed common law principles to be modified in accordance with the unique needs of the new nation. Nevertheless, it was not the only means used to accomplish this end.

Nathaniel Chipman and David Hoffman taught their readers to judge precedents according to the standards of logic. Chipman applied logical standards to substantive law. For example, he exposed the logical lapses in the rationale behind a provision of the English law of lunacy which stated that a lunatic's acts could be voided by his heirs but not by himself, even after he recovered his reason. Chipman noted that this doctrine was based on the illogical statement that "a person could not plead, that he was insane, when he did such an act; for if he was insane, how could he remember that he did the act."[40] Hoffman concentrated on procedural law, choosing to uncover "fictions in various departments of the law": for example, he noted that "the distinction between *assumpsit* and *tort* is perhaps not always well founded in the reason of things, when by merely varying the form from one to the other, a man shall succeed in vindicating a claim which he had otherwise failed in. . . ."[41] Through their treatises, Chipman and Hoffman helped to fix into American legal thought the idea that logic could be used to determine the validity of legal precedents.[42]

The most controversial standard applied to the judgement of precedents was that of morality, for there was considerable debate about its use. James Wilson argued that morality could be used to judge legal precedents so long as only a single system of moral philosophy was accepted by the American judiciary. Wilson favored the adoption of the moral sense philosophy of the Scottish Enlightenment, which he had studied while a student at the University of St. Andrews.[43] Citing the foremost publication of this school of thought—Thomas Reid's *An Inquiry into the Human Mind, on the Principles of Common Sense*[44]—Wilson explained moral sense philosophy as follows:

> This philosophy will teach us, that first principles are in themselves apparent; that to make nothing self evident, is to take away all possibility of knowing anything; that without first principles, there can be neither reason nor reasoning; that discussive knowledge requires intuitive maxims as its basis; that if every truth would admit of proof, proof would extend to infinity; that, consequently, all sound reasoning must rest ultimately on the principles of common sense—principles supported by original and intuitive evidence.[45]

Moral sense philosophy held, according to Wilson, that intuition is the foundation of knowledge and that the premises for logical deduction are self-evident truths. Man's reasoning powers are not employed until these truths, derived from the will of God, are realized. Wilson further explained:

> Having thus stated the question—what is the efficient cause of moral obligation?—I give it this answer—the will of God. This is the supreme law. His just and full right of imposing laws, and our duty in obeying them, are the sources of our moral obligations. If I am asked—why do you obey the will of God? I answer—because it is my duty so to do. If I am asked again—because I am told so by my moral sense or conscience. If I am asked a third time—how do you know that you ought to do that, of which your conscience enjoins the performance? I can only say, I *feel* that such is my duty. Here investigations must stop; reasoning can go no farther. The science of morals, as well as other sciences, is founded on truths, that cannot be discovered or proved by reasoning. Reason is confined to investigation of unknown truths by the means of such as are known. We cannot, therefore, begin to reason, till we are furnished, otherwise than by reason, with some truths, on which we can found our arguments.[46]

Wilson believed that in judging precedents one must first discover, through one's own intuition, the natural rights of the parties. Once established, one must use reason to apply these rights to the facts of the case so as to determine if the moral outcome is consistent with the judicial outcome.

Gulian C. Verplanck and Nathaniel Chipman were typical of a number of authors who adopted Wilson's suggested use of moral sense philosophy as a means of criticizing legal precedents. Verplanck relied on moral sense philosophy in his discussion of the case of *Laidlaw v. Organ*[47] where the plaintiff, through special circumstances, learned of the Treaty of Ghent before news of it had reached the general public in New Orleans. Realizing that the British blockade of New Orleans, which had depressed the price of tobacco by severely restricting its export, would be lifted, he immediately purchased a large quantity of tobacco from the defendant at his New Orleans trading company. Shortly thereafter, when news of the treaty became public, the price rose substantially and the seller sought to avoid the sale. The United States Supreme Court held that the plaintiff as vendee was not bound to communicate to the defendant as vendor facts of extrinsic circumstances which might influence the value of the commodity being purchased. Verplanck commented:

> However correct this judicial decision may have been in point of law, and however strong the expediency of the law, as laid down, may seem to be recommended by considerations of public policy and the necessities of trade, yet I believe, most of those who, without much speculation or deliberate reasoning, form their moral judgements from their unstudied impressions of right and wrong, will find it somewhat revolting to their notions of sound morality.[48]

The rationale behind this case was contrary to the moral outcome derived through the use of moral sense philosophy, leading Verplanck to consider it bad precedent and to encourage the legal community to ignore it.[49] Chipman employed moral sense philosophy to discredit an interpretation of precedent that allowed a person, who knew that another had already recorded a deed to property, to obtain title to that property by filing his own deed before it was learned that the first filer's deed contained an error, on the grounds that the first filer was prevented from challenging the deed of the second filer due to laches. Laches bars legal action because of neglect, for an unreasonable length of time, to do what in law, should have been done. Chipman wrote: "The rules of law ought never to be so construed, as to oppose the nicest sense of moral obligation. As moralists, we condemn the transaction."[50]

In spite of the wide-spread acceptance of Wilson's suggested use of moral sense philosophy, there were a sufficient number of analytical treatise authors who opposed it, to prevent it from becoming a universally recognized aspect of American jurisprudence. John Anthon was representative of this group in that he did not consider any moral philosophy to be a sound enough science to provide the law with judicial predictability. He stated: "It may be here objected, that too high an estimate is given . . . , of the value of metaphysical science in making it one of the vantage grounds of professional knowledge . . . [for] . . . the practical value of that science it must be admitted may be very justly doubted."[51] Although the fact that a particular precedent is contrary to morality has never been recognized by the American legal system as a sufficient basis by itself for ignoring such precedent, the ability of a court to rule a precedent invalid because it was contrary to generally accepted notions of morality survives (e.g., through the use of equity powers in a common law case, by determining aspects of cases "unconscionable" or by reading into the Constitution rights not previously recognized and then ruling the precedent unconstitutional).

The final standard employed to judge precedents was the standard of compatible law and public policy. George Hay utilized this standard to determine the applicability of English common law precedents regarding expatriation to American citizens. The issue he addressed was how a person could acquire the right to relinquish English citizenship when it was deemed by English common law, according to Blackstone, to be permanent and unalterable. Hay addressed this problem by noting the existence of a number of English laws that, on the contrary, recognized the loss of citizenship. For example, pursuant to the laws of territorial cession, people of an acquired territory become citizens of the acquiring nation and lose the citizenship of their former sovereign. In addition, since citizenship is composed of rights and duties, under the terms of the Treaty of Ghent, England's acknowledgment of the renouncement by Americans of their duties to England and their rights as British citizens constituted a recognition of the right of citizens to forfeit their citizenship. Given this, Hay reasoned that since there were many laws that recognized expatriation and only one that prohibited it, the common law precedent that held citizenship permanent and unalterable was void as being incompatible with other law.[52] Gulian C. Verplanck described how the standard of compatible public policy could be used by the judiciary to modify precedents. He wrote: "with respect to real estate and mortgages, nothing can be more plain than the contract between the mortgagor and the mortgagee; but what public policy may require, for the prevention of frauds, and the protection of *bona fide* purchasers or subsequent mortgagees, is another question. This may require . . . judicial regulations."[53]

The standard of legal compatibility attained its greatest role when applied within the circumstances of the American political system. Unlike the English context, in which the common law could only be compared to a Parliamentary Act or to itself, in America it would have to be compared to local ordinances, state court decisions, state statutes, the state constitution, federal court decisions, federal statutes and the federal constitution. Moreover, it was realized that because the words of a written constitution are inherently ambiguous, American judges would always be empowered to disregard a precedent under the guise of it being contrary to their conception of the original intent of the framers of the constitution.[54]

Regardless of which standard was used to judge legal precedents, once a common law principle was determined to be invalid, a substitute would have to be found. A number of analytical treatise authors recommended the use of civil law as a guide to determining what new legal principles should be adopted. Samuel Livermore observed: "I have stated the rules of the civil law, to confirm and illustrate the principles of our own law; I have endeavoured to shew [*sic*] in what they agree and in what they differ; and in questions which appeared to be doubtful or undecided at common law, I have had recourse to the opinions of the great *Roman* jurists, as the surest guide to a correct solution."[55] Daniel Chipman concurred: "Although it be true, that we cannot refer either to the ancient law of France, or to the Napoleon Code, as authorities, yet it may be useful to recur to them for the purposes of illustration."[56] The existence of a system for judging precedents meant that foreign law could be considered without fearing the introduction of principles alien to American values. This contributed to the coopting of substantial amounts of foreign law by the American legal system during the ante-bellum period.[57]

American analytical law treatises were written in response to a variety of problems caused by the American Revolution including a need to educate large numbers of prospective lawyers, a need to settle and unify the American legal system and a need to educate the American people about their rights and obligations as citizens. Since much of what was being explained concerned principles of law based on circumstances foreign to most Americans, analytical treatise authors emphasized the use of a scientific legal method, transported to America predominantly through Blackstone's *Commentaries*, to explain the law. During the post-Revolutionary and early-National periods, American jurists considered aspects of the common law ill-suited to American circumstances. Analytical treatise writers responded, building on their scientific approach to the study of law, by developing a unique American legal methodology designed to question the soundness of common law precedents.

The approach they developed, justified on the basis of utilitarian philosophy, relied on the judgmental standards of utility, logic, morality and compatibility with law and public policy. In addition, it encouraged the use of civil law as a guide to replacing common law principles that had been judged inapplicable to American circumstances. What was so revolutionary about this uniquely American legal methodology was that it established that reason could be relied upon, within certain limitations, over common law precedents. Nathaniel Chipman noted:

> I have not the vanity to suppose, that the opinions contained in the following Dissertations, are to be considered as precedents—they are only private opinions upon points of very considerable importance in the administration of law and justice, in this State. It has been my aim to derive these opinions from principles, which coincide with the principles of our government, and the spirit of its laws; and to support them by reason, rather than by precedents.[58]

It was in this manner that analytical treatise authors instilled into American legal thought a system whereby legal precedents could be judged prior to their acceptance as controlling law and judicially replaced if they were determined to be unsound.

The influence of this new conception of legal precedents was already being recognized by the middle of the 1820s. Two generations later, Peter Du Ponceau noted: "The opinions of English jurists and the decisions of English Judges so long regarded among us with implicit deference, are now scanned with greater freedom and with the spirit becoming an independent nation."[59] David Hoffman commented: "we think we can perceive in the jurists of our day, a growing sense of the necessity of appealing to general experience, and general principles, instead of restricting themselves to the narrow limits of our own common law."[60] Through the advent of a unique legal methodology, American analytical law treatises of the post-Revolutionary and early National periods succeeded in influencing the development of a unique American legal system and a unique American legal thought.

NOTES

1. Morton J. Horwitz, *The Transformation of American Law, 1780–1860* (Cambridge: Harvard University Press, 1977), pp. 257–258.

2. Lawrence M. Friedman, *A History of American Law* (New York: Simon and Schuster, 1973), pp. 286–287.

3. William Griffith, *Annual Law Register of the United States* (Burlington, NJ: David Allinson, 1822), Vols. 3 & 4. For a list of these publications see Appendix IV.

4. *Who Was Who in America, Historical Volume 1607–1896* (Chicago: A.N. Marquis Co., 1967).

5. Tapping Reeve, *The Law of Baron and Femme . . .* (New Haven, CT: Oliver Steele, 1816), preface.

6. Nathaniel Chipman, *Reports and Dissertations* (Rutland, VT: Anthony Haswell, 1793), p. 116.

7. William Wyche, *Treatise on the Practice of the Supreme Court of Judicature of the State of New-York in Civil Actions* (New York: T. & J. Swords, 1794), p. vii.

8. Daniel Chipman, *An Essay on the Law of Contracts, for the Payment of Specifick Articles* (Middlebury, VT: J.W. Copeland, 1822), p. v.

9. The American Law Institute, *Uniform Commercial Code*, 9th ed. (Minneapolis, MN: West Publishing Co., 1978), pp. XV–LV.

10. Tapping Reeve, *A Treatise on the Law of Descents in the several United States of America* (New York: Collins & Hannay, 1825), p. ii.

11. John Milton Goodenow, *Historical Sketches of the Principles and Maxims of American Jurisprudence* (Steubenville, OH: James Wilson, 1819).

12. Zephaniah Swift, *A System of the Laws of the State of Connecticut*, 2 vols. (Windham, CT: John Byrne, 1795), 1:1.

13. Samuel Livermore, *A Treatise on the Law of Principal and Agent; and of Sales by Auction*, 2 vols. (Baltimore, MD: Joseph Robinson, 1818), 1:v.

14. Gulian C. Verplanck, *An Essay on the Doctrine of Contracts . . .* (New York: G. & C. Carvill, 1825), p. iii.

15. David Hoffman, *A Course of Legal Study* (Baltimore, MD: Coale and Maxwell, 1817), p. xv.

16. Peter Gay, *The Enlightenment: The Science of Freedom* (New York: W.W. Norton & Co., 1977), p. 126.

17. Swift, *A System of the Laws*, 1:2–3.

18. Reeve, *Baron and Femme*, preface.
19. Swift, *A System of the Laws*, 2:94.
20. Reeve, *Baron and Femme*, p. 311.
21. Swift, *A System of the Laws*, 1:4; For a concurring opinion see: James Wilson, *The Works of the Honourable James Wilson, LL.D.*, ed. Robert Green McCloskey, 2 vols. (1804; reprinted Cambridge: The Belknap Press of Harvard University Press, 1967), 1:73.
22. Reeve, *Baron and Femme*, p. 98.
23. Swift, *A System of the Laws*, pp. 367–368.
24. Daniel J. Boorstin, *The Mysterious Science of the Law* (Cambridge: Harvard University Press, 1941), p. 105.
25. Sir Matthew Hale, *The History of the Common Law of England*, ed. Charles M. Gray (1739; reprinted Chicago: The University of Chicago Press, 1971), p. 46.
26. Jack P. Greene, "The Reappraisal of the American Revolution in Recent Historical Literature," in *The Reinterpretation of the American Revolution 1763–1789*, ed. Jack P. Greene (New York: Harper & Row, 1968), p. 56.
27. Friedman, *History of American Law*, p. 94; Gordon S. Wood, *The Creation of the American Republic, 1776–1787* (New York: W.W. Norton & Co., 1972), p. 300.
28. Wilson, *Works*, 1:82; James Wilson addressed this subject as part of a series of law lectures presented at the College of Philadelphia in 1790–1791. Wilson's ideas, however, had their greatest impact through the posthumous publication of his lectures under the editorship of his son in 1804. This work constructively places James Wilson among the ranks of post-Revolutionary American legal treatise authors.
29. St. George Tucker, *Blackstone's Commentaries: with Notes of Reference, to the Constitution and Laws, of the Federal Government of the United States; and of the Commonwealth of Virginia*, 5 vols. (Philadelphia: William Young Birch and Abraham Small, 1803), 1:405–406.
30. Nathaniel Chipman, *Reports and Dissertations*, pp. 123–124; For concurring opinions see: Hugh Henry Brackenridge, *Law Miscellanies* . . . (Philadelphia: P. Byrne, 1814), pp. 54–70; Reeve, *the Law of Descents*, pp. 1–2.
31. Peter S. Du Ponceau, *A Dissertation on the Nature and Extent of the Jurisdiction of the Courts of the United States. being a valedictory address delivered to the students of the Law Academy of Philadelphia, at the close of the academical year, on the 22nd April, 1824.* (Philadelphia: Abraham Small, 1824), pp. 174–175.
32. David Hume, *A Treatise of Human Nature*, ed. L.A. Selby-Bigge (1739; reprinted Oxford: Oxford University Press, 1975), p. 561.
33. James Wilson, *The Works of the Honourable James Wilson, LL.D.*, ed. Bird Wilson, 3 vols. (Philadelphia: Bronson and Chauncey, 1804), p. 353.
34. Ibid., p. 82.
35. William R. Brock, *Scotus Americanus* (Edinburgh: Edinburgh University Press, 1982), p. 127; Michael Ignatieff, "John Millar and Individualism," in Istvan Hont and Michael Ignatieff, eds., *Wealth & Virtue: The Shaping of Political Economy in the Scottish Enlightenment* (Cambridge: Cambridge University Press, 1983), p. 324; David Lieberman, "The Legal Needs of Commercial Society: The Jurisprudence of Lord Kames," in Hont and Ignatieff, eds., *Wealth & Virtue*, p. 229.
36. C. Paul Rogers III, "Scots Law in Post-Revolutionary and Eighteenth Century America: The Neglected Jurisprudence," 8 LAW & HIST. REV. 205–235 (1990).

37. Anthony Laussat, Jr., *An Essay on Equity in Pennsylvania* (Philadelphia: Robert Desilva, 1826), p. 103.

38. Swift, *A System of the Laws*, 2:131.

39. Du Ponceau, *Dissertation*, pp. 113–114.

40. Nathaniel Chipman, *Reports and Dissertations*, p. 149.

41. David Hoffman, *A Lecture Being the Second of a Series of Lectures Introductory to a Course of Lectures Now Delivering in the University of Maryland* (Baltimore, MD: John D. Toy, 1825), p. 28. Assumpsit is a common law form of action which lies for the recovery of damages for the nonperformance of an oral or simple contract. Tort is a private civil wrong or injury, other than breach of contract, for which the court will provide a remedy in the form of an action for damages.

42. For a modern analysis of the importance of logic in judging legal precedents see: Karl N. Llewellyn, *The Bramble Bush* (New York: Oceana Press, 1951), pp. 70–75.

43. Geoffrey Seed, *James Wilson* (Millwood, NY: KTO Press, 1978), p. 4; William F. Obering, "The Philosophy of Law of James Wilson: A Study in Comparative Jurisprudence," *Philosophical Studies of the American Catholic Philosophical Association* 1 (1938): 9.

44. Thomas Reid, *An Inquiry into the Human Mind, on the Principles of Common Sense* (Edinburgh: Kincaid & Bell, 1764).

45. Wilson, *Works*, ed. McCloskey, 1:200, 213.

46. Ibid., pp. 132–133.

47. 2 Wheat. (15 U.S.) 178 (1817).

48. Verplanck, *Essay on Contracts*, p. 5.

49. For other American examples of the reception of moral sense philosophy see: Daniel J. Boorstin, *The Lost World of Thomas Jefferson* (Chicago: The University of Chicago Press, 1981), pp. 163–165; Brock, *Scotus Americanus*, pp. 92–93.

50. Nathaniel Chipman, *Reports and Dissertations*, pp. 162–163.

51. John Anthon, *The Law of Nisi Prius* . . . (New-York: Gould and Banks, 1820), p. vii.

52. George Hay, *A Treatise on Expatriation* (Washington, DC: A. & G. Way, 1814), pp. 1–31.

53. Verplanck, *Essay on Contracts*, pp. 164–165.

54. Tucker, *Blackstone's Commentaries*, 1: Appendix, pp. 411–413; Brackenridge, *Law Miscellanies*, p. 74; For a modern discussion of the standard of legal compatibility see: Edward H. Levi, *An Introduction to Legal Reasoning* (Chicago: The University of Chicago Press, 1949).

55. Livermore, *Principle and Agent*, 1:xi.

56. Daniel Chipman, *Law of Contracts*, p. 78.

57. Peter Stein, *The Attraction of the Civil Law in Post-Revolutionary America*, 52 Va. L. Rev. 403–434 (1966).

58. Nathaniel Chipman, *Reports and Dissertations*, p. 115.

59. Du Ponceau, *Dissertation*, p. xxii.

60. David Hoffman, *A Lecture Being the Third of a Series of Lectures Introductory to a Course of Lectures Now Delivering in the University of Maryland* (Baltimore, MD: J.D. Toy, 1826), pp. 16–17.

4

The Redaction of a Modified Doctrine of *Stare Decisis* into American Legal Practice, 1782–1830

Although a considerable amount of common law was deliberately retained by the American states, a predominant aim of American legal educators during the fifty-year period following the American Revolution was to expunge the unquestioning acceptance of English common law from American legal thought. American law students had been exposed to the method for accomplishing this aim at new American institutions of vocational legal instruction and through the publication of distinctly American legal treatises. No intellectual movement, however, can be considered successful until its ideas become institutionalized. With regard to legal ideology, it must be employed by lawyers and judges in the day-to-day practice of law.

As is shown here, during America's post-Revolutionary and early National periods, a distinctly American legal methodology was employed by American lawyers and judges to question the soundness of English precedents. No doubt, there was some movement in England during the second half of the eighteenth century, particularly at the hands of Lord Mansfield, to adopt a less severe adherence to precedents.[1] However, this was short lived. In the years following Mansfield's position as Lord Chancellor, "the English doctrine of precedent hardened."[2] What set the American movement apart from this was the great extent to which American jurists were willing to question precedents through the use of a clearly defined methodology created and institutionalized in centers of early American legal education.

This position is at odds, in part, with the recent work of Shanon C. Stimson. While she agrees that there were significant changes in legal thought which occurred during the period in question, she argues that this was fostered by the efforts of lay jurors, who extended the power of the jury: "British and American jurisprudence," Stimson wrote, "are separated not only historically by differing court practices which commentators have frequently observed but . . . by essentially different theoretical conceptions of sovereignty, the nature of law, and the extent of ordinary citizens' power to judge the legitimacy of law."[3] This argument is incomplete in that it ignores the role of the lawyer in persuading the jury to question precedents, what Stimson calls the legitimacy of law, and of the judge in accepting the jury's verdict. The catalyst in this development was not the citizen juror but the advocate and jurist trained in a new American legal methodology.

The first step in this methodology was to limit the application of the doctrine of *stare decisis*, which tied American law to English law. The doctrine of *stare decisis* provided that courts were obliged to adhere strictly to a principle of law, developed in a case with similar facts, established by a prior court of equal or higher jurisdictional authority. If *stare decisis* were strictly followed, there would never be an opportunity for questioning precedents established under English law. If disregarded, the American legal system would lack the predictability necessary in a democratic society. The compromise position adopted was to preserve a modified version of the doctrine of *stare decisis*, which required a strict adherence to precedents established by American courts while permitting English precedents to be questioned against a number of recognized comparative standards, either because they had not yet been adopted or sanctioned by American courts or because it was determined that they were in conflict with each other.

The movement to modify the doctrine of *stare decisis* took place throughout the United States. For the purposes of this work and as a result of the limitation of resources, however, only three states will be considered—Connecticut representing New England, Virginia representing the South and New York representing the middle Atlantic states.

Connecticut was the first state to witness the success of this movement. It was the home of America's earliest vocational law schools, and the first American legal treatise to encourage a revision of the English common law was published in Connecticut and tailored to a Connecticut readership.[4] Thus, Connecticut was the first state to absorb large numbers of lawyers into its legal and judicial ranks who had been exposed to the intellectual movement that favored the modification of *stare decisis* and the questioning of common law precedents.

The first recorded Connecticut case to adopt and explain a significant modification of the doctrine of *stare decisis* was the 1786 decision of *Wilford et al. v. Grant*.[5] This was an action of trespass against six men for assault and battery committed upon a woman. Three of the defendants failed to appear for the trial. Nevertheless, the jury found for the plaintiff against all the defendants in the amount of seventy-five pounds. The defendants then filed a writ of error *coram nobis* ["our court"—addressing the very court which renders the judgement in which injustice is alleged to have been done, in contrast to appeals or reviews directed to another court], arguing that the plaintiff withheld from the court the vital fact that two of the defendants who failed to appear at the trial were minors who were thus legally incapable of arranging for their own defence. Before the appeal was decided, the plaintiff died, and her husband assumed the defence of the appeal. The Superior Court of Connecticut determined that the minor defendants should have been represented by guardians, but it questioned whether it could reverse the trial court decision as to them while affirming it against the others.

In determining the answer to this question, the Superior Court began by postulating, based on "rerum natura," that there was no reason why the trial court's decision should be reversed as to the adult defendants. The Court noted that "they were fairly tried and convicted" and, if the "judgement must be reversed as to all," there would be a failure of justice "For the right of action being merely personal, and the original plaintiff dead, the action cannot be commenced again de novo." In examining relevant case law, the Court determined that "the common-law rules of England are indeed against a reversal in part only, in a case like this. . . ." Faced with a choice between the dictates of precedents and the requirements of natural justice, the Court stated its decision to use a modified version of the doctrine of *stare decisis*, allowing English legal principles to be questioned:

> The common law of England we are to pay great deference to, as being a general system of improved reason, and a source from whence our principles of jurisprudence have been mostly drawn: The rules, however, which have not been made our own by adoption, we are to examine, and so far vary from them as they may appear contrary to reason or unadapted to our local circumstances, the policy of our law, or simplicity of our practice; which, for the reasons above suggested, we do in this case, and reverse the judgement as to the minors only. The Court established here a means by which English precedents which had not yet been adopted by Connecticut courts could be disregarded under certain circumstances on a case-by-case basis.[6]

In *Bush v. Bradley*,[7] Justice Tapping Reeve of the Connecticut Supreme Court of Errors, proprietor of the Litchfield Law School and author of two legal treatises in which he advocated limiting America's strict adherence to English precedents,[8] expanded the approach adopted in *Wilford et al. v. Grant* to the entire English law of real property. The case before the Court was an action of ejectment for a parcel of land in New Haven. Mary Woodhouse took over the property after the death of her father, Robert Woodhouse, and sold it, while still a minor, to the defendant. Prior to reaching the age of majority, she married and after her marriage remained a feme covert, which denied her the right to be seised in property. After her death, action was brought by other living relatives of Robert Woodhouse against the defendant, claiming that since Mary Woodhouse was never seised in the property, she could not sell it, and therefore that it should belong to them.

The issue at stake was whether Mary Woodhouse herself had to be seised in the property in order to sell it. English precedents required the use of the maxim *seisina facit stipitem* which provided that a person must be seised in property before he could impart it to another. Judge Reeve used the arguments presented by attorneys David Bryan Ingersoll (graduate of Litchfield, 1792) and Nathan Smith (graduate of Litchfield, 1790) to disapprove of this maxim—but would have been prevented from deciding in defendant's favor by the doctrine of *stare decisis*. Reeve chose to ignore the doctrine:

> It is said that unnecessary departures from the common law of England are not to be favored; that by such means everything is rendered uncertain. I am fully of opinion, that few maxims of our law are more important than that of *stare decisis*; but it must be acknowledged by all, that our system of law respecting real property is, in many instances, very different from the English system. We have in some instances, when we have adopted the principles of the English law, extended them to cases which, by the adjudications of the English courts, have not been supposed to fall within the governing principle; in others, we have adopted entirely different principles; and in all such cases where this has been done, which are *pari ratione* with those already settled, if we reject our own and adopt theirs, we shall mar the symmetry of our law; and the preservation of symmetry in our system, I also view as a most important consideration.[9]

As a result, Reeve decided to ignore English precedents and relied instead on the Connecticut custom and law that property descends to the heirs of the one who last owned the property regardless of whether it was seised in or not. Writing the opinion for the Court, Reeve held that Mary's husband, as her heir, had legally become seised in the property upon her death. As her husband, he was obliged to uphold the sales contract with the defendant which Mary had made as a minor. Reeve therefore found for the defendant and, in doing so, redacted into Connecticut legal practice the idea that the modified doctrine of *stare decisis* should be applied to the entire law of real property because a strict adherence to precedents would have prohibited consideration of local customs and laws that were different from those in England.[10]

Stare decisis was also modified when it was determined that English precedents were in conflict with each other. This required a suspension of the doctrine in order to permit an inquiry into the validity of each precedent so as to determine which, if any, should be adopted. In their haste to Americanize the common law, American jurists often perceived conflict of precedents where English judges did not. *K. & E. Townsend v. Bush*,[11] decided by the Connecticut Supreme Court of Errors, is a case on point. It concerned an action of assumpsit against Bush as acceptor of a bill of exchange drawn by Ebenezer and Atwater Townsend, and payable to K. & E. Townsend. Bush offered usury as a defense based on the fact that Ebenezer and Atwater Townsend obtained a usurious loan from W. Leffingwell in New York in exchange for the bill in question, without providing notice to Bush.

At issue in the case was whether Ebenezer and Atwater Townsend could appear as witnesses for Bush to testify that Bush had no effects of theirs in hand, given the likelihood that they would have to admit their own criminal activity in entering into the usurious loan. It had already been shown that they had no interest in the suit, having been discharged from all liability on the bill pursuant to an act of insolvency in the state of New York. Seth P. Staples (proprietor of Staple's Law School) and Charles Denison, for the plaintiffs, argued, citing *Walton v. Shelley*,[12] that Ebenezer and Atwater Townsend could not appear as witnesses because they would be forced to disclose their own criminal culpability with regard to the loan.[13] Nathan Smith and Roger Minott Sherman (graduate of Litchfield, 1794), representing Bush, contended that *Walton v. Shelley* should be ignored because it had been contradicted by *Jordaine v. Lashbrooke*[14] and thus the issue should be decided on the "principles of the common law" which only prevented parties to a suit from testifying as to their own criminal acts.[15]

In spite of Lord Kenyon's decision in *Jordaine v. Lashbrooke* not to overrule *Walton v. Shelley* but merely to limit it to negotiable instruments, Justice Trumbull found the English cases to be contradictory and thus decided the case on the basis of fundamental principles. He wrote: "As the decisions of the highest court and ablest judges at *Westminster Hall* have been thus directly contradictory, and as their principle . . . has never till now come directly in question before the highest courts in this state, it is our duty to decide it according to the general rules and principles of law respecting admissibility of testimony. . . ." He continued: "The only fundamental principle of the common law, applicable to the present question, is this, that no man can be a witness in his own cause; and this rule hath ever been considered as applicable to every case in which he is a party, or is interested, and to no others." Thus, Trumbull held that *Walton v. Shelley* was not valid precedent and there was no bar to the admission of Ebenezer and Atwater Townsend as witnesses on Bush's behalf.[16] These cases demonstrate that the modified doctrine of *stare decisis* had become firmly established in Connecticut law.[17]

In Virginia, where the preferred method of modifying the common law was to redact it into codes, courts were apparently not as willing as in Connecticut to allow major modification of the doctrine of *stare decisis*.[18] Nevertheless, this did not stop attorneys from trying, with occasional success, to persuade the courts to accept some change. John Wickham, a graduate of the College of William and Mary where he studied under George Wythe, was a leading advocate in favor of modifying the doctrine. The case of *Boswell & Johnson v. Jones*[19] is representative of his early initiatives. Boswell and Johnson were charged with trespass. Johnson was found guilty and fined fifteen pounds and Boswell was found not guilty. Johnson alone obtained a new trial in the District Court, which awarded a verdict against both Johnson and Boswell in the amount of sixty pounds.

Boswell and Johnson brought the case before the Virginia Court of Appeals, questioning whether the District Court properly granted a new trial. Appellants' attorney sought to have the District Court's decision overturned, citing a series of English decisions which held that where one defendant is acquitted, a new trial cannot be granted upon the motion of the other defendant. Wickham, representing the appellee, Jones, contended that the English decisions should be ignored because they were unsound. He argued: "It is possible, that the jury may erroneously find a verdict against the wrong defendant, whom they intended to acquit. In such a case, it would neither be just nor reasonable, that the Court should not have a power of setting aside the verdict."[20] While Wickham was unsuccessful on behalf of his client, he did succeed in convincing at least one of the justices that the precedents relied on by appellants' counsel should not be strictly followed under all circumstances. The President of the Court wrote:

> One Judge doubted as to the reason of it [the rule of law according to English precedents], since the ground of new trials being to attain real justice, if the Court perceive that injustice has been done in the acquittal of one defendant, upon principle it would seem right to grant a new trial, from whosoever the motion might come. And as to authority, the same Judge is of opinion, that though uniform decisions, which establish the rules of *property*, ought to be adhered to, yet he does not view them as sacred in points of *practice*, which may be varied, as experience shall evince their convenience or inconvenience.[21]

Another time Wickham was presented with an opportunity to question directly the role of English precedents in Virginia, he had greater success in convincing the Court of the need to modify the doctrine of *stare decisis*. *Baring v. Reeder*[22] concerned the loan by Baring of some articles of personal property to the wife of Richard Claiborne. Richard Claiborne later made out a bill of sale to Reeder for merchandise including these articles. Baring found out about this bill of sale and recovered his property from Claiborne before it was to be delivered to Reeder. Consequently, Reeder filed an action of trover [a possessory action wherein the plaintiff must show that he has either a general or special property in a thing converted and the right to its possession at the time of the alleged conversion] against Baring. At the trial, Baring's counsel offered to prove by the deposition of Mrs. Claiborne that several articles covered by the bill of sale had been lent to her by Baring and that she had informed Reeder of this before he accepted the bill of sale, which would disqualify his action of trover. The District Court barred the testimony of Mrs. Claiborne on the grounds that she was "interested, and an incompetent witness."[23] The jury found for Reeder and Baring appealed.

The issue considered by the Virginia Supreme Court of Appeals was whether a wife can serve as a witness in a case in which her husband may be, but is not yet, interested. The Attorney-General of the Commonwealth of Virginia, appearing on behalf of Reeder, cited the English case of *King v. Cliviger*[24] which held that a "wife could not be permitted to give evidence *even tending to any degree* to criminate her husband," arguing that Mrs. Claiborne must be prevented from testifying because the evidence she would present would implicate her husband in a fraud.[25] John Wickham, representing Baring, argued that while a "wife cannot give evidence tending to criminate her husband, yet between third persons, she may be called to prove facts which may eventually charge him."[26] As for *King v. Cliviger*, Wickham urged the Virginia court not to rely on it stating, "The decision of the Court, in the *King v. Cliviger* was right upon the main question; but some loose *dicta* of the Judges have been quoted, which were not warranted by the case before them: and even the authority of that case has since been doubted."[27]

Justice Spencer Roane, a fellow graduate of the College of William and Mary and student of George Wythe, writing for the majority, not only refused to rely on *King v. Cliviger*, but also took the opportunity to explain that some areas of the English common law could not be strictly adhered to in America. Roane wrote:

> I consider myself bound to *pare down* the governmental part of the common law of *England* to the standard of our free republican constitution; . . . I am free to admit that from the *progressive* and *mutable* state of the common law . . . on *some subjects*, that law ought not to be received here . . . in the same *extent* that it is admitted in *England*, the circumstances and character of which nation varying from ours, produces (imperceptibly perhaps) a correspondent variation in the rules of their common law . . . with respect to the *ancient* decisions in *England*. . . . Who will contend that they are *binding authorities* upon us, in all cases whatsoever? . . . Shall we go back to the *Gothic* days of Lord *Coke*, and reject every man as a witness who is not *Christian*?[28]

While Justice Roane's statement does not amount to an abandonment of the doctrine of *stare decisis*, it does represent a willingness on the part of the Virginia Supreme Court of Appeals to limit the application of the doctrine in certain circumstances.[29]

Virginia courts were more willing to adopt a modified doctrine of *stare decisis* where English precedents were deemed to be in conflict with each other. In *Newton v. Wilson*,[30] the Virginia Supreme Court of Appeals set aside the dictates of the doctrine of *stare decisis* on the grounds that there were contradicting English precedents. This was an action of debt brought by James Wilson against William Newton on an agreement in which the defendant agreed to pay the plaintiff four hundred dollars, annually, for the use of his mills, two tracts of land adjoining the mills, a miller and a stock of hogs for a term of ten years. The defendant used the property specified for one year, but refused to make payment. At trial, the defendant tendered a bill of exceptions [a formal statement in writing of the objections or exceptions taken by a party during a trial of a cause to the decisions, rulings, or instructions of the trial judge] in which he stated that the miller was a negro, who had been held as a slave by the plaintiff but was emancipated by him before the date of the agreement, and, shortly after its commencement, the miller refused to work for the defendant and left. The trial court refused to admit this evidence and issued a judgement for the plaintiff. The issue before the Virginia Supreme Court of Appeals was how far the doctrine of apportionment should apply to this particular case.

St. George Tucker, former Professor of Law and Police at the College of William and Mary and author of a treatise through which he encouraged American lawyers to question English precedents,[31] was presented by both litigants' counsels with conflicting English precedents. While these precedents were ambiguous, they could have been interpreted so as to establish a firm rule of law. However, Tucker, writing on behalf of the Court, used this opportunity to abandon the doctrine of *stare decisis*, noting: "Where authorities are uncertain and contradictory, we must have recourse to *principle* as our guide."[32] In search of the principle behind those English precedents which opposed apportioning damages in cases similar to the one before the Court, Tucker considered Baron Jeffrey Gilbert's reasoning in his *A Treatise on Rents*[33] that the concept of apportionment should not apply to an action for rent on a lease of land with a stock of sheep where the sheep all die, because it would be too difficult to allot the rent. Tucker accepted this concern over the difficulty of apportioning rent as the fundamental principle he was seeking. However, he considered it unsound noting that "a jury of farmers would probably be able, very easily, to estimate the profits which might have arisen from the stock of sheep."[34] Thus, he rejected those cases built upon it and held that an apportionment should apply to an action of debt on a lease where not everything promised in the lease was delivered.[35] While Virginia courts were unwilling to adopt a wholesale modification of the doctrine of *stare decisis*, they were willing to modify it where English precedents where perceived to be in conflict with each other and where American circumstances prevented English precedents from being equitably applied.

New York, perhaps because it perceived itself to have suffered a rich history of abuses pursuant to English common law authority, adopted and exceeded the same types of modifications incorporated into Connecticut and Virginia law.[36] In *Silva v. Low*,[37] the New York Supreme Court of Judicature decided to ignore the doctrine of *stare decisis* on the ground that it required the application of unjust and irrational rules. The case before the Court was an action on a policy of insurance covering cargo on a ship voyaging from North Carolina to Great Britain via Falmouth. The ship's captain intended to stop at Sandy Hook, New York, in order to pick up additional seamen, but before reaching the point where the vessel needed to alter its course from a direct route to Falmouth, it sank.

The significant issue before the Court was whether the intended stop-over in New York constituted a "distinct voyage" under the policy. This would have voided coverage. A series of English cases held that so long as the destination was the same, an intent to deviate from a direct route not yet implemented would not void the policy. Justice Jacob Radcliff, writing for the Court, wished to ignore these cases but would have been prevented from doing so by the doctrine of *stare decisis*. He responded to this dilemma as follows: "Should we implicitly follow precedents, on occasions like the present, we must hope for little improvement in our commercial code. A single decision, though founded on mistake, would become of binding force, and by repetition, error might be continued, or heaped on error, until the common sense of mankind, and the necessity of the case oblige us to return to first principles, and abandon precedents. These considerations, I think, are sufficient to authorize a freedom of opinion."[38] Having placed the control of prior authority aside, Justice Radcliff arrived at what he considered to be "a just and rational rule, consistent with itself, and which may not lead to future embarrassment."[39] He found for the insurance company, concluding that the mere intention to stop at New York was sufficient to transform the trip from North Carolina to New York into a "distinct voyage" not covered under the policy.[40] In this manner, the New York Supreme Court of Judicature explained its willingness to recognize that a strict adherence to English common law principles could on occasion be incompatible with New York's notions of justice and rationality.

This relaxed view of English precedents was taken to the extreme in *Goix v. Low*[41] where Chief Justice John Lansing, Jr., of the New York Supreme Court of Judicature announced, in a minority opinion, that he no longer considered English cases binding authority in New York courts. The case was an action on a policy of insurance which covered the American ship Minerva on a voyage from New York to Guadaloupe. An exception to coverage under the policy included the lawful seizure of the ship and/or its cargo. The ship was captured on the insured voyage by a British ship of war, brought to the island of Antigua and there condemned by a court of admiralty as a lawful prize. No reason for the condemnation was stated in the sentence of the Court.

The issues before the New York Court were: (1) whether the description in the policy of the ship as being American constituted a warranty that she was transporting American property, and (2) whether a judgement of condemnation by a foreign court of admiralty, absent a statement of reason, could be presumed to be a factual determination that the ship was carrying a non-neutral cargo. The first issue was answered in the affirmative by all the justices. With regard to the second issue, however, Chief Justice Lansing parted with his fellow judges by disregarding the English case of *Saloucci v. Woodmass*[42] where Lord Mansfield held that it could be presumed from the condemnation of an Italian ship by a Spanish court of admiralty, absent a stated reason, that the ship's cargo belonged to an enemy of Spain. Lansing reasoned: "I cannot satisfy myself on what ground this presumption ought to prevail in preference to any other. The opinions of Lord Mansfield merit, and will always command a respectful attention; but at a period when they cease to be binding as authority, I can follow them so far only, as they tend to convince my mind that they are correct."[43] It was the opinion of Lansing that since no factual evidence existed to indicate that the Minerva's cargo was not neutral, the seizure of the ship must be considered unlawful. Thus, the owners of the Minerva had a valid claim for compensation under the policy. While this was not the holding adopted by the majority, the majority did not take issue with the Chief Justice's discussion of the value of English precedent.

The opinion that English precedents were no longer binding authority in New York was soon confirmed by the institution of a practice whereby English opinions were not to be relied upon prior to being sanctioned by either a New York or a federal court. In *Ward v. Center*,[44] Justice William W. Van Ness, a frequent correspondent of Peter Van Schaack (proprietor of the Kinderhook Law School), criticized an attorney's use of an English case noting that "the case of *Pa[i]sley v. Freeman*,[45] seems to have been taken for law, but it never has, to my knowledge, received the sanction of this court."[46] In *Wetmore v. Henshaw*,[47] Chief Justice Smith Thompson noted that "the principles upon which these [English] decisions are bottomed, have been sanctioned and affirmed by Judge *Washington*, in the circuit court of the *United States*."[48] The implications of this practice were summarized by William Johnson, Reporter for the New York Supreme Court of Judicature from 1799 to 1823. He wrote: "notwithstanding the declaration in the constitution, no lawyer can pronounce, with absolute certainty, that the principles he has learned from the English jurists, or the opinions of English judges, however accomplished and venerable, are the *law* of this state, until they have been recognised and sanctioned by our own courts."[49] Thus, sanctioning of English cases became a necessary prerequisite to their being relied upon by a New York court.

Carpenter v. Butterfield[50] represents an example of a case where there were conflicting English precedents. The case was an action of covenant by which Butterfield promised to pay Carpenter ninety-six pounds on 1 May 1798. At trial, the defendant offered a set-off in the form of a promissory note made by the plaintiff to Joseph Dickson and endorsed by him to the defendant. It was disclosed that the defendant procured the note to be endorsed to him after he received notice of the issuance of writ for his arrest and before it could be carried out. The issue presented before the New York Supreme Court of Judicature was whether a promissory note purchased by the defendant after the issuance of a writ for his arrest, but before the return of it, might be admitted as a set-off against the plaintiff's demand.

Justice James Kent, former Professor of Law at Columbia College and a close friend of Peter Van Schaack, considered the relevant English precedents and found them to contradict one another. He commented: "I have looked into the English authorities on this subject, and they are found to differ . . . it will appear that they cannot afford decisive ground, *as authorities*, for the determination of the present action." Having seized this opportunity to determine that he could no longer be bound by precedents because of their conflicting opinions, Kent turned his attention to the rationale behind the doctrine of set-off. He noted that it was adopted from the civil law "to advance justice and prevent a circuity of action" and thus it would never be "permitted for the purposes of fraud." In applying these principles to the case before him, Kent concluded that the defendant could not be allowed to prevail, for his purchase of the promissory note with the sole intention of defeating the plaintiff's action constituted fraud and was contrary to the doctrine of set-off.[51]

The three representative jurisdictions of Connecticut, Virginia and New York all adopted modifications to the doctrine of *stare decisis* which permitted English precedents to be questioned. What remained was to integrate into American legal practice the systematic and predictable method for judging precedents introduced by America's first generation of legal educators. The foundation of this approach was the reduction of precedents to their fundamental principles so as to make them easier to judge. The movement to instill this approach into American law was spearheaded in each of the representative states by legal educators who succeeded in gaining high appointments in their state court systems.

The Connecticut case of *Brown v. Union Insurance Co.*[52] presented an opportunity for Zephaniah Swift, proprietor of the Windham Law School and author of a treatise in which he recommended the use of a systematic method for the consideration of precedents,[53] to use his position as a judge on the Connecticut Supreme Court of Errors to implant into Connecticut law the idea of reducing questioned precedents to fundamental principles. Swift began his analysis of the case before the Court by noting: "It is conceded, that the decisions in Great Britain have no binding authority on us: and, as the question never has been decided in this court, it is open for examination on original principles; and it is in this point of view that I shall consider the subject."[54] The rule of law presented for consideration was an English practice of accepting, as conclusive evidence, a decree of a foreign court of admiralty that, under certain circumstances, the nature of the cargo of a vessel could constitute a breach of neutrality. Swift determined that this precedent was based upon principles of the law of nations which recognized the right of capture on the high seas by nations at war and the right of nations to create courts to determine questions of prize according to the law of nations. Given this, he reasoned that Connecticut courts were obliged to recognize this practice, not so much as an English precedent, but because it was founded upon the law of nations which had already become a part of American common law.[55]

In Virginia, in *Newton v. Wilson*,[56] St. George Tucker used his position as a judge on the Virginia Supreme Court of Appeals to implant the same method advocated by Swift. As noted earlier (see p. 74), Tucker stated in that case a willingness to reduce precedents to fundamental principles so as to judge more easily their soundness whenever he considered them ambiguous or contradictory.[57] In the action before the Court, he rejected a rule of law that prohibited the apportionment of rent where a lessee was not provided with services promised by a lessor in a commercial lease on the grounds that it was based upon the incorrect principle that a jury would be unable to estimate the loss of profits.[58]

One of the foremost judicial advocates in New York of the reduction of questioned precedent to its fundamental principles was Justice James Kent of the New York Supreme Court of Judicature. *Winton v. Saidler*[59] presented an early opportunity for Kent to show how this approach could be used to judge the soundness of an English precedent. The case before the Court presented conflicting English common law rules which Kent used as an opportunity for dispensing with the requirements of *stare decisis* and for reducing the rules to the general principles they were founded upon. He explained: "This court has never given any opinion on the question, and as the recent and contradictory decisions in England afford us no positive guide, we must examine the rule upon the general principles of the law of evidence."[60] Kent chose to consider the case of *Walton v. Shelley*[61] for it was representative of the school of thought with which he instinctively had problems. He determined that the general principle it was based upon was derived from the civil law maxim, *nemo allegans suam turpitudinem est audiendus* ["no one alleging his own turpitude is to be heard as a witness"], which he concluded should "be received with many limitations; for as a general rule, it is contradicted by daily experience," noting the common practice of having witnesses testify as to their own depravity in a case.[62] Based on this, Kent held that *Walton v. Shelley* and the line of precedents it represented were flawed and that the opposing rule of law was valid.[63]

Through the efforts of these prominent legal educators in their capacity as judges, the method for reducing issues of legal precedents to questions of legal principles was firmly established into American legal practice. The next step was to gain acceptance for a process whereby these principles could be judged against comparative standards. This was an essential aspect of the modified doctrine of *stare decisis* for it provided the legal system with the predictability necessary to protect a society from governmental harassment. The comparative standards used to judge precedents introduced by America's first generation of legal educators and successfully integrated into American legal practice were: utility, logic, morality and conflicting American law and the policy behind the law.

The standard employed most widely throughout the three states under consideration was that of utility. In *Sheldon v. Lemuel Kibbe*,[64] Chief Justice Stephen T. Hosmer of the Superior Court of Connecticut used the standard of utility to overrule an English precedent. The case before the Court was an action of assault and battery. The defendant sought to bar the action on the grounds that the plaintiff had obtained a former recovery against another individual for the same trespass. The plaintiff responded that he had never received satisfaction for that judgement because the individual was sent to prison, took the poor prisoner's oath and was discharged later, under the act for the relief of insolvent debtors, without having paid damages.

The fundamental issue presented before the Court was whether an unsatisfied judgement [an obligation created by a court which has not been complied with] against a joint trespasser is a bar to an action against his co-trespasser. The trial court decided in favor of the defendant, citing the English case, *Brown v. Wootton*,[65] which held that a judgement against an individual involved in a joint trespass is a bar to a suit against his co-trespasser. On appeal, Hosmer challenged this precedent by first establishing the role of utility in judging the law. He wrote: "The common law, founded as it is upon reason, and allowing nothing that is nugatory, much less that is pernicious, will sanction no inutility. . . ."[66] With reference to the specifics of *Brown v. Wootton*, Hosmer noted that its rule of law would also have to apply to a situation where joint trespassers were sued separately, for a person injured by a joint trespass maintained the choice under the common law to institute suit against the trespassers either jointly or severally. The result would be, wrote Hosmer, that the common law would, for example, "authorize the pendency and proceeding of twenty separate actions against persons concerned in a joint trespass, and after the accumulation of vast expense, . . . [would] . . . hold, that the first judgement bars the other suits!"[67] Since, under these circumstances, *Brown v. Wootton* would foster utility by making costly legal actions useless, Hosmer held that the trial court should not have considered it valid precedent.[68]

A similar argument was used in *Downman v. Downman's Executors*[69] where the Virginia Court of Appeals ruled a precedent invalid on the basis of utility. The case concerned an action of debt brought by Downman's executors against Downman. At trial, Downman's executors obtained a conditional judgement from the Clerk of the Court, and, at a later date, Downman petitioned the trial court for leave to set the judgement aside, and to file a plea of tender. A plea of tender is a common law pleading wherein the defendant states that he has been always ready to pay the amount demanded, and before commencement of the suit, tendered it to the plaintiff, and now brings it into court ready to make payment. The trial court refused to admit the plea, in part on the grounds that it was not pleaded immediately as required by common law precedent as noted in a decision by Lord Holt in *Idle v. Coke*[70]. The issue before the appellate court was whether an office judgement could be set aside in order to allow the filing of a plea of tender. In considering the English precedent relied upon by the trial court, the President of the Court of Appeals wrote: "Considering the circumstances of this country, and the dispersed situation of the attorneys and their clients, who can seldom communicate with each other but at Court, justice seems to require a relaxation in these rules of practice."[71] Thus, the Court determined that the precedent relied on by the trial court was incompatible with the realities of America's vast distances and held that the plea of tender should have been accepted so long as no delay was intended by the appellant.[72]

The standard of utility was also widely adopted in New York as a result of *Jackson, ex dem. Benton v. Laughhead*[73] where Justice Brockholst Livingston of the New York Supreme Court of Judicature employed it to judge an English legal practice unsuited to American needs. The case concerned an action of ejectment: Laughhead had mortgaged the land in question to Benton but had failed to keep up his mortgage payments, so Benton leased the land to Jackson, who sought to have Laughhead removed from the property. The trial court granted a verdict for the plaintiff, Jackson, subject to an opinion of the appellate court as to whether the defendant, Laughead, was entitled to a notice to quit prior to the ejectment action.

Justice Livingston determined that the English cases on point were "not sufficiently uniform to be of much service" and chose instead to decide the case on the basis of the utility of the situation. He reasoned that requiring a notice to quit prior to filing an action of ejectment would create "no hardship on the mortgagee, while a contrary practice may be much abused, in a country where so many thousand estates are held in this way." Furthermore, he believed that since the mortgagor usually had a much greater interest in the property than the mortgagee, requiring a notice to quit would at least allow the mortgagor the opportunity to "protect himself against an action by payment of the money due."[74] Justice Smith Thompson of the Court disagreed with this position on the grounds that it contradicted settled English practice noting that "in the case of *Keech v. Hall*, (Doug. 21.)[75] Lord *Mansfield* says, when the mortgagor is left in possession, the true inference to be drawn, is an agreement that he shall possess the premises at will, in the strictest sense, and therefore no notice is ever given him to quit." Livingston responded: "The case of *Keech v. Hall*, in *Douglas*, 21. is not an authority here, and it is enough to say that we may be permitted to regulate a mere matter of practice, even in opposition to what may, under other circumstances, be deemed a better course in Westminster-Hall." The majority of the Court sided with Livingston's utility-based argument and held that a mortgagor must receive a notice to quit at least six months before an action for ejectment can be brought by a mortgagee.[76]

James Willard Hurst described this use of utility as an American responsiveness to social circumstance which in turn fostered attempts to control the environment.[77] He noted: "In its structures and processes, law promoted such interplay of attention to general and particular aspects of experience as sharpened men's perception and cultivated their will to act."[78] Furthermore: "In many fashions thus the press and tug of general and particular in law encouraged us to try to command circumstance."[79] In making these claims, Hurst did not substantially rely on developments in early American legal education. Nevertheless, the evidence presented herein supports his conclusions.

In addition to utility, the standard of logic was used to judge precedent by examining whether it was based upon a logical foundation or by determining its logical consistency with similar cases. *Douglas v. Satterlee*[80] is a noteworthy example in which the New York Supreme Court of Judicature condemned a precedent by revealing that it lacked a logical foundation. The case was an action of assumpsit [an action which lies for the recovery of damages for the non-performance of an oral or simple contract or a contract that is neither of record nor under seal] against the administrators of an estate for payment of a promissory note made by the intestate. In answering the complaint, the administrators admitted the existence of the promissory note but refused to compensate the plaintiff because the estate would lack sufficient funds after settling previously submitted claims. The plaintiff responded with a general demurrer and joinder contending that the existence of other debts alone was no bar to his recovery in the cause and that the defendants answer was inappropriate for they should have pleaded *plene administravit praeter* ["plea of full administration"—a plea by an executor or administrator of an estate that he has fully administered all assets of the estate, except assets that are not sufficient to satisfy the plaintiff]. The issue before the Court was whether a plea admitting assets sufficient to settle plaintiff's claim should be judged bad *in toto*, allowing the plaintiff to be fully compensated, merely because the plea listed other claims that formed no protection to the assets.

In considering this case, Chief Justice James Kent was confronted by the English case of *Parker v. Atfield*[81] where Chief Justice Holt held that if an administrator incorrectly pleaded three judgments, while not having assets sufficient to satisfy one, it constituted an admission of assets to satisfy all three, in spite of a replication to the contrary, allowing the plaintiff to receive compensation for the judgments pleaded (in other words, the administrator would be liable for all three amounts). Kent disagreed, for he considered it illogical to judge a plea admitting one thing when the concluding part of the plea stated another. He wrote: "If the conclusion was just, the rule would be applicable, but when the plea contains an explicit averment of assets, it is equally illogical and unjust to let the implied admission of assets prevail over the express averment to the contrary, *expressum facit cessare tacitum*."[82] As a result, Kent, writing on behalf of the Court, granted judgement for the defendants on the grounds that an implied admission of assets to satisfy a recognized claim is superseded by an express statement to the contrary, even if this statement is not in proper form.

Another means of determining that a case lacked a logical foundation was to demonstrate that the application of one of its rules of law to certain factual circumstances would lead to absurd results. In *K. & E. Townsend v. Bush*,[83] Justice Zephaniah Swift of the Connecticut Supreme Court of Errors determined a rule of law espoused by Lord Mansfield—that no party who had signed an instrument should ever be permitted to give testimony to invalidate it—to be illogical because it could serve to shield criminal conduct. This became apparent in the case before him where the testimony of signatories of an instrument was necessary to prove it usurious. In determining the application of the Mansfield rule to the facts of the case, Swift commented: "If this principle should be carried to its full extent, it would furnish an effectual shield for usury, gambling, fraud, and illegal contracts. Let all who are concerned in the transaction, or who have knowledge of it, become parties to the writings made use of, and there will be neither danger nor possibility of detection."[84] Swift reasoned that since the rationale behind the Mansfield rule could only have been to preserve legal contracts, the fact that illegal contracts were sometimes preserved through the application of this rule indicated that the foundation of the precedent was illogical.[85]

The case of *Martin v. Payne*[86] is representative of another use of the standard of logic. Here, the New York Supreme Court of Judicature concluded that a precedent was inconsistent with all other cases on the same point. The case was an action of trespass on the case for debauching and impregnating the plaintiff's daughter causing the plaintiff to lose her services and to incur the cost of her pregnancy. At the time of the seduction, the daughter was nineteen years of age and lived with and worked for her uncle. Although she often visited her father, she stated at the trial that she did not intend to return to his house on a permanent basis for she had believed that the defendant wished to marry her.

The issue before the Court was whether the plaintiff could maintain an action based on a relationship of master and servant given the fact that the daughter worked for another and stated that she did not intend to return to live with her father. In considering the case, Justice Ambrose Spencer was presented by defendant's attorney with the English decision of *Dean v. Peel*[87] which held that since the daughter was in the service of another and had no intention of returning to the household of her father, the relationship of master and servant between her and her father did not exist. Spencer objected to this case noting, "That is the only case which has ever denied the right of the father to maintain an action for debauching his daughter whilst under age; and I consider it as a departure from all former decisions on this subject."[88] As a result of this use of the method of logical consistency, Spencer refused to sanction *Dean v. Peel* and held that the plaintiff could maintain an action based on master and servant in spite of his daughter working for another because she was under the age of majority and he was still responsible for her.[89]

Likewise, in *Griswold v. Penniman*,[90] Chief Justice Zephaniah Swift of the Superior Court of Connecticut evaluated English precedent by its logical consistency with other precedents. This case was an action brought by a creditor on a probate bond rendered by the defendant when she took administration of the estate of her husband. It was alleged in the complaint that the defendant breached her probate bond by failing to inventory a portion of the estate of her husband which consisted of the personal property of the defendant's father who had recently died intestate. The plaintiff contended that this property had vested in the defendant's husband upon the death of her father. The defendant argued that it had vested in her as a chose in action [a personal right not reduced into possession, but recoverable by a suit at law] and since it had not reduced to possession during the coverture, it survived to her on the death of her husband. The trial court found for the defendant and the plaintiff appealed.

The trial court's reasoning was based on the authority of an opinion by Lord Hardwicke in *Garforth v. Bradley*[91] which held that a chose in action coming to the wife during coverture, not reduced to possession by the husband by bringing an action in his own name, will survive to the wife. Swift compared this case to other unspecified relevant decisions and found it to be inconsistent with them. He wrote: "This opinion is contradictory to the whole current of authorities; and the concession, that the husband may sue in his own name, proves that the property absolutely vested in him, so that it could not survive, without some act done by him."[92] Having discovered this logical inconsistency, Swift concluded that the trial court was wrong in relying on *Garforth v. Bradley*.[93] Logic was thus the second standard employed to judge the soundness of English court opinions.

The dictates of morality were employed to rule precedents invalid when these precedents were deemed to be unjust, opposed to common or good sense or against natural law or justice. Believing that one should strive to make law indistinguishable from morality, American jurists were willing to use moral principles to resolve ambiguous domestic precedents.

In *Jones v. The Commonwealth*,[94] Justice Carrington, writing on behalf of the Virginia Supreme Court of Appeals, overruled a Virginia precedent which permitted juries to assess damages on a joint process because he considered it unjust. The case concerned four people who were jointly indicted for assaulting a magistrate. One died before trial and the remaining three were jointly convicted and jointly fined one hundred and six pounds. The issue presented for consideration was whether the rendering of a joint judgement and fine was proper. Carrington ruled that the trial court should have imposed separate fines of differing amounts depending upon each defendant's wrongdoing. He reasoned:

> If the case be considered on principle, the injustice of a contrary doctrine will be rendered more obvious. Where several persons are concerned in a trespass, the probability is, that some one of them is either from wealth, situation or talents, a man of more influence than the rest; and, therefore, that he does, by these adventitious circumstances, prevail upon the others to unite with him in it. Now, in such a case as that, would it not be the highest injustice to oblige one of the others of less capacity, poorer circumstances, and, therefore, liable to all the influence of his companion, to undergo as severe punishment as him who was more guilty, and perhaps in event a greater? It strikes me, that nothing could be more unreasonable; and therefore, I shall be very loth to yield my assent to such a position.[95]

The Virginia Court of Appeals extended this application of moral principles in *Waller v. Armistead's adm'rs*[96] by applying it to a rule of law established by the highest court of another state. The case before the Court concerned two deeds that were executed by a woman minutes before her marriage without the knowledge of her intended husband. One deed acquitted her brother, who served as her guardian after the death of their parents, of all claims pertaining to his investment of her inheritance. The other deed provided a gift of part of her inheritance to her brother's son in consideration of "natural love and affection." Her brother, who had previously drafted the deeds, presented them to her for the first time at her wedding. The question before the Court was whether the deeds were valid. A New York opinion by Chancellor James Kent was the only precedent considered which supported the validity of the deeds. In *Kirby v. Taylor*,[97] Kent drew a distinction between a deed that compensates a guardian for an antecedent duty and a deed of "release, acquittance or discharge." He considered the former void against "the policy of the law" and the latter "*prima facie*" valid. Justice Cabell, writing on behalf of the Virginia Court, disagreed: "We cannot perceive the justness of this distinction. A simple release, by which the guardian is exonerated from accounting, and consequently from paying a just balance which may be in his hands, is as much a gratuity as a direct gift by formal conveyance." As a result, the Court ruled both deeds invalid as being contrary to public policy and reprobated by fraud.[98]

Another form of the standard of morality redacted into American law was common or good sense. In *Filly v. Brace*,[99] common sense was used to reject a principle espoused by Lord Mansfield. The case before the Connecticut Supreme Court of Errors was an action on a note whose terms included an indemnification of Filly by Brace for warranting the credit worthiness of Brace to a third party who, as a result, accepted two other notes from Brace. When Brace failed to pay the two other notes, the third party sought payment from Filly on the basis of his warranty of Brace. Prior to compensating the third party, Filly sought payment from Brace under the terms of his notes' warranty provision. The majority of the Court held that Filly's suit was insufficient because his liability to the third party was not a cause of action. Justice Jesse Root, who had provided Tapping Reeve with legal instruction and remained a close friend, differed with his colleagues, however, noting that the rationale for their opinion was based on a statement of Lord Mansfield's in *Taylor v. Mills & Magnall*[100] which violated common sense. Root wrote of Mansfield's opinion: "But his assertion, if it be so understood, that an action never could be brought by the surety before he had paid the debt of his principal, was a mere obiter opinion, and not applicable to the cause then before him; and besides is contradictory to common sense and to other judicial determinations on the subject."[101]

This use of the notion of good sense as a standard against which to judge precedent was also applied by the New York Supreme Court of Judicature in *Cunningham v. Morrell*.[102] This was an action of covenant concerning an agreement for the construction of a turnpike road. The covenant provided for payment in installments, as work progressed. The dispute arose when, after work had commenced and after having received an installment payment, the builder sought final compensation before completing the project. The issue before the Court was whether performance under the covenant was a condition subsequent to final payment. A condition subsequent pertaining to a contract is one in which performance of a part of the contract by one party to the contract is a prerequisite to payment by another party. In considering this case, the Court was presented by counsel with two New York cases which, in application to the facts at hand, required that the completion of work should not be considered a condition subsequent to final payment. Chief Justice James Kent, writing on behalf of the Court, questioned the soundness of this precedent.

Kent established that both cases were governed by the English case of *Terry v. Duntze*,[103] which concerned a covenant for the construction of a building. The covenant provided that the building be completed by a given day and compensation be rendered in installments as the building proceeded, according to a prescribed state of progress, with final payment made when the building was completed. The Common Bench held that, because two installments were to be paid before completion of the building when only part of the construction was performed, the covenants were independent and the plaintiff could receive the entire consideration without showing that he had completed the building. Kent considered this decision contrary to the understanding of the parties, which required that final payment be made only after the building was completed. He reasoned that "the good sense and justice of the case . . . required this construction, and the meaning of the parties could not have been mistaken. The error in that case, and in the two cases in this court which followed it, consisted in holding the covenants to be independent *throughout*, because a part of the consideration money was to be paid before the entire service was to be performed." As a result, Kent overruled the two New York cases based on *Terry v. Duntze* and held that completion of the turnpike was a condition precedent to final compensation.[104]

The final form of the standard of morality against which precedents were judged was natural law or justice. Its use was most noteworthy in the Virginia Supreme Court of Appeals case of *Read v. Read*.[105] This was an action of ejectment brought by a citizen of Ireland, who took an oath of abjuration and allegiance to America on 21 November 1787, against an American citizen seeking real property in Virginia claimed to have been inherited as a result of the intestate death in October 1787 of the American citizen's husband. Pursuant to the common law, an alien was barred from inheriting real property. The plaintiff, however, argued that *Calvin's case*[106] authorized his inheritance of American property for it held that those born under obedience to one sovereign cannot be considered aliens. Justice Spencer Roane reasoned that this was based upon the principle that "allegiance is perpetual, and cannot be renounced by the subject" which he considered in opposition to natural law.[107] Roane stated that *Calvin's case*:

> denied the existence of a great natural right; I mean the right of expatriation. . . . Shall we not . . . correct the mistakes of a municipal code, touching a question of general law, by referring to the fountain from which itself has drawn? Shall we decide a question of natural right, and of general law, by referring to the most approved writers, and to the sense of the world, on that subject, or be governed by the particular municipal codes of a particular country? I believe, sir, that this position of the English judges has always stood condemned by the most enlightened writers upon natural law.[108]

As a result, the Court held that since the plaintiff was not an American citizen at the time of the death of the intestatus, he could not inherit the Virginia property in question.

This standard was also applied by the New York Supreme Court of Judicature in *Upton v. Vail*[109] where an action on the case was brought against Upton for "falsely and deceitfully" inducing Vail to give credit to one Daniel Brown, Jr. Upton had a judgement bond against Brown for five hundred and fifty dollars when he recommended Brown to Vail as a man of property so as to cause Vail to sell Brown ten dollars worth of goods on credit. Subsequently, Upton enforced his judgement and took possession of Brown's property including the goods purchased on credit from Vail.

The issue on appeal was whether the action could lie absent written evidence of the inducement. Chief Justice James Kent, delivering the opinion on behalf of the Court, did not find any binding precedent to assist in addressing this question. However, the nonbinding case of *Paisley v. Freeman*[110] supported the action. In determining whether or not to sanction the case, Kent reduced it to its underlying principle which he judged sound because it was consistent with natural justice. Kent wrote: "I have carefully examined the reasoning of the judges in that case, and in the subsequent cases, which go to the question, or support the soundness of that decision; and I profess my approbation of the doctrine on which it was decided. The case went not upon any new ground, but upon an application of a principle of natural justice, long recognized in the law, that fraud or deceit accompanied with damage is a good cause of action."[111] Thus, based upon the use of the standard of natural justice, the Court held that Vail could sustain an action against Upton in this case absent written proof of the inducement.[112]

The most far-reaching category of standards employed to judge precedents was conflicting American law and policy. It included American common law principles and their underlying policy and American constitutional requirements and the institutional values implied within them. While issues of conflicts of law occasionally found their way into British courts, the American federal system with its multiple jurisdictions presented much greater opportunities for legal comparison. In addition to conflicts between principles of American and English common law, the existence of written American constitutions, compared to the unwritten English constitution, made it easier for American judges to identify conflicts between common law principles and supreme constitutional requirements. The use of America's various constitutions as standards against which to judge precedents proved so powerful that it was almost immediately extended to domestic statutes through the exercise of the power of judicial review.

One of the earliest cases to use American common law principles to overrule the authority of English precedent was the Connecticut case of *Starr v. Starr*.[113] This was an appeal from a judgement of a court of probate which approved a last will and testament that granted property to the city and citizens of Middletown, Connecticut. The appellants contended that the will should have been ruled void because the appellees, as residents of Middletown, constituted legatees and, as a result, their witnessing of the will was invalid. The appellees responded that according to English law they were allowed to serve as witnesses to those portions of the will which did not directly affect them. In considering English precedent as applied to this case, the Connecticut Supreme Court of Errors questioned its compatibility with American legal principles. The Court reasoned:

> And although by some British authorities, executors and even legatees, who have released their legacy, and no party in the suit, have been admitted under certain circumstances (for there are adjudications both ways,) yet such adjudications are incompatible with the laws of Connecticut; the simplicity of which excludes the possibility of introducing that speculative metaphysical refinement which so

> much embarrasses the British courts, without deranging our whole system. . . . Further, witnesses interested in the question only, are there not excluded, but in Connecticut they are—so that according to the British practice witnesses may be admitted to prove a will as to one piece of land, although they hold other lands by the same will, and equally interested in the same question; but in Connecticut, such witnesses are wholly inadmissible.[114]

As a result, the Court ruled that the English authorities on this point were void, being incompatible with Connecticut law. Thus, the decision of the probate court was overruled.

This approach was followed in *Naylor v. Fosdick*[115] where the Connecticut Supreme Court of Errors disallowed a deed of assignment [the instrument of transfer by a party of all of his rights to some kind of property, usually intangible property such as rights in a lease, mortgage, agreement of sale or a partnership] authorized under English law because it would have constituted a change in Connecticut bankruptcy law. The case concerned an action of *scire facias* [a judicial writ, founded upon some matter of record, such as judgement or recognizance, and requiring the person against whom it is brought to show cause why the party bringing it should not have advantage of such record] brought by a creditor against a garnishee of an absent debtor. The debtor, in failing circumstances, had entered into an agreement with an agent of several of the creditors whereby the debtor executed a deed of assignment of debts due him to the agent as a trustee, instructing him to collect the debts and distribute the proceeds to the creditors equally and proportionally according to the respective amounts owed them. The plaintiff objected to this arrangement and pressed a claim against the defendant for garnishment of the debtor's assets in his possession. A garnishment is a statutory proceeding whereby a person's present and future assets are applied to payment of his debt to a third person by statutory process. Defendant's attorneys answered that, since his debt had been assigned to the trustee in accordance with English precedent, citing, in part, *Atkins v. Berwick*,[116] *Tarback v. Marbury*[117] and *Holbird v. Anderson*,[118] the plaintiff had no claim against him. Plaintiff's attorneys, Lyman Law (graduate of Litchfield, 1791) and William Pitt Cleaveland (graduate of Litchfield, 1794), responded that the deed of assignment was invalid because it prevented a creditor, without his consent, from exercising rights guaranteed by Connecticut bankruptcy law to secure debts through the attachment of property.

The issue presented before the Court was whether a debtor could make a binding assignment of his estate to a trustee for the benefit of creditors without the consent of all the creditors. In deciding this case, Justice Zephaniah Swift, writing on behalf of the Court, focused on the conflicts of law issue raised by the plaintiff. Swift reasoned: "by our law, the body and the estate both real and personal, of debtors, are responsible for their debts; and creditors are entitled to avail themselves of their superior vigilance in the attachment of property to secure their debts. To admit the assignment in question to be valid would be directly repugnant to the prominent principle in our jurisprudence."[119] Relying on the standard of conflicting law, Swift overruled the English precedents that authorized the above deed of assignment.[120]

The standard of comparative law was not limited to instances where clearly stated principles of law conflicted; it was also extended to circumstances in which precedent contrasted with the policy behind the law. In *Chappel v. Brewster*,[121] the Connecticut Superior Court held a series of principles of English property law void because they were opposed to the policy behind Connecticut's property law. The case before the Court was an action of disseisin [an action to dispossess the possessor of a freehold in deed] brought by the heirs of a testator against the possessor of land which had been willed to the plaintiffs. In 1733, Caleb Chappel died and in his will bequeathed the land in question to his "son Noah, and his male heirs forever; so that it may remain in the name of the Chappels forever." Noah died intestate leaving three sons who conveyed their rights to Joshua Chappel and his heirs with covenants of seisin and warrantee. Joshua conveyed the property to his daughter who in turn conveyed the property to the defendant. The plaintiffs, grandchildren of Noah Chappel, claimed that, according to the terms of the original will, none of the donees in tail [the lawful issue of a testator] had the right to alien the property for longer than their own lives. The defendant responded that the restrictions of the original will could only be deemed applicable to the first generation of heirs because otherwise it would conflict with Connecticut's rule against perpetuities.[122]

While the Court found that the restrictions of the will ceased to operate by the time the property came into the possession of Noah's sons, it was not satisfied that the wording of Connecticut's rule against perpetuities clearly applied. Instead, the Court decided the case on the policy behind the rule. It noted "that the doctrine of fee-simple [*sic*] conditional, and fee-simple [*sic*] absolute, as they were anciently held in England, and entailments, by virtue of the statute *de donis*, could never have any force in this state, being opposed to the nature of our tenures, and against the reason and policy of our law."[123] As a result, by relying on the standard of the policy behind the law, the Court found for the defendant on the grounds that the restrictive covenant in the will was contrary to the policy behind Connecticut's property law.

The Virginia Supreme Court of Appeals adopted this same approach in *Austin's Adm'x v. Winston's Ex'x*.[124] This was an action for specific performance [the remedy of performance of a contract in the specific form in which it was made, or according to the precise terms agreed upon] brought by the executrix of a debtor against the administratrix of one of his creditors to redeem slaves transferred from the debtor to the creditor. The slaves had been transferred as part of an agreement whereby the debtor exchanged the slaves for a fictitious debt, higher than his actual debt, on the condition that the debtor could have free use of some of the slaves or redeem them at a future date. This agreement was designed to defraud other creditors and the Commonwealth of Virginia by protecting the debtor's slaves from attachment. The Virginia High Court of Chancery decreed that the defendant was obliged to return those slaves or their value in excess of the original debt to the plaintiff. The defendant appealed to the Virginia Supreme Court of Appeals, which overturned the chancery court's opinion and ruled, citing *Walker v. Perkins*,[125] that relief should be apportioned according to the degree of criminality of both parties so as to discourage fraud and prevent extortion.

Justice St. George Tucker disagreed, arguing that *Walker v. Perkins* was contrary to the policy behind the common law. He wrote: "the doctrine contended for by Mr. *Blackstone*, in the case of *Walker v. Perkins*, above mentioned, has prevailed: but I incline to the contrary opinion, as thinking that all contracts founded on motives or considerations against the policy of the common law . . . are void both in law and equity, and ought not to have the aid of a Court to carry them into effect."[126] While this argument constituted a dissent, it did influence the Court to state that "it is not to be considered that any principle is here fixed so as to operate as a precedent in other cases."[127] The use of the standard of the policy behind the law here succeeded in limiting the application of an English precedent to future cases.

Another form of the standard of conflicting American law implanted into American legal practice involved using American constitutions as a standard against which to question the validity of precedents. The first American case to adopt this approach was *Commonwealth v. Caton*[128] where the Virginia Supreme Court of Appeals ruled a pardon voted by the Virginia House of Delegates unconstitutional. The case involved three men who had been convicted of treason under a statute passed in 1776 by the General Court. In 1782, the Virginia House of Delegates voted them a pardon and sent it to the Senate for concurrence, which the Senate refused. The Attorney-General moved in the General Court that the condemned be executed in accordance with their sentence. The prisoners pleaded the pardon granted by the House of Delegates. The case was adjourned to the Court of Appeals for "novelty and difficulty."

Justice George Wythe of the Court considered the case by entertaining arguments concerning the validity of the pardon under the terms of the Virginia Constitution. The Attorney-General contended that the pardon was void because the Senate had not concurred with the resolution as required by the Constitution. The attorneys for the prisoners argued that the language of the Constitution takes the power of pardoning from the executive branch and gives it to the "assembly" which they suggest is the House of Delegates. Wythe considered these arguments by referring to the Constitution itself. He wrote:

> These arguments receive some illustration from the twentieth section of the constitution, recognizing the power of the whole legislature, and not one branch, to abolish penalties and forfeitures: which is contravened by the other construction; for, if the house of delegates can remit part of the penalty, they may the whole, as well as the forfeiture of the goods, as the corporal suffering. An idea utterly inconsistent, with the recognition of a power, in the whole legislature, to do it.[129]

By judging the authorization of the pardon against the standard of the Virginia Constitution, Wythe ruled the pardon invalid. This was the first recorded American case where the question of the unconstitutionality of a resolution or law was discussed before a judicial tribunal and thus it constituted an important step in the development of the concept of judicial review.

The New York Supreme Court of Judicature also considered American constitutions as a standard against which to judge domestic precedents in *Dash v. Van Kleeck*.[130] The case was an action of debt for an escape. Jason Rudes, a debtor of the plaintiff, was imprisoned for his debts in the Albany County jail. The defendant, as Sheriff of Albany County, was responsible for the prison. On 18 May 1807, Rudes escaped to the northern part of the city of Albany and returned to incarceration immediately thereafter. The plaintiff did not find out about the escape until several years later. Subsequently, he commenced the above action. On 5 April 1810, after the filing of this suit but before the Court heard the case, the New York Legislature passed a statute that provided that a return or recapture of an escaped prisoner before a suit is brought for the escape, constitutes a good defence at common law.[131] The defendant pleaded *nil debet* ["he owes nothing"] and argued, in part, that the return of Rudes to prison prior to the commencement of the suit barred the plaintiff's recovery pursuant to the 5 April 1810 statute. The plaintiff responded that the statute could not be interpreted so as to have a retrospective effect because its language was prospective and because common law precedent provided that no statute was to have a retrospect beyond the time of its commencement. The relevant issue presented before the Court was whether the 5 April 1810 statute could be interpreted so as to apply retrospectively to the action of debt for an escape before the Court.

In deciding for the plaintiff, the Court was reluctant to accept his attorney's reliance on the common law to prohibit a retrospective interpretation of the Statute. Instead, the Court favored judging the Statute against several American constitutions. Chief Justice Kent, writing with the majority, interpreted the United States Constitution's prohibition against *ex post facto* laws so as to prevent a retrospective application of the New York Statute. He wrote: "An *ex post facto* law, in the strict technical sense of the term, is usually understood to apply to criminal cases, and this is its meaning, when used in the constitution of the *United States*; yet laws impairing previously acquired *civil rights* are equally within the reason of that prohibition, and equally to be condemned."[132] While the *ex post facto* clause of the United States constitution was sufficient to prevent a retrospective application of the New York statute, Kent was still faced with the problem of considering the Statute as an attempt by the legislature to inform the courts that they had been misinterpreting prior statutes.

In resolving this problem, Kent relied on a very liberal interpretation of judicial review by extending the use of constitutional standards to include policy implied within constitutions. Kent reasoned that this interpretation of the Statute could not be valid because the legislature "would then be taking cognizance of a judicial question" in violation of the doctrine of separation of powers. In support of this assertion, Kent surprisingly referred to other state constitutions in order to explain the rationale behind the doctrine of separation of powers applicable to New York. He wrote: "The constitutions of several of the United States, and among others, those of Massachusetts and Virginia, have an express provision, that the legislative and judicial powers shall be preserved separate and distinct, so that one department shall not exercise the functions belonging to the other."[133] Kent concluded that these express statements of other state constitutions explained the theory implied, but not written, in New York's constitution. Thus, the doctrine of separation of powers implied within the New York Constitution prohibited the legislature from requiring the judiciary to interpret a statute in a particular manner. In this case, Kent used expressed and implied provisions of a number of American constitutions as a standard against which to challenge a retrospective application of a New York statute.[134]

The use of policy implied within American constitutions as a standard against which to judge precedent was also adopted by the Virginia Supreme Court of Appeals in *Jones v. The Commonwealth*[135] where Justice Spencer Roane used the spirit behind the United States Bill of Rights to rule a Virginia precedent unconstitutional. In the same case, as noted earlier, Justice Carrington had overruled a precedent on the ground of morality, thus coming to the same conclusion as Justice Roane by a different route (see p. 83). This case concerned an assault by four people upon a magistrate in the execution of his office. Before trial, one of the accused died. At trial, the District Court rendered a joint judgement against the three remaining defendants and jointly fined them one hundred and six pounds.

The Virginia Supreme Court of Appeals granted a writ of supersedeas [a command to stay the proceedings at law] and took up the issue of whether the District Court ought not to have assessed separate fines against the several defendants in accordance to their degree of fault. The Virginia Attorney General argued that the District Court's assessment of a joint fine was authorized by Virginia precedent which allowed damages to be assessed on a joint process. Justice Spencer Roane, writing for the Court, judged this practice to be contrary to the policy behind that portion of the Bill of Rights which prohibited excess fines—a policy which, according to Roane, provided that one man should not be punished for the fault of another. He reasoned: "This is so unjust and contrary to the spirit of the Bill of Rights, that even if it were established by adjudged cases to be the law, nay even if an act of Assembly should pass authorizing it, in express terms, I should most probably be of opinion, that the one should be exploded, and the other declared unconstitutional and not law."[136]

Justice Roane broadened his use of constitutional policy as a means of voiding precedent in *Read v. Read*,[137] a case in which he had also applied the standard of morality to judge precedents (see p. 85). The issue presented before the Court was whether a British subject born before the American Revolution could inherit land in the United States before the treaty of 1794. The appellees argued that the appellant could not inherit the land in question because, as an alien, according to the common law, he was barred from inheriting real property in Virginia. The appellant responded that according to *Calvin's case,*[138] which held that persons born in Scotland after the accession of the James I to the crown of England were no longer aliens to England and were thus capable of inheriting land in England, Virginians still held allegiance to the British King and as such the appellant could not be considered an alien.

Roane addressed the issue presented before the Court by analyzing the reason behind *Calvin's case*. He began by explaining, citing St. George Tucker's, *Blackstone's Commentaries,*[139] that it "was bottomed upon three main principles": "1st. That allegiance is perpetual, and cannot be renounced by the subject; 2dly. A supposition of the continuation of the same sovereignty to which this perpetual allegiance was originally due; and, 3dly. The character of that allegiance, by the English law, is, that it is due to the person of the sovereign, and not to his political character." Roane proceeded by showing that each principle was "heterogeneous to our republican institutions." He considered the first principle in contrast to "the sublime principles contained in the declaration of independence [*sic*], and in the Virginia bill of rights [*sic*], consecrating the right of expatriation." He spoke of the second position as being contradicted by the fact that "the American people have erected a different as well as a new government." He judged the third principle to be exploded because "we have, happily, no king, to whose sacred person this allegiance may be said to be due. It is the government only, which affords protection to the citizen, and to this government only, which is perpetually changing, as to the persons who administer it, though itself is permanent, the allegiance of the citizen is due." As a result, in part, of this use of the policy behind the constitution, Roane rejected *Calvin's case* and concluded that the appellant could be barred from inheriting lands in Virginia because he was an alien.[140]

During America's post-Revolutionary and early National periods, American lawyers and judges, rather than citizen jurors as argued by Stimson, successfully integrated into American legal practice a modified doctrine of *stare decisis*, introduced by America's first generation of legal educators, which provided that precedents established by American courts should be strictly adhered to while permitting English precedents to be questioned against the standards of utility, logic, morality and conflicting American law and policy either because they had not yet been adopted or sanctioned by American courts or because they were determined to be in conflict with each other. Justice Tapping Reeve noted:

> The law of England . . . must with great propriety be deemed our law; for our ancestors came from that country, bringing with them the legal notions which there prevailed; which have ever been considered the common law of this country, unless altered by our own legislative acts, or so manifestly improper to be received, arising from widely differing local circumstances, that our courts have been obliged to reject them, to attain the ends of justice, for which all laws are made. But in a case where the reason is the same, and as strong in this country as

that, and of equal applicability to our circumstances as theirs, the law is the same.[141]

As attorneys and judges became more familiar with the use of this method, they also developed a willingness to question domestic precedents against the powerful comparative standards of morality and constitutional law. While this willingness to judge domestic precedents removed some predictability from the American legal system, it instilled a dynamic whereby laws could be more rapidly adapted to new and changing circumstances.

NOTES

1. David Lieberman, *The Province of Legislation Determined* (Cambridge: Cambridge University Press, 1989), pp. 99–143. Even Blackstone admitted in the *Commentaries*, 1:69, that precedent could be questioned if it were determined to be "most evidently contrary to reason; much more if it be contrary to the divine law."
2. Jim Evans, "Changes in the Doctrine of Precedent during the Nineteenth Century" in Laurence Goldstein, ed., *Precedent in Law* (Oxford: Clarendon Press, 1987).
3. Shanon C. Stimson, *The American Revolution in the Law* (London: Macmillan, 1990), p. 3.
4. Zephaniah Swift, *A System of the Laws of the State of Connecticut*, 2 vols. (Windham, CT: John Byrne, 1795).
5. 1 Kirby 114 (1786).
6. Id. at 116–117.
7. 4 Day 298 (1810).
8. Tapping Reeve, *The Law of Baron and Femme* . . . (New Haven, CT: Oliver Steele, 1816); Tapping Reeve, *A Treatise on the Law of Descents* (New York: Collins & Hannay, 1825).
9. Bush v. Bradley, 4 Day 298, 305 (1810).
10. Id. at 307.
11. 1 Conn. 259 (1814).
12. 99 Eng. Rep. 1104 (1786).
13. Id. at 266.
14. 30 Eng. Rep. 1154 (1798).
15. Id. at 261.
16. Id. at 266.
17. See also: Starr v. Starr, 2 Root 303 (1795); Babcock v. Huntington, 2 Day 392 (1806).
18. William E. Ross, *History of Virginia Codification*, 11 Va. L. Reg. 79 (June, 1905).
19. 1 Va. (1 Wash.) 417 (1794).
20. Id. at 418.
21. Id. at 420. See also: Eldridge and Another v. Fisher, 11 Va. (1 Hen. & M.) 559, 560 (1807), where attorney G.K. Taylor argued "*Stare decisis* is a rule which I hold in as much respect as any man in the Commonwealth, but there are cases in which it may be necessary to depart from it. . . ."

22. 11 Va. (1 Hen. & M.) 154 (1806).

23. Id. at 154.

24. 100 Eng. Rep. 143 (1788).

25. Id. at 156.

26. Id. at 155.

27. Id. at 156.

28. Id. at 161–163.

29. See also: Thornton v. Smith, 1 Va. (1 Wash.) 106, 109 (1792), where the president of the Virginia Court of Appeals refused to be bound by an English precedent because it was grounded upon circumstances foreign to Virginia.

30. 13 Va. (3 Hen. & M.) 470 (1809).

31. St. George Tucker, *Blackstone's Commentaries: with Notes of Reference, to the Constitution and Laws, of the Federal Government of the United States; and of the Commonwealth of Virginia*, 5 vols. (Philadelphia: William Young Birch and Abraham Small, 1803).

32. 13 Va. (3 Hen. & M.) 470, 480 (1809).

33. Baron Jeffrey Gilbert, *A Treatise on Rents* (London: Henry Lintot, 1758), pp. 187–188.

34. Id. at 481.

35. Id. at 482. See also: Braxton v. Winslow, 4 Call 308, 314–317 (1791), where Justice Spencer Roane and Chancellor George Wythe independently noted that conflicting English decisions presented an opportunity for ignoring the dictates of precedents.

36. Stanley N. Katz, ed., *James Alexander's Brief Narrative of the Case and Trial of John Peter Zenger, Printer of the New York Weekly Journal* (Cambridge: Harvard University Press, 1963).

37. 1 Johns. Cas. 184 (1799).

38. Id. at 191.

39. Id. at 190.

40. Id. at 196.

41. 1 Johns. Cas. 341 (1800).

42. 99 Eng. Rep. 688 (1784).

43. Id. at 359.

44. 3 Johns. Cas. 269 (1808).

45. [100 Eng. Rep. 450 (1789)].

46. Id. at 278.

47. 12 Johns. 324 (1815).

48. Id. at 336.

49. William Johnson, *Reports of Cases Adjudged in the Supreme Court of Judicature of the State of New York . . .*, 3 vols., 2nd ed. rev. (New York: Banks, Gould & Co., 1846), I:viii.

50. 3 Johns. Cas. 144 (1802).

51. Id. at 153–155. See also: The People v. Herrick, 13 Johns. 82 (1816), where Justice Ambrose Spenser, a close friend of Peter Van Schaack, resorted to a fundamental principle, in the face of conflicting English precedents, to hold that a prisoner could serve as a witness in a court of law; Denton v. Noyes, 6 Johns. 296, 311 (1810), in which Justice William W. Van Ness of the New York Supreme Court of Judicature wrote: "But I think I shall be able to show, that the weight of authority is against the opinion of the court [that an attorney was permitted to appear for a person who had not

employed him], or, at least, that the law is so far doubtful, as to leave us at liberty to establish a rule for ourselves."

52. 4 Day 179 (1810).

53. Swift, *A System of the Laws.*

54. 4 Day 179, 186 (1810).

55. Id. at 186–187. See also: Fish v. Fish, 1 Conn. 559, 561 (1816), where Justice James Gould of the Superior Court of Connecticut, a 1795 graduate and joint proprietor of the Litchfield Law School, refused to follow an English precedent because, in reducing it to its underlying principles, he judged it contrary to reason.

56. 13 Va. (3 Hen. & M.) 470 (1809).

57. 13 Va. (3 Hen. & M.) 470, 480 (1809).

58. Id. at 481–482. See also: Hoyle v. Young, 1 Va. (1 Wash.) 188, 190 (1793), where the Virginia Court of Appeals stated, in reference to a question about when a demurrer to evidence could be received at trial: "We have been able to derive but little aid upon this subject from the *English* books, and have therefore taken it up on principle."

59. 3 Johns. Cas. 185 (1802).

60. Id. at 190.

61. 99 Eng. Rep. 1104 (1786).

62. 3 Johns. Cas. 185, 191 (1802).

63. See also: Le Roy v. Servis, 1 Cai. Cas. 1, 4 (1801), where the New York Court for the Trial of Impeachments and Correction of Errors wrote: "The cases on this question [of whether the Chancellor could retain jurisdiction on the point of relief in a cause referred to a law court] are contradictory. The law is not bound down by a series of uniform decisions, in a manner not to be shaken, and so as to preclude the consideration of the reason of the rule."

64. 3 Conn. 214 (1819).

65. 79 Eng. Rep. 62 (1605).

66. Id. at 219.

67. Id. at 219.

68. See also: Halsey v. Brown, 3 Day 346 (1809), where the Connecticut Supreme Court of Errors ruled that the English case of Ellis v. Turner, 101 Eng. Rep. 1529 (1800), which held the owners of a vessel liable for goods received by the ship's master for transport, was not valid precedent in the case before them in light of useful local custom which provided that the freight of money received by the master of a vessel was his perquisite; Fish v. Fish, 1 Conn. 559, 563 (1816), where Justice James Gould of the Superior Court of Connecticut ruled an English precedent invalid, which provided that a widow could not have dower in an equity of redemption, because "the practical hardship of the rule established in *England*, is, in that country, comparatively small: whereas, in this state, it would be very severe."

69. 1 Va. (1 Wash.) 34 (1791).

70. 91 Eng. Rep. 525 (1705).

71. Id. at 37.

72. See also: Ross v. Poythress, 1 Va. (1 Wash.) 155 (1792), where then attorney John Marshall, a graduate of the College of William and Mary and a student of George Wythe, successfully argued that goods and chattels could be used to satisfy judgments, in violation of English precedent which required judgments to be settled in cash, because, contrary to the circumstances of England, most American wealth was held in

real property and currency was scarce; Slaughter v. Green, 22 Va. (1 Rand.) 3 (1821), where Justice Spencer Roane employed the standard of utility to uphold an interpretation of a bailment, whereby wheat provided to a grist mill by multiple suppliers could be held in a common stock and milled into a common mass of flour, on the grounds that it was generally convenient.

73. 2 Johns. 75 (1806).

74. Id. at 75–76.

75. [99 Eng. Rep. 17, 18 (1778)].

76. Id. at 76–77. See also: Salstonstall ads. White, 1 Cole. & Cai. Cas. 86 (1799), where the New York Supreme Court of Judicature held: "The strict principles applicable to proceedings as for a vacant possession in England, cannot, without manifest inconvenience, be applied to unlocated lands in this country"; Hassenfrats v. Kelly, 13 Johns. 466, 469 (1816), where Justice Ambrose Spenser of Supreme Court of the State of New York held invalid a precedent, which made the seller of land liable for damages caused by the existence of an adverse possessor who the seller had no knowledge of, because "it would be impossible for any man, owning lands in the unsettled part of our country, to convey them with safety; for, peradventure, some man may have intruded upon them, who would have the hardihood to give a warranty deed."

77. James Willard Hurst, *Law and the Conditions of Freedom* (Madison: The University of Wisconsin Press, 1956); James Willard Hurst, *Law and Social Process in United States History* (Ann Arbor: University of Michigan Press, 1960); James Willard Hurst, *Law and Social Order in the United States* (Ithaca, NY: Cornell University Press, 1977).

78. Hurst, *Law and Social Process*, p. 152.

79. Ibid., p. 167.

80. 11 Johns. 16 (1814).

81. 91 Eng. Rep. 1351 (1701).

82. 11 Johns. 16, 20 (1814).

83. 1 Conn. 259 (1814).

84. Id. at 270.

85. See also: Denton v. Noyes, 6 Johns. 296, 316 (1810), where Justice William W. Van Ness dissented from the holding of the Court by listing the injustices that would result by applying the holding to other circumstances; Cunningham v. Morrell, 10 Johns. 203, 205 (1813), where Chief Justice Kent overruled an English decision because it "misapplied, or carried to an unreasonable length" a rule of law; Pinto v. Atwater, 1 Day 193, 199 (1804), where attorney John Stark Edwards (graduate of Litchfield, 1796) successfully argued: "When a general rule is not correctly applied, we may reject the application and resort to the rule. . . ."

86. 9 Johns. 387 (1812).

87. 102 Eng. Rep. 986 (1804).

88. Id. at 389–390.

89. See also: Denton v. Noyes, 6 Johns. 296, 314 (1810) where Justice Van Ness used the method of logical consistency to question a precedent noting: "If we were right in that case, of which I have no doubt, the court must be wrong in this; for it is impossible for both decisions to be right."

90. 2 Conn. 564 (1818).

91. 28 Eng. Rep. 430 & 570 (1755).

92. Id. at 567.

93. See also: Fitch v. Brainerd, 2 Day 163, 183 (1805), where attorneys David Bryan Ingersoll (graduate of Litchfield, 1792) and David Daggett (proprietor of Staple's Law School) argued that a *feme covert* could legally devise her real estate with the consent of her husband because this rule of law was logically consistent with her power to devise personal property.

94. 5 Va. (1 Call) 555 (1799).

95. Id. at 558–559.

96. 29 Va. (2 Leigh) 11 (1830).

97. 6 Johns. Ch. 242 (1822).

98. 29 Va. (2 Leigh) 15 (1830).

99. 1 Root 507 (1793).

100. 98 Eng. Rep. 1221, 1223 (1777).

101. Id. at 513.

102. 10 Johns. 203 (1813).

103. 126 Eng. Rep. 611 (1795).

104. Id. at 205–206. See also: Markle v. Hatfield, 2 Johns. 455, 458 (1807), where attorney F. Tallmadge successfully argued that Lord Coke's opinion in Vane v. Studley (cited in Wade's case, 77 Eng. Rep. 232, 234 (1601) "is against every principle of justice and common sense."

105. 3 Va. (5 Call) 160 (1804).

106. 77 Eng. Rep. 377 (1608).

107. Id. at 200.

108. Id. at 201.

109. 6 Johns. 181 (1810).

110. 100 Eng. Rep. 450 (1789).

111. Id. at 182.

112. See also: Jones v. The Commonwealth, 5 Va. (1 Call) 555, 556 (1799), where Justice Spenser Roane sanctioned Godfrey's case, 77 Eng. Rep. 1199 (1614) because it was "bottomed upon . . . the principles of natural justice."

113. 2 Root 303 (1795).

114. Id. at 306–307.

115. 4 Day 146 (1810).

116. 93 Eng. Rep. 450 (1719).

117. 23 Eng. Rep. 926 (1705).

118. 101 Eng. Rep. 132 (1793).

119. Id. at 157.

120. See also: Nash v. Tupper, 1 Cai. R. 402, 412–413 (1803), where the New York Supreme Court of Judicature ruled against the well-settled English principle that contracts, with few exceptions, are to be construed according to the laws of the country in which they are made, on the grounds that a seventeen-year statute of limitations prescribed in Connecticut where two promissory notes under dispute were signed was inapplicable to a case filed in a New York court given New York's six-year statute of limitations.

121. 1 Kirby 175 (1786).

122. Id. at 175.

123. Id. at 176–177.

124. 11 Va. (1 Hen. & M.) 33 (1806).

125. 96 Eng. Rep. 299 (1764).

126. Id. at 37.
127. Id. at 51.
128. 3 Va. (4 Call) 5 (1782).
129. Id. at 13.
130. 7 Johns. 477 (1811).
131. 1810 N.Y. Laws c. 187.
132. 7 Johns. 477, 505 (1811).
133. Id. at 508.
134. See also: Turner v. Turner's Ex'x., 4 Call 234 (1792), where the Virginia Supreme Court of Appeals ruled a 1787 Virginia statute unconstitutional in that it violated the *ex post facto* and separation of powers clauses of the Virginia Constitution.
135. 5 Va. (1 Call) 555 (1799).
136. 5 Va. (1 Call) 555 at 557.
137. 3 Va. (5 Call) 160 (1804).
138. 77 Eng. Rep. 377 (1608).
139. Tucker, *Blackstone's Commentaries*, 1:371.
140. 3 Va. (5 Call) 160, 200–202.
141. Peck v. Lockwood, 5 Day 22, 26 (1811).

5

The Effect of a Uniquely American Legal Thought on the Americanization of Law

In 1977, Morton J. Horwitz published *The Transformation of American Law 1780–1860* in which he argued that judges during the post-Revolutionary and early National periods instigated a change in legal thought. He demonstrated that they developed a perception of law which allowed them to play a role, along with legislators, in governing society, promoting socially desirable conduct and bringing about social change.[1] Although Horwitz recognized this change, he believed that it was solely fostered by an economically influenced judiciary which sought to enable "emergent entrepreneurial and commercial groups to win a disproportionate share of wealth and power in American society."[2] While he considered the possibility that there was another influence behind this development, noting that "judges and jurists had begun to convert the old natural law justification of the common law into a theory of legal 'science'," he concluded, "except for the identification of 'science' with systematization and classification . . . there is no coherent content or methodology to be found in these persistent claims to the scientific character of law," and thus the intellectual influences on this changing conception of law were minimal at best.[3]

This position, however, is in need of revision. It has been already shown herein that there was indeed a coherent content and methodology associated with the scientific perception of law and that this perception, rooted in ideas propounded by European natural law writers, developed into a uniquely American legal thought. What remains is to trace the impact the intellectual influences embodied in this new American legal thought had on the Americanization of English statutory and common law.

As is shown below, post-Revolutionary and early National period American lawyers employed this new legal thought to persuade judges to mould principles of law, particularly in the areas of property law, commercial law and family law, to the economic needs and republican values of the new nation. This new legal thought opened the door for civil law which gained entrance into American jurisprudence as jurists sought models for replacing laws they had judged unsound or inapplicable. Judicial activists extended this questioning of the law to statutes and executive orders through the advent of judicial review. Those lawyers who were committed to extensive reformation of the law changed their forum to state legislatures where, through the passage of statutes, the law could be more actively modified. This legislative activity came to a head in the form of the American codification movement. Although this movement was unsuccessful in accomplishing its goal of replacing the entire common law with a comprehensive code, complete areas of the law, most notably concerning property and crime, were replaced with subject-specific codes.

The implications of these activities were profound. The tension that developed between those who advocated the expansive use of courts to modify the law and an aggressive use of judicial review and those who sought to limit this power was the origin of the modern conflict of judicial activism versus judicial conservatism. Armed with the ability to question the law, American lawyers encouraged the litigiousness of the American people and were instrumental in creating a legal system that would settle political, as well as legal, disputes. Examination of this progression and development of ideas reveals that the influence of post-Revolutionary and early National period legal education in America was much greater than has previously been supposed, not only in the field of the law proper, but in the extent of its influence on American society and politics.

Reformation of the law in accordance with ideas put forth by early American legal educators first came about in the common law court room. Equity courts, which had traditionally adapted the law to new circumstances, were no longer accomplishing this task because of skepticism about the role of equity which had developed from colonial experiences.[4] As a result, the power of equity courts was restricted to the point where it could not Americanize the law. Instead, instances of the incompatibility of the English common law to American circumstances were exposed by the presentation of personal disputes to common law courts for resolution. Lawyers who had been educated to question legal precedents brought such conflicts to the attention of the courts, using arguments based on standards of reason rather than precedent to persuade judges to resolve disputes by modifying or replacing the law in question. The aspects of the common law most significantly altered in this fashion were property law, commercial law and family law.

English property law was the primary focus of reform by post-Revolutionary American jurists because they believed it to be aristocratic and opposed to republican values, in that it was designed to preserve what Americans perceived as the feudal system. Thomas Cooper wrote: "what harmony is there between allodial property and feudal law?"[5] [Allodial, which is the opposite of feudal, is defined as property owned without obligation of vassalage or fealty.] The complexity of the English law of real property was seen as preventing most Americans from knowing their legal rights and from enforcing them. Henry Dwight Sedgewick complained that there was nothing "more simple than the ownership of real property," but the common law relating to it was so plagued by "subtleties, quibbles, refinements, and false analogies . . . that it can excite little admiration except in the eyes of a thoroughbred common lawyer."[6] The restraint placed by the English law of real property on the free exchange of property was particularly problematic in a country where land was the major source of wealth. Due to the lack of a stable hard currency through much of the post-Revolutionary period, land was often a necessary means for securing debt. As such, it was imperative that people be allowed to buy and sell it freely. To prevent this through legal restraints was perceived as preserving the existence of an American landed gentry whom American jurists called aristocratic and whom they considered anti-republican (see p. 31).

New York courts considered English property law a likely target for reform because it was viewed as not being suited to American circumstances. In *Jackson v. Brownson*[7], attorney Joseph Kirkland convinced the Supreme Court of New York of the necessity of questioning against the standard of utility the English precedent that provided that timber should not be removed from land by a tenant as it is considered an injury to the inheritance of the heirs of the owner of the property. Justice William Van Ness, writing on behalf of the Court, adopted Kirkland's argument almost word-for-word, noting that New York was heavily forested, unlike England, so that it was usually necessary to clear land so as to render it fit for cultivation. Thus, the Court decided to abandon the English rule of law, holding instead that where wild and uncultivated land, wholly covered with timber was leased, the tenant might cut down part of the timber, in order to make the land suitable for cultivation; but he could not fell all the timber, so as to permanently injure inheritance. *Hassenfrats v. Kelly*[8] also provided the Supreme Court of New York with an opportunity to judge a principle of English common law inapplicable to American circumstances. The principle provided that a person who conveyed real property that was adversely possessed [the acquisition of real property by possession for a statutory period under certain circumstances] by another could be held liable for selling a pretended title. The Court reasoned that holding a conveyer of real estate liable for failing to disclose an adverse possession was unreasonable in America, where large tracts of land were often held by absentee owners who would not easily come by knowledge of trespassers on their land. As a result, the Court established the rule that a person who conveys land, without knowledge that there is a subsisting adverse possession, is not liable for selling a pretended title.[9]

The Americanization of property law was not the exclusive domain of New York. Connecticut courts often modified English common law because they believed it to be corrupted by anti-republican principles. The Connecticut Superior Court, in *Chappel v. Brewster*,[10] was successfully convinced by attorneys Elkanah Tisdale and Hezekiah Huntington to conclude that the English tenures of fee-simple conditional, fee-simple absolute and entailments had no force in Connecticut because they were deemed "opposed to the nature of our tenures, and against the reason and policy of our law."[11] The Court ruled that a 1733 will which bequeathed real property to the testator's male heirs forever so that it would remain in the name of his family constituted an invalid fee tail estate which was prohibited because it would lead to the creation of an American aristocracy based upon property ownership. [Fee tail is an estate of inheritance given to a man and the heirs of his body, or limited to certain classes of particular heirs.] As a result, the Court ordered that the property be transferred to the heir as a fee simple estate which incorporates no restrictions.

The same type of argument was applied to the case of *Bush v. Bradley*[12] where David Bryan Ingersoll and Nathan Smith successfully argued that the Connecticut Supreme Court of Errors should reject an English law that prevented an heir-at-law from acquiring a testator's property because, while it was owned by the testator, it was never seised in by him. Justice Tapping Reeve wrote for the Court: "The English law distinguishes betwixt a right of possession and a right of property; but our law does not. Wherever there is a right to real property, there is, of course, a right of possession, and the statute, which takes away the right of possession, takes away the right of property. . . ."[13] The grounds for this rejection were, in part, based on the notion that any law that prevented the free transfer of property because of a mere technicality was contrary to America's republican values.

The second area of law to be Americanized was commercial law. Changes were fostered by America's sense of commercial utilitarianism and the government's need to assist economic development. In *Mayell v. Potter,*[14] the New York Supreme Court of Judicature modified the English common law rule that a common carrier is bound to deliver goods according to their engagement, on the grounds of commercial utilitarianism. This was a special action on the case concerning a bill of lading signed by the defendant, for failing to deliver merchandise that was ultimately intended for the plaintiff. The defendant, the master of a schooner, acknowledged receipt of four cases of merchandise which he agreed to deliver from New York to Najah Taylor in Norfolk, Virginia. Mr. Taylor was visiting Norfolk on business, but no specific address was given for his whereabouts. Taylor alleged he never received the goods. The defendant proved that, according to local custom, he sent the shipment via a Hampton pilot from City Point to Thomas Allen for delivery to Taylor, who could not be located. The Court chose to ignore English precedent, which would have required the defendant to adhere strictly to the terms of the bill of lading. Instead, the Court modified the English rule so as to permit a common carrier to leave such goods with someone who knew the person intended to receive the goods, if the intended receiver could not be located, because this was according to the usage of trade.

This utilitarian approach was also adopted in *Cunningham v. Morrell*[15] where attorney Allen Fisk persuaded the New York Supreme Court to dismiss the English case of *Terry v. Duntze*[16] because it "carried too far the principle of mutual and independent covenants" at the expense of the economic well being of the parties.[17] In that case, the covenant provided that the plaintiff should complete a building by a given day and the defendant should pay consideration in installments as construction progressed. Two separate sums of money were to be paid before completion of the building. When only part of the service had been performed, the English court had held the covenants independent of the progress of the work and permitted the plaintiff to maintain an action for the entire consideration, without any averment of performance. This was contrary to the intention of the parties. The error in that case, according to the New York court, was in holding the covenant to be independent throughout, "because a part of the consideration money was to be paid before the entire service was to be performed." Chief Justice James Kent, writing on behalf of the Court, commented: "The good sense and justice of the case, as it appears to us, required this construction, and the meaning of the parties could not have been mistaken." Thus, the New York Supreme Court adopted the position, contrary to English precedent, that in order for the plaintiff to be entitled to the whole consideration, he was required "to aver and show a performance of the whole work."[18]

Connecticut also modified English commercial law as is noted in *Halsey v. Brown*[19] where the Connecticut Supreme Court of Errors was persuaded by Calvin Goddard to reject the English case of *Ellis v. Turner*[20] as it applied to "the freight of money received by the master of a vessel."[21] That case held that the owners of a vessel were liable for goods received by its master for transportation. Justice Zephaniah Swift disagreed, claiming that the custom and usage of merchants in Connecticut and New York provided that any payment for the transport of money received by the master of a vessel was his own perquisite. Swift argued that this constituted an exception to the common law rule. He explained:

> The general law applicable to the commercial world, that owners of vessels are answerable for the contracts and conduct of their masters, when acting within the scope of their authority, must be admitted. But as it is a principle, that the general common law may be, and in many instances is, controlled by special custom; so the general commercial law may, by the same reason, be controlled by a special local usage, so far as that usage extends; which will operate upon all contracts of this nature, made in view of, or with reference to, such usage.[22]

The Court accepted Swift's argument and held that the owners of the vessel were not liable for the loss of gold and silver accepted as freight by the ship's master. Instead, the Court ruled the ship's master was liable since the contract was personal and an individual obligation.[23]

Virginia continued this trend in *Newton v. Wilson*[24] where the Virginia Supreme Court of Appeals was encouraged by William Wirt and James Randolph to contest the English practice of not apportioning rents in a situation where a person rented land with cattle and some of the cattle died. St. George Tucker, writing for the Court, believed that the stated reason behind the English rule—that determining the amount of apportionment would be too difficult—was erroneous, for a jury of farmers "would probably be able, very easily to estimate the profits which might have arisen" from the cattle if none had died.[25] Thus, the Court held that the apportionment of rents in similar cases, while invalid in England, was valid in Virginia.[26]

A third area of law targeted for Americanization was family law, which included the liberalization of divorce law and the extension of legal rights to married women. The American Revolution had affected how women perceived themselves and how men perceived women. In *Women of the Republic*,[27] Linda Kerber showed that the Revolution sped the integration of women into the civil polity—their services in a guerilla war were much sought after, to provide food and shelter, to contribute funds and to act as spies. This raised the consciousness of women generally, a factor that may be illustrated by the increase in divorce rate.

Norma Basch has documented that the majority of American states and territories adopted liberal divorce laws during the post-Revolutionary period.[28] Linda Kerber noted a direct connection between the ideas and imagery of the Revolution and the changed attitudes towards divorce. She wrote: "The principles of the Revolution, after all, had laid great stress on the right to be free of burdensome masters, and the rhetoric of the Revolution had drawn heavily on the imagery of the happy and the unhappy family."[29] Women in unhappy marriages issued their own declarations of independence through American divorce proceedings. The number of per capita divorces in the thirteen colonies and later states filed by women nearly doubled from 1775–1786 as compared to 1765–1774.[30] Although this was fostered by the desires of women, they were empowered by the enactment by men in state legislatures of liberal divorce laws.

Changes specifically addressing the rights of women were not enacted into law for approximately another twenty years. During those years, a new generation of men had been brought up by women who took a more active role in the family. The Revolution had led to the creation of the image of the "republican mother" who was in charge of rearing republican children and of instilling republican values in children. Such women could not continue to be regarded as mere chattels, but as individuals with rights of their own.[31]

Between 1815 and 1830, a married woman's right to possess and control property independent of her husband had been firmly established in American law. In *Fish v. Fish*,[32] for example, the Connecticut Supreme Court of Errors addressed the issue of whether a widow can be endowed of an equity of redemption. An equity of redemption is a right a mortgagor is given after a foreclosure to redeem his property from default by paying the amount of debt, interest and costs. Pursuant to the English common law, it had been held that a widow could not have dower in an equity of redemption.[33] Justice James Gould (graduate of Litchfield, 1795, and co-proprietor of the Litchfield Law School), writing with the majority, was encouraged by attorney Jonathan Walter Edwards (graduate of Litchfield, 1794) to consider this rule inapplicable to Connecticut on the basis of a utilitarian argument. Gould accepted Edwards' position, noting:

> the practical hardship of the rule established in *England*, is, in that country, comparatively small: whereas, in this state, it would be very severe. In *England*, a mortgage in *fee* is rarely made; security upon lands being usually effected, by creating a large term for *years*, by way of mortgage, and thus leave the right of dower unimpaired; a consideration, which may have prevented the interposition of Parliament, to alter the rule. Our mortgages, on the other hand, are almost universally in fee.[34]

In other words, since English mortgages were effectively equivalent to long-term leases, the widow could retain her right of dower provided that she made such payments as were required. In America, however, since the mortgage would have transferred title to the property in fee simple to her husband, she would not be able to redeem a foreclosed mortgage in his name. As a result, the Court established the rule that a widow could be endowed of an equity of redemption.[35] This Connecticut case is representative of changes in the law which occurred in a number of other states. Marylynn Salmon has noted: "In New York, Maryland, Virginia, and South Carolina, chancellors applied and developed a body of law allowing *femes coverts* to own separate property. Over time, the degree of independence granted to women in these jurisdictions increased, and by the end of the period studied [1750–1830], the right to separate property was exercised with relative ease."[36]

The final area of the law regarding womens' rights to be changed during the early National period concerned wife-beating. In *People v. William Winters*,[37] the New York Circuit Court considered whether a husband had the right to beat his wife or to inflict corporal punishment upon her. English common law precedent permitted a husband the right to give his wife moderate correction. However, Circuit Judge Walworth was urged by District Attorney J. Palmer to rule that the English rule of law was invalid as being contrary to public policy. Consequently, Walworth instructed the jury that "a husband has no right to beat his wife or to inflict punishment upon her. But he may defend himself against her, and may restrain her from acts of violence towards himself or towards others, for he is accountable for her acts which injure others."[38] New York was not alone in its condemnation of wife-beating. Suzanne Lebsock has shown that this attitude was also prevalent in the American South.[39]

Another aspect of the movement to Americanize the common law involved the use of foreign or civil law. As common law precedents were questioned, American jurists looked to foreign law, usually based on Roman or civil law, as a model for determining new law. An anonymous contributor to the *North American Review* wrote: "it is by comparison of our own rules and practice with those of foreigners, that we become fully sensible of what is defective or excellent, and therefore of what is to be cherished and upheld, or to be disapproved and abolished in our institutions."[40] He went on to argue that civil law provided five principal benefits to the new American legal system: (1) its clear understanding of personal rights served as a guide to applying the American Bill of Rights to American circumstances; (2) it provided guidance regarding the reformation of the laws of inheritance and probate; (3) it was considered by courts in the exercise of equity jurisdiction to be an alternate source of precedents once the application of common law was ruled unjust; (4) it was considered a repository of principles concerning national intercourse which was particularly applicable to the American federal system; and (5) it was viewed as the origin of mercantile and maritime law.[41] It was in consideration of these uses of the civil law that post-Revolutionary American legal educators decided to incorporate the teaching of it into American legal education.

Civil law played an essential part in the curricula of vocational law schools and was also recommended reading for law students receiving their legal educations through clerkships. No doubt, during the colonial period, the civil law was occasionally studied alongside the common law. But its greatest impact and proliferation was achieved after the Revolution when its usefulness in helping to create new law was realized. Among the civil law treatises most frequently read in America's post-Revolutionary law schools, in order of the number of copies published, were: Cesare Beccaria, *An Essay on Crimes and Punishments*;[42] Jean Jacques Burlamaqui, *The Principles of Natural Law*;[43] Emmerich de Vattel, *The Law of Nations . . .* ;[44] Georg Friedrich von Martens, *Summary of the Law of Nations . . .* ;[45] Charles Louis de Secondat, Baron de la Brède et de Montesquieu, *The Spirit of Laws*;[46] Hugo Grotius, *The Right of War and Peace*;[47] Samuel Freiherr von Pufendorf, *The Law of Nature and Nations . . .* ;[48] Jean Domat, *The Civil Law in its Natural Order . . .* ;[49] and Henry Home, Lord Kames, *Principles of Equity*.[50,51] These texts were widely available in America either through the publication of American editions or through the importation of British editions, and all of the foreign language texts were available in English translations. As a result, law students who did not attend vocational law schools also frequently read these treatises. The importance of these works to the American lawyer has been summarized by Peter Stein who noted that "all these works adopted the position that Roman law, though no longer authoritative by reason of the (Holy Roman) Empire (*ratione Imperii*), should still be followed in the empire of reason (*imperio Rationis*)."[52]

The proof of the direct impact of the civil law on the American judiciary is in the frequency in which the above texts were cited in reported cases as an aid to modifying English law. In the celebrated case of *Pierson v. Post*,[53] the New York Supreme Court relied on the writings of civilians to assist in the establishment of new American law because the English law was deemed unhelpful. The case was an action of trespass on the case brought by a pursuer of a fox against the killer of the fox. Trespass on the case is an action for recovery of damages for an injury caused to a party from the wrongful act of another, unaccompanied by direct or immediate force, or which is the indirect or secondary consequence of the defendant's act. Post commenced a fox hunt on an uninhabited stretch of land.

While he was in pursuit of the fox, Pierson, with the intent of stopping the fox hunt, captured and killed the fox in the sight of Post.

The question before the Court was whether Post, by the pursuit of the fox in the manner described in the declaration, acquired property in the fox sufficient to sustain an action against Pierson for capturing and killing his property. The only English case cited, which was from *Keble v. Hickringill*,[54] held that an action was sustainable for "maliciously hindering and disturbing the plaintiff in the exercise and enjoyment" of duck hunting where the defendant rescued ducks from a decoy pond owned by the plaintiff. Justice Tompkins, writing on behalf of the New York Court, noted that "it is obvious the [English] court laid much stress in their opinion upon the plaintiff's possession of the ducks, ratione soli." Since the fox was not killed on land owned by the plaintiff, Justice Tomkins concluded that "little satisfactory aid can, therefore, be derived from the English reporters."[55]

Attorney Cadwallader D. Colden suggested to Tompkins that he consider the writings of the civilians. Tompkins agreed and noted that Justinian, Fleta and Breton adopted the principle that "pursuit alone vests no property or right in the huntsman; and that even pursuit, accompanied with wounding, is equally ineffectual for that purpose, unless the animal be actually taken" and that Puffendorf and Bynkershock believed that "actual corporal possession" of a beast *ferae naturae* ["wild animal"] was necessary in order to establish occupancy. As a result, Tompkins concluded that "mere pursuit gave Post no legal right to the fox, but that he [the fox] became the property of Pierson, who intercepted and killed him." This rule of law was based on civil law because the English common law was unclear.[56]

New York courts were not the only ones to incorporate civil and foreign law into the common law. In *Bourke v. Granberry*,[57] the Court of Appeals of Virginia stated a preference for civil law over English law in deciding an issue under the law of nations. The case before the Court was an action of debt against the President of a marine insurance company by the owner of an insured vessel seeking compensation for the seizure and condemnation as prize of the vessel by the Vice-Admiralty Court of Great Britain in Jamaica. The Vice-Admiralty Court found that the vessel was not neutral and was not American. If this were recognized by the Virginia court, it would limit coverage under the policy. At trial, the vessel's owner was allowed to admit evidence that the ship was an American vessel and that he was an American citizen. The trial court found for the vessel's owner, and the insurance company appealed.

The issue before the Court of Appeals was whether the trial court had erred in admitting evidence as to the American ownership of the vessel. The vessel's owner argued that the admission of proof of ownership was valid because the Vice-Admiralty Court's finding was erroneous. The insurance company contended, citing *Anonymous*[58], that the evidence should have been suppressed because the Vice Admiralty Court's decree was conclusive of the facts of ownership. Justice Spencer Roane (a former student of George Wythe's at the College of William and Mary), writing on behalf of the Court, was persuaded by attorney William Wirt, to ignore the dictates of the English precedent and instead to follow the law of nations. Roane wrote:

> If, on the contrary, this be a question under the law of nations, the British courts are not the exclusive arbiters of it. On a question of national law, we refer to other, and more impartial, authorities. We consult the learned on that subject, and resort to the concurring testimony of general jurists. . . . It is not new for this court to differ from the courts of England, on questions of general law. It was done in the case of Reed and Reed, in favour of the great natural right of expatriation. . . . If, therefore, Britain has decided this question one way, France and other nations have decided it in another; and we are to chuse [*sic*] between them. In making this decision, we are to go by great principles, and not by the conflicting and unsatisfactory decisions of British Judges.[59]

Thus, Roane determined that, according to principles of general jurisprudence, questions of prize between citizens of different nations are governed by the law of nations rather than by local or municipal laws. Regardless of the countries from which courts of admiralty derived their jurisdictions, all admiralty courts were required to apply the same international law.

Justice Roane further determined that as a result of "comity, reciprocity, and general convenience," the decrees of any court of admiralty which decided a case pursuant to the law of nations "should be respected by the others." However, citing the laws "of the nations of Europe" in contradiction to English precedent, Roane coopted into American law an exception, for he concluded that he had the power to reconsider the British court's factual determination that the ship in question was not American. He explained that "a contrary doctrine would tend to diminish the actual price for which the property might be sold, and thus, in the event of restitution, or otherwise, throw an actual loss upon the owner of the property himself." The utilitarian nature of this argument was the standard by which Roane questioned the English case cited by the insurance company. Foreign law was used as a model for the creation of a substitute rule of American law which was distinct from English law and which allowed him to reverse, as far as Virginia was concerned, the decree of the Vice-Admiralty Court of Great Britain.[60]

The use of civil or foreign law by American lawyers and judges not only made the task of Americanizing the common law easier but also built up their confidence in the power of reason over precedents. American jurists did not approach the questioning of English law without doubts. In judging aspects of such an ancient and revered institution, they could not help but wonder if their perceptions of unsoundness were correct. The discovery of civil law principles that were either clearer than or contrary to the common law rules they were questioning helped confirm their suspicions that the English rule in question might be less than ideal. Consequently, the use of civil or foreign law by post-Revolutionary and early National period American jurists reinforced their confidence in the superiority of their reasoning powers over precedents.

Concurrent with the remolding of the common law, American jurists expanded their questioning of precedents to include American statutes, executive orders and civil practices, through the development of the doctrine of judicial review. As the methodology for Americanizing the common law was developed, jurists borrowed the same arguments to judge encoded law, gaining confidence from their civil law studies.

Virginians were in the forefront of the judicial review movement largely because they had been previously exposed, more than any other state, to an early model of the doctrine. In colonial times, the Privy Council had utilized a limited form of what would later be called judicial review to judge colonial legislation against the standard of the State's charter.[61] Given Virginia jurists' familiarity with this technique, it was much easier for them, as compared to jurists in other jurisdictions, to employ and expand its use to judge the soundness of Virginia statutes.

The earliest case in Virginia, and indeed in the United States, to utilize the modern doctrine of judicial review, albeit in a modest form, was *Commonwealth v. Caton*[62] where the Virginia Court of Appeals ruled unconstitutional a resolution of the Virginia House of Delegates granting a pardon. Although the House of Delegates had approved this pardon, the Virginia Senate had not concurred. Justice George Wythe, who was Professor of Law and Police at the College of William and Mary and was instrumental in the development of a distinct American legal methodology, wrote: "These arguments [as to whether a pardon could be granted by only one house of the legislature] receive some illustration from the twentieth section of the constitution, recognizing the power of the whole legislature, and not one branch, to abolish penalties and forfeitures: which is contravened by the other construction; for, if the house of delegates can remit part of the penalty, they may the whole. . . ." In concluding that the state constitution barred the pardon pleaded by the prisoners, Wythe gave an impassioned explanation of the circumstances under which he would exercise judicial review:

> [It is my duty] to protect one branch of the legislature, and, consequently, the whole community, against the usurpations of the other: and, whenever the proper occasion occurs, I shall feel the duty; and, fearlessly, perform it. Whenever traitors shall be fairly convicted, . . . , if one branch of the legislature, without the concurrence of the other, shall attempt to rescue the offenders from the sentence of the law, I shall not hesitate, sitting in this place, to say, to the general court, Fiat justitia, ruat coelum; and, to the usurping branch of the legislature, you attempt worse than a vain thing; for, although, you cannot succeed, you set an example, which may convulse society to its centre. Nay more, if the whole legislature, . . . , should attempt to overleap the bounds, prescribed to them by the people, I, in administering the public justice of the country, will meet the united powers, at my seat in this tribunal; and, pointing to the constitution, will say, to them, here is the limit of your authority; and, hither, shall you go, but no further.[63]

While the Court's holding in *Commonwealth v. Caton* only established precedent for a limited application of judicial review, George Wythe's dictum leaves no doubt about the potential power of the doctrine and the likelihood of its increased use.

In 1792, the Virginia Court of Appeals was presented with its first opportunity since *Commonwealth v. Caton* to expand on its earlier use of judicial review. In *Turner v. Turner's Ex'x,*[64] the Court used the doctrine of judicial review to rule a retroactive application of a state statute unconstitutional. The Act of 1787 respecting parol gifts of slaves was designed to amend a previous statute enacted in 1758. The question before the Court was whether the 1787 act applied to a gift of slaves which took place in 1783. The attorney for the plaintiff argued that the state legislature had intended the amendment to apply retroactively. Edmund Pendleton, as President of the Court, held that the state legislature "cannot prescribe a rule of construction, as to the past. For a legislative interpretation, changing titles founded upon existing statutes, would be subject to every objection which lies to *ex post facto* laws, as it would destroy rights already acquired under the former statute, by one made subsequent to the time when they became vested. A power to be deprecated, as oppressive and contrary to the principles of the constitution."[65] Thus, in holding the Act of 1787 prospective only, the Court expanded judicial review to include ruling an application of a state statute unconstitutional.

Jones v. The Commonwealth[66] presented the Virginia Court of Appeals with yet another chance to develop judicial review. The Court overruled a Virginia practice which provided that in a joint indictment, a jury could fine the defendants as a group, rather than assess separate fines against each of them. John Wickham (a graduate of the College of William and Mary, where he had studied under George Wythe), representing the plaintiff, argued that the practice in question could result in a defendant, who had paid his proportionable part of damages, remaining in jail until all the others had paid theirs. This would result in him being punished for the offence of others. Judge Spencer Roane accepted Wickham's point and ruled this practice unconstitutional, noting: "This is so unjust and contrary to the spirit of the [U.S.] Bill of Rights, that even if it were established by adjudged cases to be the law, nay even if an act of Assembly should pass authorizing it, in express terms, I should most probably be of opinion, that the one should be exploded, and the other declared unconstitutional and not law."[67] In ruling this practice unconstitutional, Justice Roane could not find a specific provision in the Constitution which expressly established the notion that a person could not be punished for someone else's crime. So he determined that this notion was implied within the Bill of Rights as a whole and as such it could be used to judge the practice in question unconstitutional. This was the ultimate expansion of the doctrine of judicial review, for now a judge could rule a statute unconstitutional on the basis of his own determination of concepts implied within the Constitution. Since constitutions are often ambiguous and unspecific, a judge could almost always see something implied within it to rule a statute, executive order or civil practice unconstitutional.

Virginia was not alone in the development and expansive use of the doctrine of judicial review. A limited form of it was introduced into New York law in 1784. In *Rutgers v. Waddington,*[68] the Mayor's Court of New York City was urged by Alexander Hamilton, Brockholst Livingston and Morgan Lewis to rule a state statute void as being contrary to the Treaty of Peace of 1782. While the Court determined that they lacked the power to nullify the statute, they interpreted it in such a way that it was made impotent. In 1786, the Rhode Island Supreme Court held a state statute unconstitutional. The case of *Trevett v. Weeden*[69] concerned legislation that made it illegal not to accept the state's currency as payment for goods and services. Moreover, the act provided that a person charged with violating it had no right of jury trial or appeal. Weeden's attorney, James M. Varnum persuaded the Court to rule the statute in violation of the State's unwritten Constitution on the grounds that the denial of a jury trial or appeal was contrary to those laws of nature and ancient rights that were instilled in the Constitution.

Even the federal bench developed and expanded the doctrine of judicial review. In *Hayburn's Case,*[70] Chief Justice John Jay wrote that an act of Congress, which authorized Revolutionary War veterans to file pension claims in United States circuit courts so that judges could certify to the Secretary of War the degree of the claimant's disability and recommend the proper percentage of monthly pay to be awarded, was unconstitutional because the requirement that judges assume administrative duties for the executive branch was contrary to the separation of powers. The Court expanded the use of judicial review, in opposition to the arguments of defense attorney John Marshall, in *Ware v. Hylton*[71] where it voided a Virginia statute that provided for the confiscation of British property, on the grounds that it violated the Treaty of Peace of 1782. A Supreme Court justice made a broad statement concerning the doctrine of judicial review in *Calder v. Bull*[72] where, while the Supreme Court held that the *ex post facto* clause of the Constitution could not be used to rule a noncriminal Connecticut statute unconstitutional, Justice Samuel Chase stated that he would be willing in an appropriate case to rule a statute that intruded upon private contract or property rights unconstitutional even if it were not "expressly restrained by the Constitution."[73] Justice Chase was here advocating the position espoused, as noted earlier, by Judge Spencer Roane of Virginia; a use of judicial review as the ultimate expression of judicial power, through a veto of statutes.

While some judges were increasingly using the doctrine of judicial review to expand the power of the judiciary as compared to the other branches of government, opposition to this trend was brewing both in and out of the court house. In response to *Trevett v. Weeden*, the state legislature deplored the Rhode Island's Supreme Court's broad exercise of judicial review, and at the next election all the judges who voted in favor of the decision were voted out of office by the people.[74]

Even the United States Supreme Court was split over the issue. In *Calder v. Bull*, where Justice Chase had argued in favor of a broad use of judicial review, Justice James Iredell opposed Chase's position:

> If any act of Congress, or of the Legislature of a state, violates those constitutional provisions [which define the objects of legislative power], it is unquestionably void; though, I admit, that as the authority to declare it void is of a delicate and awful nature, the Court will never resort to that authority, but in a clear and urgent case. If, on the other hand, the Legislature of the Union, or the Legislature of any member of the Union, shall pass a law, within the general scope of their constitutional power, the Court cannot pronounce it to be void, merely because it is, in their judgement, contrary to the principles of natural justice. The ideas of natural justice are regulated by no fixed standard: the ablest and purest men have differed on the subject; and all that the Court could properly say, in such an event, would be, that the Legislature (possessed of an equal right of opinion) had passed an act which, in the opinion of the judges, was inconsistent with the abstract principles of natural justice.[75]

Recently, Elizabeth McCaughey has argued that the case of *Marbury v. Madison,*[76] widely recognized as the first United States Supreme Court case to clearly articulate under what circumstances judicial review could be exercised,[77] can be interpreted as an expression of this movement to limit, rather than expand, judicial powers.[78] Sylvia Snowiss, to the contrary, has contended that, in *Marbury v. Madison*, Marshall

> did not, as is widely assumed, simply reinforce or extend ideas partially or wholly accepted. He built instead a new practice, and did so by effecting a radical transformation in existing conceptions of the Constitution and of the judicial relationship to it. Marshall achieved this transformation, moreover, with no public discussion or acknowledgement of his purposes or methods.[79]

Of these two opposing views, the evidence presented herein is most inconsistent with that presented by Snowiss. While she accepts that any "discussion of judicial review in America must start with William Blackstone" and that there was "early American resistance to Blackstone's ideas . . . manifested in the actual exercise of judicial review in some state courts," she dismisses the relevance of these early incidents of judicial review because they were "not accompanied by any uniform or coherent defence of the practice or by any systematic attempt to refute Blackstone's reasoning [on the subject of parliamentary supremacy]."[80] Why these arguments must necessarily be contained in these cases in order to claim the existence of a recognized practice of judicial review prior to *Marbury v. Madison*, she does not explain. The facts remain that the practice of judicial review was employed on numerous occasions prior to *Marbury v. Madison* and Blackstone's position on parliamentary supremacy was refuted by St. George Tucker in a publication that appeared several months prior to *Marbury v. Madi-*

son.[81] While arguments persist about John Marshall's intentions in *Marbury v. Madison*, the popular outcry to the decision in *Trevett v. Weeden* and the concerns expressed by Justice James Iredell in *Calder v. Bull* were forerunners of a later movement to curtail judicial modification of the law.

This movement by judicial conservatives was most forcefully expressed in state court opinions of the 1820s and early 1830s. In *Card v. Grinman*,[82] the Connecticut Supreme Court considered the issue of whether a parol revocation of a will was valid under Connecticut law. Attorneys William Pitt Cleaveland (graduate of Litchfield, 1794) and D. Young argued that the common law of England which provided that wills were revocable by word only had been altered in Connecticut prior to the Revolution to require a written revocation. Thus the Court should not accept an application of the English common law rule. In concluding that there were insufficient reasons to overturn the English precedent, Chief Justice Stephen Titus Hosmer, writing for the Court, took the opportunity to explain a much more conservative role for the courts than had been exercised before. He wrote:

> Undoubtedly, by an assumption of legislative power, this Court can promulge as law, any provision, which will meet a particular mischief; but with a very eminent judge I take pleasure in declaring, "It is my wish and my comfort to stand *super anteguas vias:* I cannot legislate; but by my industry, I can discover what our predecessors have done, and I will servilely tread in their footsteps." . . . The *English* common law, so far as it was not unadapted to the local circumstances of this country, our ancestors, on their emigration hither brought with them; and until it is abrogated, by statute, I must, with the exception mentioned, consider it as the common law of this state. I deprecate a departure from the old highway of the common law, by the indulgence of a disposition to decide on principles of equity and convenience, which often are notional and imaginary.[83]

Justice J. Carr of the Court of Appeals of Virginia also espoused judicial conservatism in *Foreman v. Lloyd*[84] where the Court considered whether a recently enacted state statute concerning the disposition of property to settle a judgement debt should be applied to the circumstances of the case even though it would result in a severe hardship. Justice Carr expressed a strongly conservative minority opinion, stating: "The law, however harsh, however unwise, is, to my understanding, expressed in terms too plain to be changed by construction, or judicial action in any form."[85] In part, the inception of the conservative movement may be attributed to the success of the activist movement, since judges who had once supported legal reform were transformed, as their initial goals were realized, from activists to preservationists.

This movement by judicial conservatives to restrict judicial activists from using the court system as a tool for Americanizing the law gained some success during the early National period. It failed, however, to curtail the Americanization of the law, for although some attorneys had used the judiciary to reform the legal system, other lawyers, many of whom were members of state legislatures, had used state legislatures to accomplish the same end. While the use of the judiciary to conform the law to new circumstances continued, this legislative activity, which dated from 1776, was expanded in the 1820s in response to the success of judicial conservatives. The resultant American codification movement was the principal means by which American lawyers continued their efforts to Americanize the law in spite of opposition. The use of this method only decreased in the 1840s when its own success rendered it obsolete, since any additional refinements to meet the changing needs of society could be made through the more gradual reforms available in the court room.

Soon after the signing of the Declaration of Independence, state legislatures began to enact statutes designed to replace English and Colonial statutes and some select areas of the common law in force in America before the Revolution. New York was the first state of common law jurisdiction to codify all its statutory law and some of its common law, over the period from 1824 to 1828. Among the states that followed New York's lead to codification, in at least a limited form, were: Georgia, Massachusetts, Maine, Tennessee, Pennsylvania, Maryland, New Jersey, South Carolina, Vermont, Virginia, California, the Dakota Territory, Idaho and Montana.[86]

Some attempts were made at codification prior to New York's success. In 1776, the Virginia legislature appointed a commission to revise the state's laws. The result, which was adopted in 1785, most importantly abolished the law of primogeniture, reformed the criminal law by abolishing the death penalty except for treason and murder and established freedom of religion.[87] The New Jersey legislature undertook a similar revision between 1780 and 1799, which led, in part, to the passage of an "Act to Abolish Primogeniture and Entails"; an "Act to Punish Crimes," which voided the death penalty except for treason and murder, lessened the penalty for minor offenses and established independent regulation of the state's prison system; and an "Act Respecting the Court of Chancery," which, among other things, allowed appeals to be taken from Chancery to the Court of Appeals and Errors.[88] Virginia and New Jersey were typical of most states in the union in their revision of colonial statutes and selected common law principles.[89]

The most significant legislative activity, however, was the revision of a state's complete body of law. Beginning in the 1820s, reform-minded lawyers used the rationale behind the modified doctrine of *stare decisis* and the example of European civil codes to commence an American codification movement that was designed to revise a jurisdiction's entire body of law. They were able to foster this movement for, in addition to practicing law, a substantial number of vocational law school graduates and other lawyers who had been exposed to the teachings of these law schools through the publication of analytical law treatises, swelled the ranks of the legislative branch of government.[90] The results of their labors was a much more extensive Americanization of the law than was able to be achieved within judicial forums.

William E. Ross has suggested that Thomas Jefferson was the first to propose codification, as a member of Virginia's commission of revision in 1777. However, Jefferson is reported to have advocated the abandonment of the English system of laws and the creation of a new American system, a process that goes beyond the concept of codification of existing laws.[91] Ultimately, Virginia's statutory revision was concerned solely with unifying the law, without attempting to present it in a clear and concise manner. St. George Tucker, one of the revisors, said Virginia's revision was, "the parent of new complexities, by the introduction of new law; and the reenaction, omission, or suspension of former acts, whose operation is thus rendered *doubtful* even in the most important cases."[92] Consequently, codifiers did not consider it a model for their own movement.

The American codification movement, as such, can be traced back to James Wilson, who in March 1791 was appointed Reviser of Pennsylvania statutes by the Pennsylvania House of Representatives. In response to this appointment, on 24 August 1791 Wilson delivered a proposal to the Speaker of the Pennsylvania House of Representatives in which he advocated reducing both statute and common law into a digest in which the law would be "collected in a natural series, and reduced to a just form" so as to produce a legal system noted for its "simplicity and plainness and precision."[93] While the Pennsylvania legislature did not approve Wilson's proposal, its thorough discussion in the legal community helped influence the later codification movement. Hugh Henry Brackenridge, who advocated the codification of Pennsylvania laws twenty-two years after Wilson, identified Wilson's proposal as his inspiration. He wrote that the abandonment of Wilson's project "was considered a great loss by intelligent men."[94]

Although Wilson had suggested codification in 1791, it did not become a reasonably successful movement until the 1820s. Up until this point, the primary forum for legal reform was the court room. However, as time progressed, many lawyers became impatient with trying to change the law one case at a time, particularly since they now had to confront a more organized judicial conservatism. As a result, they sought another forum and means to reform the common law. The American publication of English translations of the Code Napoléon (the widely acclaimed French post-Revolutionary codification) between 1811 and 1823, suggested a potential solution to their problem.[95]

New York was the first common law jurisdiction to attempt codification of its own laws.[96] In 1824, the New York state legislature provided for a revision of its statutes. A commission consisting of Erastus Root, Benjamin F. Butler and John Duer was appointed. Butler and Duer argued for a substantial revision of the statutes noting that "the existing laws should be entirely rewritten with a view to placing the topics in a logical order under titles and subtitles."[97] In the 1825 session of the state legislature, their suggestion was passed. Root, who opposed it, resigned and John C. Spencer took his place.

The methodology adopted by the commission was rooted in the new system of American legal thought, based on the application of ideas, rooted in the works of European natural law writers, to the analysis of law. First the law was to be systematized and categorized in a manner similar to that used by Blackstone, to bring it into the realm of a pragmatic science. The law would then be reduced, in simplified language, to its primary rules and fundamental principles and judged against the standards of utility, logic, morality and conflicting American law and policy so as to determine what was in need of revision or abolition. Lastly, these rules and principles were to be rewritten, regardless of whether they needed revision, incorporating all the changes this application of method suggested. In an address given before the state legislature on 4 January 1825, the commissioners indicated their intention "to free our written code from the prolixities, uncertainties, and confusion incident to the style and manner in which it has hitherto been framed, and to apply to the elucidation of this branch of the noblest of all sciences, those principles of an enlarged philosophy, which now obtain in every other department of knowledge."[98] As the commissioners saw it, this new system of American legal thought was the key to unlocking the complexities of the law.

The commissioners began their work by classifying and systematizing the state's statutes along the lines suggested by William Blackstone, to bring the law into the rank of the sciences. They wrote: "The general distribution of the subjects of the whole revision . . . has been made conformable to the admirable system of judge Blackstone's *Commentaries* . . . the same arrangement which had reduced to order and system, the floating and complicated principles of the *unwritten* common law, must necessarily be sufficient to comprehend the written laws, which are in their nature, merely *supplementary* to that common law."[99] There were two principal reasons for modeling their work after Blackstone. The first was a desire to reduce their work to a science, for they noted that they "were led to this general arrangement, as the most natural, and at the same time the most scientific, of which the subject was capable."[100] The second was because they believed that the imperfections in the law would become more apparent through such an organization. They noted that, by adopting Blackstone's categorization, the law "can be viewed as a whole, and its defects at once perceived and supplied."[101] Thus, New York's laws were grouped into five broad categories: (1) constitutional and administrative matters, (2) private rights, (3) civil procedure, (4) criminal law and procedure and (5) public law.

Once statutes were organized into these categories, the commissioners determined that they would need to include within these groups common law precedents that either elucidated or altered the written law. The commissioners noted that statutes "have been conformed in express terms, to the constructions given them by the decisions of our courts; and . . . in numerous instances . . . rules of the common law have been reduced to a written text . . . whilst in other instances those rules have been enlarged, modified, or varied, the more fully to conform them to the nature of our government, and to the habits and exigencies of the people."[102] Thus, the commissioners did not focus exclusively on statutes, but extended their work to the common law, and hence achieved codification rather than simply revision.

The codifiers reduced statutory law and common law that pertained to the statutes into simplified expressions of primary rules and fundamental principles so as to make their judgement of the law easier. They explained:

> It has been our study in the chapters we have commenced, to adopt the most simple arrangement; to confine the sections to short propositions; to omit unnecessary words; and to avoid, as far as practicable, all ambiguities of expression . . . to facilitate . . . In performing that part of our duty, which required us to suggest to the legislature "such contradictions, omissions or imperfections" as may be found in the acts to be revised, with the mode in which they may be "reconciled, supplied or amended"; and to recommend "the repeal of such acts or parts of acts" as ought in our judgement to be repealed. . . .[103]

These simplified rules and principles were then judged against the standards of utility, logic, morality and conflicting American law and policy and were rewritten, regardless of whether they needed revision, incorporating all the changes this application of method suggested.

This approach was most extensively applied to the criminal law. In the area of medical malpractice, the codifiers employed the standard of utility to suggest a law providing for charges of manslaughter against a doctor who through intoxication or gross ignorance killed a patient, since recent common law cases had indicated that such a law was necessary, and the existing law was unclear.[104] On arson, the codifiers felt that the intention of the statute had not been clearly stated, and that it was logically inconsistent in that the penalties established depended upon the motive of the arsonist—if he was trying to defraud his insurers, the punishment was much more severe than if his aim was purely destructive. The statute was modified by the insertion of words in italics, so that the changes made could be clearly distinguished.[105] The codifiers also changed the laws on petty larceny to limit prosecutions for theft of produce to those in which more than five dollars worth of goods had been stolen, on the grounds that prosecution for lesser offenses was immoral.[106] In addition to these individual modifications, the codifiers proposed an entire new body of law concerning the administration of prisons so as to place the state's prison law in conformity to the federal and state constitution and to the concerns of public policy.[107]

Another subject to which they applied this method was property law, which was targeted for revision by the commissioners because they considered it to be inconsistent and nonuniform. While the common law of real property was "connected throughout with the doctrine of tenures, and meant and adapted to maintain the feudal system, . . . an elaborate system of expedients [had been] devised . . . for the express purpose of evading the rules of the common law." The result was the success of "technical and arbitrary constructions . . . over reason and common sense," and its revision was deemed essential.[108]

The areas of property law that were most significantly altered as a result of these concerns and the application of judgmental standards were the laws of contingent remainder and ejectment. Contingent remainders [the restriction of a legacy to depend upon some uncertain future event, commonly, the leaving of property to people as yet unborn] was abolished by the codifiers on the grounds of utility because they believed "that where a rule of law is found by experience to be inconvenient or unjust, its direct abolition is preferable to its circuitous evasion, not only because a needless complexity is thus avoided, but because the means of evasion are always attended with expense, and productive of litigation."[109] Ejectment, an action which was dependent on the creation of fictitious parties to recover possession of land and obtain damages for the unlawful detention of its possession, was abolished on the grounds that its complexity and wastefulness was contrary to utility and that its dependence on fictitious parties was illogical.[110] In all, New York's law of real property was transformed from a system based on what was perceived to be feudal relationships to one geared to fostering economic growth within a democratic society. In the words of the codifiers: "all technical rules and distinctions, having no relationship to the essential nature of property and the means of its beneficial enjoyment, but which are derived from the feudal system" were abolished.[111]

In 1828, the last sections of the revision of New York's laws were approved. The end result, called the *Civil Code of New York*, was the first true codification of law in the common law world. While it did not codify all of New York's laws, it did systematize and digest laws relating to a wide variety of subjects. Its influence over the other states was profound. Ernest Henry Breuer has written: "As the newer states were admitted to the Union many of them adopted the New York Revised Statutes with but minor changes, to suit local conditions; others adopted great parts of them verbatim. Others adopted the general outlines with modifications. In a short space of three years the Revisers had taken a handful of disconnected laws and with principles taken from the mysterious and intangible common law had fabricated a complete whole, both tangible and intelligible."[112] News of New York's noble experiment even reached far beyond America's shores. Sir Henry Maine wrote: "But for its success and popularity, we should not probably have had the advantage of watching the greatest experiment which has ever been tried on English jurisprudence—the still-proceeding codification and consolidation of the entire law of New York."[113]

There has been disagreement as to why the codification movement went into decline during the second half of the nineteenth century. Charles M. Cook argues that the codification movement dissipated as "the ranks of its advocates thinned" in the face of "a persistently strong opposition"[114] and Roscoe Pound wrote that "more than anything else the books of our great nineteenth century text writers defeated the urge of a code."[115] These positions fail, however, since opposition and precodification law treatises did not prevent the movement from developing.

An hypothesis more consistent with the evidence is that the movement's decline was a product of its own limited success. Codification provided such a drastic means of Americanizing the law that once it had been accomplished with regard to key subject areas there was little need to continue it. Most supporters of codification were content with the idea that the adaptation of the law to the changing needs of society could be accomplished, in spite of opposition from judicial conservatives, within the court room and through individual statutory enactments. The movement was also diminished because codification made the law easier to criticize. So long as the law was in an unwritten form, it possessed a certain mystique and respectability. Once redacted into an easily readable and accessible code, it lost its mystery and could be judged. It was one thing for fault to be found with English and colonial law or American law when it was judged in conflict with the Constitution, but to see an abundance of error in American common and statutory law was frightening to many. The diminution of the American codification movement was a result of its own limited success and the availability of acceptable alternative methods for adapting the law to changing circumstances. To suggest, however, that the movement was totally defeated ignores America's continuing reliance on codes, as indicated, for example, by the adoption of the Federal Code of Civil Procedure in 1938 and the Uniform Commercial Code in 1967.

While the Americanization of the law was the most significant direct achievement that resulted from the development of a uniquely American legal thought, more far-reaching implications can be traced to it. Changes in American legal thinking had a substantial impact on the phenomenal litigiousness of American society.[116] The perception within the new American legal thought of the law as a series of concepts that could be rapidly changed to fit the developing needs of a society has contributed to the litigiousness of American as compared to English society. In England, where this perception has not been embodied in legal thought, a lawyer has been restrictive in how he views a potential case. When a client enters a solicitor's office and presents a dispute, the solicitor pigeon-holes the facts into the law to determine whether the potential client has a sustainable action. His American counterpart approaches the circumstances differently. When he is presented with a client's dispute, he determines, based on his own sense of morality *or greed*, whether the potential client deserves to be represented, for the attorney believes that he can always make an argument that some law should be adapted to resolve his client's wrong. A society in which anyone who feels wronged can find a legal argument to support his position and a court willing to listen which has the willingness to act is prone to litigiousness.

As Americans increasingly turned to the courts to settle their disputes, the power of the legal profession and the judiciary substantially increased. This development, however, was not the exclusive result of litigiousness. The doctrine of judicial review would not have developed if it were not for the belief in the power of reason over precedents and in the fallibility of law, as expounded in vocational law schools and in early analytical treatises. The frequent adoption of legislative powers by courts would not have been accepted if it were not for the need to Americanize the law and the success of the American bar in persuading the judiciary to adopt a reasonably predictable method for accomplishing it. As a result of the advent of a distinct American legal thought which fostered the litigiousness of the American people, the power of judicial review and a willingness on the part of judges to make law, the American legal system assumed a unique equal partnership with the legislative and executive branches in governing the United States. Examination of the progression and development of American legal thought reveals that the influence of post-Revolutionary and early National period legal education was much greater than has previously been supposed, not only in the field of the law proper, but in the extent of its influence on American society and politics.

NOTES

1. Morton J. Horwitz, *The Transformation of American Law 1780–1860* (Cambridge: Harvard University Press, 1977), p. 30.
2. Ibid, p. xvi.
3. Ibid, pp. 18, 257.
4. Stanley N. Katz, ed., *James Alexander's Brief Narrative of the Case and Trial of John Peter Zenger, Printer of the New York Weekly Journal* (Cambridge: Harvard University Press, 1963); Anthony Laussat, Jr., *An Essay on Equity in Pennsylvania* (Philadelphia: Robert Desilva, 1826).
5. *New York American*, 8 October 1824.
6. Henry Dwight Sedgewick, "The Common Law," 19 *North American Review* 424 (Boston, MA: Cummings and Hillard, 1824).
7. 7 Johns. 227 (1810).
8. 13 Johns. 466 (1813).
9. See also: Jackson v. Laughhead, 2 Johns. 75, 75 (1806), discussed earlier, where the New York Supreme Court of Judicature adopted the requirement that a mortgagee, before he brings an action of ejectment against the mortgagor, must give notice to quit the premises six calendar months before service of the declaration because this would not constitute a "hardship on the mortgagee, while a contrary practice may be much abused, in a country where so many thousand estates are held in this way."
10. 1 Kirby 175 (1786).
11. 1 Kirby at 177.
12. 4 Day 298 (1810).
13. 4 Day at 306–307.
14. 2 Johns. Cas. 371 (1801).
15. 10 Johns. 203 (1813).
16. 126 Eng. Rep. 611 (1795).
17. 10 Johns. at 204.
18. Id. at 205.
19. 3 Day 346 (1809).
20. 101 Eng. Rep. 1529 (1800).
21. 3 Day at 346.
22. Id. at 349.
23. See also: K. & E. Townsend v. Bush, 1 Conn. 259, 270 (1814), where the

Connecticut Superior Court held that a party to a negotiable instrument, who is divested of his interest, is a competent witness to prove it usurious in its creation for otherwise a principle of law could be established that would serve as "an effectual shield for usury, gambling, fraud, and illegal contracts."

24. 13 Va. (3 Hen. & M.) 470 (1809).

25. 13 Va. (3 Hen. & M.) at 481.

26. See also: Downman v. Downman's Executors, 1 Va. (1 Wash.) 34, 37 (1791), where the Virginia Court of Appeals refused to adopt a number of English rules of practice because "considering the circumstances of this country, and the dispersed situation of the attorneys and their clients, who can seldom communicate with each other but at Court, justice seems to require a relaxation in these rules of practice."

27. Linda Kerber, *Women of the Republic* (Chapel Hill: University of North Carolina Press, 1980), pp. 235, 269.

28. Norma Basch, "From the Bonds of Empire to the Bonds of Matrimony: The Emerging Right of Divorce in the Context of American Independence," Paper Delivered at the 1990 meeting of the Organization of American Historians.

29. Kerber, *Women of the Republic*, p. 10.

30. Nancy Cott, "Divorce and the Changing Status of Women in Eighteenth-Century Massachusetts," *William & Mary Quarterly*, 3d. Ser. 33 (1976), 592, table 1.

31. Kerber, *Women of the Republic*.

32. 1 Conn. 559 (1816).

33. Burgess v. Wheate, 96 Eng. Rep. 67 (1759).

34. 1 Conn. at 563.

35. See also: Lowry et ux. v. Tiernan and Williamson, 2 H. & G. 34 (1827), where the Maryland Court of Appeals held that a *feme covert* entrusted with stock could not order her trustees to sell the stock and reinvest the proceeds according to the directions of her husband; and, one earlier case, Bethune v. Beresford, 1 S.C. Eq. (1 Des.) 174 (1790), where the South Carolina Court of Equity protected a married women from her husband's coercion when he attempted to put up his wife's estate as collateral for a loan for the couple's living expenses.

36. Marylynn Salmon, *Women and the Law of Property in Early America* (Chapel Hill: University of North Carolina Press, 1986), p. 185.

37. 2 Parker's Crim. R. 10 (1823).

38. 2 Parker's Crim. R. at 10.

39. Suzanne Lebsock, *The Free Women of Petersburg: Status and Culture in a Southern Town, 1784–1860* (New York: W.W. Norton & Company, 1984), pp. 34–35.

40. Anonymous, "On the Study of the Civil Law," 11 *North American Review* 407 at 408 (Boston, MA: Cummings and Hillard, 1820).

41. Id. at 409–410.

42. Cesare Beccaria, *An Essay on Crimes and Punishments* (Charlestown, NC: David Bruce, 1777; Philadelphia: Robert Bell, 1778; Philadelphia: William Young, 1793).

43. Jean Jacques Burlamaqui, *The Principles of Natural Law*, trans. Thomas Nugent (Boston, MA: Joseph Bumstead, 1792; Cambridge: Harvard University Press, 1807).

44. Emmerich de Vattel, *The Law of Nations . . .* (New York: Samuel Campbell, 1796; Northampton, MA: S. Butler, 1820).

45. Georg Friedrich von Martens, *Summary of the Law of Nations . . .*, trans. William Cobbett (Philadelphia: Thomas Bradford, 1795).

46. Charles Louis de Secondat, Baron de la Brède et de Montesquieu, *The Spirit of Laws*, trans. Thomas Nugent (London: Nourse, 1750).

47. Hugo Grotius, *The Right of War and Peace* (London: W. Innys, 1738).

48. Samuel Freiherr von Pufendorf, *The Law of Nature and Nations . . .* (London: J. & J. Bonwicke, 1749).

49. Jean Domat, *The Civil Law in its Natural Order . . .* (London: J. Bettenham, 1722).

50. Henry Home, Lord Kames, *Principles of Equity*, 2 vols., 2nd ed. rev. (Edinburgh: Kincaid & J. Bell; London: A. Millar, 1767).

51. Peter Van Schaack, "The Sciences necessary for a Lawyer are. . . ." , Van Schaack Family Papers, Rare Book and Manuscript Library, Columbia University, New York, New York; the Library of the Litchfield Law School, Litchfield Historical Society, Litchfield, Connecticut; the Law Library of Transylvania University, Oceana Publications, Inc., Dobbs Ferry, New York; Abiel A. Loomis, "Hebron Law Lectures (1814)," Connecticut State Library, Hartford, Connecticut; "'the Founders' Collection being the library of Staple's Law School," Yale University Law Library, New Haven, Connecticut; "A System of Readings on the Subjects of Politics & Law Recommended by Mr. Tucker, Professor of Law & Politics in the College of William and Mary," Cabell Deposits, University of Virginia Library; "List of Subscribers," in Georg Friederich von Martens, *Summary of the Law of Nations . . .* , trans. William Cobbett (Philadelphia: Thomas Bradford, 1795), pp. 366–375.

52. Peter Stein, "The Attraction of the Civil Law in Post-Revolutionary America," 52 Va. L. Rev. 403 at 404 (1966).

53. 3 Cai. R. 175 (1805); Pierson v. Post is standardly one of the first cases taught in modern American property law courses.

54. 88 Eng. Rep. 898 (1706).

55. 3 Cai. R. at 178–179.

56. 3 Cai. R. at 177–178; See also: Seton & Co. v. Low, 1 Johns. Cas. 1, 9 (1799), where Justice Lewis of the New York Supreme Court of Judicature relied on Grotius and Bynkershoeck and the "ordinances of France of 1543 and 1584" to define "contraband of war"; Goix v. Low, 1 Johns. Cas. 341 (1800), where Justice James Kent of the New York Supreme Court of Judicature relied on Georg Friederich Von Martens and Henry Home, Lord Kames, to rule that a plea of a foreign judgement is a bar to a second action, *exceptio rei judicata*.

57. 21 Va. (1 Gilmer) 16 (1820).

58. 91 Eng. Rep. 1382 (1698).

59. 21 Va. (1 Gilmer) at 25.

60. Id. at 22; See also: Read v. Read, 3 Va. (5 Call) 160 (1804), where Judge Spencer Roane of the Virginia Court of Appeals refused to sanction the English law of expatriation arguing:

> Shall we not under the sound sense of these [civil law] maxims, correct the mistakes of a municipal code, touching a question of general law, by referring to the fountain from which itself has drawn? Shall we decide a question of natural right, and of general law, by referring to the most approved writers, and to the sense of the world, on that subject, or be governed by the particular municipal

> codes of a particular country? I believe, sir, that this position of the English judges has always stood condemned by the most enlightened writers upon natural law.

See also: Innes v. Roane and Others, 3 Va. (4 Call) 379, 401 (1797), where Justice Lyons cites Vattel for the proposition that "the period of peace" refers to a "declaration of government" and "that infractions of it, by individuals before it is proclaimed, cannot be punished."

61. Julius Goebel, Jr., *Antecedents and Beginnings to 1801*, Vol.1, History of the Supreme Court of the United States, 11 vols. (New York: The MacMillan Co., 1971), ed. Paul A. Freund, 1:60–72.

62. 3 Va. (4 Call) 4 (1782).

63. 3 Va. (4 Call) at 8.

64. 3 Va. (4 Call) 234 (1792).

65. 3 Va. (4 Call) at 237.

66. 5 Va. (1 Call) 555 (1799).

67. 5 Va. (1 Call) at 557.

68. *The Case of Elizabeth Rutgers verses Joshua Waddington . . . August 7, 1786.* (New York: Bradstreet Press, 1866); "Arguments and Judgement of the Mayor's Court of the City of New York, in a Cause between Elizabeth Rutgers and Joshua Waddington (1784)," in Julius Goebel, Jr., ed., *The Law Practice of Alexander Hamilton*, 5 vols. (New York: Columbia University Press, 1964), 1:282–543.

69. James M. Varnum, *The Case, Trevett against Weeden . . . Superior Court in the County of Newport, September Term, 1786 . . .* (Providence, RI: John Carter, 1787).

70. 2 U.S. (2 Dall.) 409 (1792).

71. 3 U.S. (3 Dall.) 199 (1796).

72. 3 U.S. (3 Dall.) 386 (1798).

73. 3 U.S. (3 Dall.) at 386.

74. Goebel, *History of the Supreme Court*, pp. 137–141.

75. 3 U.S. (3 Dall.) at 398–400.

76. 5 U.S. (1 Cranch) 137 (1803).

77. Laurence H. Tribe, *American Constitutional Law* (New York: The Foundation Press, Inc., 1978), pp. 20–23; Lawrence M. Friedman, *A History of American Law* (New York: Simon and Schuster, 1973), pp. 107, 117, 301; John E. Nowak, Ronald D. Rotunda & J. Nelson Young, *Handbook on Constitutional Law* (St. Paul, MN: West Publishing Company, 1978), pp. 1–14.

78. Elizabeth McCaughey, "*Marbury v. Madison*: Have We Missed the Real Meaning?", *Presidential Studies Quarterly*, Vol. XIX, No. 3 (Summer 1989), pp.491–528.

79. Sylvia Snowiss, *Judicial Review and the Law of the Constitution* (New Haven: Yale University Press, 1990), p. viii.

80. Snowiss, *Judicial Review*, p. 13.

81. St. George Tucker, *Blackstone's Commentaries: with Notes of Reference, to the Constitution and Laws, of the Federal Government of the United States; and of the Commonwealth of Virginia*, 5 vols. (Philadelphia: William Young Birch and Abraham Small, 1803), 1:288.

82. 5 Conn. 164 (1823).

83. 5 Conn. at 168.

84. 29 Va. (2 Leigh) 309 (1830).

85. 29 Va. (2 Leigh) at 312 (Carr, J., dissenting).

86. See: Lawrence M. Friedman, *A History of American Law* (New York: Simon and Schuster, 1973), pp. 351–358; Charles M. Cook, *The American Codification Movement* (Westport, CT: Greenwood Press, 1981).

87. William E. Ross, "History of Virginia Codification," 11 Va. L. Reg. 79, 90 (June, 1905).

88. John E. O'Connor, "Legal Reform in the Early Republic: The New Jersey Experience," 22 Am. J. Leg. Hist. 95 (1978).

89. See also: *Acts and Laws of Connecticut in America* (Hartford, CT: Hudson and Goodwin, 1796); Louis P. Masur, "The Culture of Executions and the Conflict Over Capital Punishment in America, 1776–1860" (Ph.D. dissertation, Princeton University, 1985).

90. *Biographical Directory of the United States Congress 1774–1989* (Washington, DC: United States Government Printing Office, 1989), s.v.; The Secretary of State of Connecticut, *The Connecticut Register* (New London, CT: Samuel Green, 1820), s.v.; *The Secretary of the State of Connecticut, The Connecticut Annual Register* (New London, CT: Samuel Green, 1830), s.v.

91. Ross, "History of Virginia Codification," 11 Va. L. Reg. at 90.

92. Tucker, *Blackstone's Commentaries*, 1:xiii.

93. James Wilson, *The Works of the Honourable James Wilson, LL.D.*, ed. Robert Green McCloskey, 2 vols. (1804; reprinted Cambridge: The Belknap Press of Harvard University Press, 1967), 1:59–64.

94. Ibid., 1:60–64; Hugh Henry Brackenridge, *Law Miscellanies* (Philadelphia: P. Byrne, 1814), pp. 73–74.

95. "Penal Code of the French Empire," *American Review of History and Politics* (1811), 2:appendix, pp. 1–69; John Rodman, *Commercial Code of the French Empire Translated for the American Review, With Explanatory Notes of Commerce in General* (Philadelphia: C. Wiley, 1811); *The Commercial Code of France . . .* , trans. by John Rodman (New York: C. Wiley, 1814); [Edward Everett], "Code Napoleon," 20 *North American Review* 400 (1825); "Constitution and Penal Code of France," 1 U.S.L.J. 405 (1823).

96. While Louisiana adopted a code in 1808, it should not be considered in this category for it was a civil law jurisdiction which had simply adopted a copy of the Napoleonic code. See: Clarence J. Morrow, "Louisiana Blueprint: Civilian Codification and Legal Method for State and Nation," 17 Tul. L. Rev. 351, 388 (1943).

97. Quoted in Ernest Henry Breuer, *The New York Revised Statutes—1829* (Albany, NY: New York State Library, 1961), p. 1.

98. Quoted in Peggy A. Rabkin, *Fathers to Daughters: The Legal Foundations of Female Emancipation* (Westport, CT: Greenwood Press, 1980), p. 62.

99. *Report of the Commissioners Appointed to Revise the Statute Laws of this State . . .* (Albany, NY: Croswell and Van Benthuysen, 1827), pp. 4, 5.

100. *Report of the Commissioners Appointed to Revise the Statute Laws of the State of New-York . . .* (Albany, NY: Croswell, Barnum & Van Benthuysen, 1826), p. 8.

101. *Report of the Commissioners* (1827), p. 4.

102. *The Revised Statutes of the State of New York, Passed in the Years, 1827–1828* (Albany, NY: Gould & Banks, 1830), 1:iii.

103. *Report of the Commissioners* (1826), pp. 18–19.

104. *Chapter I. of the Fourth Part of the Proposed Revision of the Statute Laws of the State of New-York* (Albany, NY: Croswell & Van Benthuysen, 1828), §18 and §19, p. 15.
105. Ibid., §5, p. 24.
106. Ibid., §2, p. 66.
107. *Chapter III. of the First Part of the Proposed Revision of the Statute Laws of the State of New-York* (Albany, NY: Croswell and Van Benthuysen, 1827), Title II.
108. Quoted in Cook, *American Codification Movement*, p. 147.
109. *Chapter I. of the Second Part of the Proposed Revision of the Statute Laws of the State of New-York* (Albany, NY: Croswell and Van Benthuysen, 1828), §35, p. 28.
110. William A. Butler, *The Revision of the Statutes of the State of New York and the Revisers* (New York: Banks and Bros., 1889), p. 44; N.Y. Rev. Stat., ch. 4. §24 (1828).
111. *Chapter I. of the Second Part* (1828), p. 21.
112. Breuer, *New York Revised Statutes*, p. 3.
113. H.J.S. Maine, "Roman Law and Legal Education," in *Cambridge Essays* (London: John W. Parker and Son, 1856), p. 17.
114. Cook, *American Codification Movement*, p. 201.
115. Roscoe Pound, *The Formative Era of American Law* (Boston, MA: Little, Brown and Co., 1938), p. 154.
116. Peter Charles Hoffer, "Honor and the Roots of American Litigiousness," 33 Am. J. Leg. Hist. 295 (1989).

Conclusion

This work has focused on the influence of American post-Revolutionary and early National period legal education on the development of American legal thought and, through it, the shaping of American law and, ultimately, American society and politics.

In the post-Revolutionary period, leaders of the bar established proprietary law schools to meet their increasing workload. The instruction offered at these institutions, which was propagated throughout the country through the publication of analytical law treatises, was manifested into legal practice as a modified doctrine of *stare decisis*, wherein precedents could be judged against the standards of utility, morality, logic and conflicting American law and policy. Civil law gained entrance into American jurisprudence as jurists sought to replace laws they had judged unsound or inapplicable to American circumstances.

The doctrine of judicial review was developed to extend the judiciary's questioning of law to include American statutes, executive orders and civil practices. Lawyers took this movement further by shifting their activism to state legislatures where complete areas of the law were replaced with statutes as part of an American codification movement. Armed with the ability to question precedents, American lawyers helped the United States to become one of the world's most litigious societies. Conflicts between judicial activists and judicial conservatives have dominated American politics, and law has assumed a preeminent place in American society and politics.

Contrary to the assertions of Morton Horwitz, it has been shown that a coherent content and methodology was associated with American lawyers' scientific perception of law. This perception, which developed into a uniquely American legal thought, had a significant impact on the transformation of American law and on the development of a distinctly American legal system.

APPENDIX I

St. George Tucker's Reading List for Law Students at the College of William and Mary

A System of Reading on the Subjects of Politics & Law Recommended by Mr. Tucker, Professor of Law & Politics in the College of William and Mary.

Rutherford's Institutes of Nat: Law.
Turbull's on same.
Burlemaqui on same.
Puffendorf's law of Nature & Nations.
Montesquieu's Spirit of Laws.
Grotius on War & peace.
Vattel's Law of Nations.
Locke on Civil Government.
Rousseau's Social Contract.
De Lolme on the British Const.
Burgh's Political Disquisitions.
Taylor's Elements of Civil Law.
Justinian's Institutes by Harris.
Domat's Civil Law.
Smith's Wealth of Nations.
Beccaria on Crimes & Punishment.
Stuart's Political Economy.
Brown on Equality.

Godwin's Political Justice.

Prince on Civil Liberty & his political works in general.

Priestly's political works.

Publius on the American Constitutions.

Mackintosh on the French Constitution.

Jefferson's notes on Virginia.

Paine's Works.

Dickinson's Farmers Letters.

Adam's Defence of the American Constitution.

Laws of the United States.

Laws of Virginia.

Purvis's Eds: 1684.

Park's 1733.

Hunter's 1753.

Rind & Purdie's 1769.

Nicholson & Prentis's 1785.

Davis's 1794.

Sessions Acts from 1777 to 1794 inclusive.

Blackstone's Commentaries.

Hargrave's Coke upon Littleton.

Coke's Institutes: 2d, 3d & 4th parts.

Hale's History of the Common Law.

Hale's Pleas of the Crown.

Sheppard's Touchstone.

Wood's Institutes of Common Law.

Doctor & Student.

Coke's Reports by Wilson.

Plowden's reports—in English.

Hobart's reports.

Carthew's reports.

Comberbatch's reports.

Sir Thomas Raymond's reports.

Shower's reports.

Cases in H.B. William 3.

Salkeld's reports.

Lord Raymond's reports.

Strange's reports.

Hardwicke's cases.
Wilson's reports.
Burrow's reports.
Blackstone's reports.
Cowper's reports.
Douglas's reports.
Durnford & Easts reports.
Bacon's Abridgement.
Jacob's Law Dictionary.
Treatise of Equity.
Maxims in Equity.
Equity Cases abridged. 2 volumes.
Vernon's reports.
Peere Williams reports.
Vezeys reports.
Atkins reports.

[1 December 1800, Cabell Deposit, University of Virginia Library, Charlottesville, VA]

Locke's *Essays on Civil Government* was added in 1803 (St. George Tucker to the Rector of the College of William and Mary, 9 December 1803, Tucker-Coleman Collection, Earl Gregg Swem Library, College of William and Mary, Williamsburg, Virginia).

APPENDIX II

Proprietary Law Schools Founded Prior to 1830, with Biographical Information about Instructors and Graduates

Note: Names are followed by state of permanent residence, final year of attendance at school and other available biographical information. Numbers of students indicate only known attendants. However, comments are quoted when larger numbers were indicated. A "+" after the number indicates that greater numbers are known of, although names are missing.

1. Litchfield Law School, Litchfield, Connecticut, 1782–1833

Proprietors:

Tapping Reeve—B.A., LL.D., Col. N.J.; LL.D., Middlebury; Princeton, Tutor 1769–1770; Litchfield County (Conn.) State Att'y 1788–1791; Conn. Super. Ct., J. 1798–1800; Conn. Sup. Ct. Err., C.J. 1814–1816; Author: *Law of Baron and Femme . . .* (New-Haven, CT: Oliver Steele, 1816); *A Treatise on the Law of Descents* (New York: Collins & Hannay, 1825).

James Gould—B.A., LL.D.(Hon.), Yale; Litchfield; Yale, Tutor 1793–1795; Conn. Super. Ct. and Ct. Err., J. 1816–1819; Author: *A Treatise on the Principles of Pleading, in Civil Actions* (Boston, MA: Lilly & Wait, 1832).

Examiner:

Jabez Williams Huntington, Conn. (1808)—B.A., Yale; Litchfield; Conn. H. of Reps. 1829; U.S. H. of Reps. from Conn. 1829–1834; Conn. Sup. Ct. Err., J. 1834–1840; U.S. Sen. from Conn. (Whig) 1840–1847.

Number of students = 1,000+

Students:

Nehemiah Abbott, Me. (1823)—Me. H. of Reps. 1842, 1843, 1845; U.S. H. of Reps. from Me. (Rep.) 1857–1859.

George Abeel, N.Y. (1823)

Charles Adams, Mass. (1812)

Elijah Adams (1794) [son of Andrew Adams: Conn. Super. Ct., C.J.].

John T. Adams, Conn. (1833)

Joseph T. Adams, Mass. (1820)

Rufus Adams (1796)

Charles Aiken, N.H. (1832)

John A. Albro, Mass. (1821)

Cyrus Alden, Mass. (1808)

Hiram O. Alden, N.H. (1823)

Alexander M. Allen, Ga. (1801)

John Allen, Mass. (1784)—Conn. H. of Reps. 1793–1796, Clerk, 1796; U.S. H. of Reps. from Conn. (Fed.) 1797–1799; Conn. Sup. Ct. Err., J. 1800–1806.

Zimri R. Allen, Vt. (1811)

J.T. Allyn, Md. (1821)

William J. Alston, S.C. (1824)

William W. Alston, S.C. (1818)

Samuel Ames, R.I. (1824)—B.A., Brown; R.I. Gen. Assembly 1841; R.I. Sup. Ct., C.J. 1856.

Franklin Anderson, Md. (1813)

John Anderson, Me. (1815)—B.A., Bowdoin; Me. Sen. 1823; U.S. H. of Reps. from Me. (Jeff. Dem.) 1825–1833; U.S. Att'y for Me. 1833–1836.

William Andrews, Mass. (1812)

William T. Andrews, Mass. (1812)

Chester Ashley, Mass. (1814)—B.A., Williams; U.S. Sen. from Ark. (Dem.) 1844–1848.

Thomas S. Aspinwall, N.Y. (1810)

Frederick Atwater, N.Y. (1814)

Jonathan Atwater (1797)

Russell Atwater, N.Y. (1815)

Charles Austin, Mass. (1812)

Ralsaman (Ralsa) C. Austin, Conn. (1801)

Seneca Austin, Vt. (1820)

Elisha Averill, Conn. (1814)

William H. Averill, Conn. (1817)

Zacheus Ayer, S.C. (1817)

Roswell Babbitt, N.Y. (1833)

Asa Bacon (1794)

David Bacon, Conn. (1806)

Ezekiel Bacon, Mass. (1794)—B.A., Yale; Mass. H. of Reps. 1805–1806; U.S. H. of Reps. from Mass. (Dem.) 1807–1813; Mass. Ct. of C.P., C.J. 1811–1814; N.Y. Ct. of C.P., J. 1818; N.Y. Assembly 1819; N.Y. Const. Conv., Del. 1821.

William Johnson Bacon, Mass. (1823) [son of Ezekiel Bacon]—B.A., Hamilton; N.Y. Assembly 1850; N.Y. Sup. Ct., J. 1854–1870; U.S. H. of Reps. from N.Y. (Rep.) 1877–1879.

Joshua Baker, La. (1821)

Walter Baker, N.H. (1812)

Everett Balcom, Mass. (1818)

Birdsey Baldwin (1806)

Charles Baldwin, Conn. (1810)

Ebenezer Baldwin, Conn. (1810)

Henry Baldwin, Conn. (1797–1798)—B.A., LL.D., Yale; U.S. H. of Reps. from Pa. (Fed.) 1817–1822; U.S. Sup. Ct., J. 1830–1844 (strict constructionist); Author: *A General View of the Origin and Nature of the Constitution and Government of the United States . . .* (Philadelphia: J.C. Clark, 1837); *Report of Cases . . .* (Philadelphia: J. Kay, 1837).

Roger Sherman Baldwin, Conn. (1812)—B.A., LL.D.(Hon.), Yale; LL.D.(Hon.), Trinity Col. (Conn.); Conn. Sen. 1837–1838; Conn. H. of Reps. 1840–1841; Conn. Gov. 1844–1846; U.S. Sen. from Conn. (Whig) 1847–1851.

Samuel S. Baldwin, Conn. (1800)

William C. Banks, Ga. (1818)

David Barclay, Jr., Va. (1832)

Enos H. Barnes, Va. (1826)

Joseph Barnes, Mass. (1801)—Pa., J.

Lauren Barnes, Conn. (1806)

William Barnwell, S.C. (1826)

Daniel Starr Bartram, Conn. (1799)

Anson Bates, Conn. (1820)

Elijah Bates (1794)

Josiah B. Battle, Conn. (1798)

Eli H. Baxter, Ga. (1818)

Horace Baxter, Mass. (1812)

Erasmus Darwin Beach, Mass. (1832)

Jesse Beach (1789)

Levi S. Beebee, N.Y. (1830)

Truman Beecher, Conn. (1816)

David B. Beers, Conn. (1829)

Frederick Beers, Conn. (1809)

Seth Preston Beers, Conn. (1803)—Conn. H. of Reps., Speaker; leading Litchfield County (Conn.) lawyer.

Hezekiah Belden, Conn. (1797)

Harvey Bell, Jr., Vt. (1812)

James Bell, N.H. (1824)—B.A., Bowdoin; N.H. H. of Reps. 1846, 1850; N.H. Const. Conv., Del. 1850; U.S. Sen. from N.H. (Whig) 1855–1857.

Joseph H. Bellamy, Conn. (1808)

Amos Benedict (1802)

Noah Bennet Benedict (1789)

William Benedict (1797)

Milo L. Bennett, Conn. (1811)—B.A., Yale; LL.D.; Vt. Sup. Ct., J.

James Beverly, D.C. (1813)

William Beverly, D.C. (1813)

Horatio Bigelow, Mass. (1810)

Silas Bigelow, Mass.(1814)

Noyes Billings, Conn. (1820)—Conn. Lt. Gov.

F.W. Bingham, N.Y. (1830)

John Bird, Conn. (1787)—B.A., Yale; N.Y. Assembly 1796–1798; U.S. H. of Reps. from N.Y. (Dem.) 1799–1801.

Jonathon P. Bishop (1814)

Edward Bissell, Conn. (1828)

John Bissell, Jr., Conn. (1826)

Alfred Bixby, N.H. (1821)

Samuel Curtis Blackman (1796)

David Blackwell, Ky. (1813)

Eli Whitney Blake, Mass. (1817) [nephew of Eli Whitney]—B.A., Yale.

Francis A. Blake, Mass. (1817)

Samuel C. Blakeley (1796)

David Sherman Boardman (1793)

George S. Boardman, Conn. (1819)

William Whiting Boardman, Conn. (1816)—B.A., Yale; Cambridge; Conn. Sen., Clerk 1820; Conn. P. Ct., J.; Conn. H. of Reps. 1836–1839, 1845, 1849, 1851, Speaker 1836, 1839, 1845; U.S. H. of Reps. from Conn. (Whig) 1840–1843.

Job S.T. Bolles, Ga. (1822)

Nathaniel P. Bond, Ga. (1819)

William Key Bond, Md. (1811)—U.S. H. of Reps. from Ohio (Whig) 1835–1841.

Virgil D. Bonesteel, N.Y. (1830)

Joseph Bonnell, Del. (1815)

James Booth, Jr., Del. (1810) [son of James Booth: author of the Del. Const. 1776; Del. Sup. Ct., C.J. 1799–1828]—Del. Sup. Ct., C.J. 1841–1855.

Charles Bosson, Mass. (1811)

Charles Bostwick, Conn. (1798)

James Boyle (1833)

John P. Brace, Conn. (1812)—B.A., Williams.

Thomas K. Brace, Conn. (1802)

Abraham Bradley, Jr. (1790)

Benjamin H. Bradley, Conn. (1818)

Edwin D. Bradley, Conn. (1827)

Stephen Row Bradley, Conn. (1775)—B.A., Yale; Cumberland County (Vt.) State Att'y 1780; Windham County (Vt.) Ct., J. 1783; Vt. H. of Reps., Speaker 1785; Vt. Super. Ct., J. 1788; U.S. Sen. from Vt. (Dem.) 1791–1795, 1801–1813, Pres. Pro Tem. 1802–1803, 1808.

Hezekiah Brainerd, Jr. (1793)

George A. Brayton, R.I. (1825)

John Breckenridge, Md. (1821)

Daniel B. Brinsmade, Conn. (1803)

Frederick Bronson, N.Y. (1824)

Whitfield Brooks, S.C. (1814)

Jacob Broome, Del. (1809–1810)

Charles R. Brown, Conn. (1813)

Franklin Brown, N.Y. (1827–1828)

George Brown, N.Y. (1814)

Nicholas Brown, Jr., R.I. (1811)

Andrew DeWitt Bruyn, N.Y. (1811)—B.A., Princeton; N.Y. Assembly 1818; N.Y. Ct. of C.P., J. 1826–1836; U.S. H. of Reps. from N.Y. (Dem.) 1837–1838.

William S. Buchanan, Pa. (1824)

William P. Buffet, N.Y. (1813)

Joseph Bulkley, Conn. (1810)

Epaphras W. Bull (1796)

Epaphras W. Bull, Conn. (1826)

Royal Bullard, Mass. (1810)

Charles Bunker, Conn. (1822)

James F. Bunnell, N.Y. (1827)

W. Arnold Burgess, R.I. (1821)

Aaron Burr, N.J. (1774)—B.A., Col. N.J.; N.Y. Att'y Gen. 1789–1791; U.S. Sen. from N.Y. (Fed.) 1791–1797; N.Y. Assembly 1797; U.S. V.P. (Rep.) 1801–1805.

William Porter Burrall, Conn. (1828)—B.A., Yale; Conn. Gen. Assembly 1861; Conn. Sen.

Timothy Burt (1796)

Chester Pierce Butler, Pa. (1818)—B.A., Princeton; Pa. H. of Reps. 1832, 1838–1839, 1843; U.S. H. of Reps. from Pa. (Whig) 1847–1850.

David B. Butler, N.J. (1825)

John Caldwell Calhoun, S.C. (1805–1806)—B.A., Yale; LL.D.; S.C. Legislature 1808; U.S. H. of Reps. from S.C. (War Dem.) 1811–1817; U.S. Sec. War 1817–1825; U.S. V.P. 1825–1829, 1829–1832; U.S. Sen. from S.C. 1832–1843, 1845–1850; U.S. Sec. State 1843–1845.

Stephen Cambreleng, N.C. (1813)

Ralph G. Camp, Conn. (1824)

Colin Campbell, S.C. (1809)

George L. Campbell, N.Y. (1826)

John Campbell, S.C. (1820)—B.A., S.C. Col.; U.S. H. of Reps. from S.C. (State's Rights Whig) 1829–1831, (State's Rights Dem.) 1837–1845.

Ezra Canfield, Conn. (1801)

Henry J. Canfield, Conn. (1808)

Joseph Canfield, Jr. (1785)

Peter L. Cantelou, Ga. (1813)

William B. Cantelou, Ga. (1813)

John W. Cardwell, Ga. (1823)

Charles Hobart Carroll, D.C. (1817)—B.A., St. Mary's Col. (Md.); Livingston County (N.Y.) Ct., J. 1823–1829; N.Y. Sen. 1827–1828; N.Y. Assembly 1836; U.S. H. of Reps. from N.Y. (Clay Whig) 1843–1847.

William Carroll, Ind. (1823)

Dyer Castor, Pa. (1825)

George Catlin, Pa. (1817)

George Smith Catlin, Conn. (1827)—Amherst; Conn. H. of Reps. 1831, 1846; Windham County (Conn.) Pros. Att'y 1842–1843; U.S. H. of Reps. from Conn. (Dem.) 1843–1845; Conn. Sen. 1850; Windham County (Conn.) Ct., J. 1850–1851.

Grove Catlin, Conn. (1806)

Mellen Chamberlain, Me. (1819)

Benjamin Lee Chambers, Md. (1822)

Joseph Chambers, Pa. (1820)

Epaphroditus Champion, Jr., Conn. (1805) [son of Epaphroditus Champion: U.S. H. of Reps. from Conn. (Fed.) 1807–1817].

Chistopher Champlin, R.I. (1810) [son of Christopher Grant Champlin: U.S. H. of Reps. from R.I. 1797–1801; U.S. Sen. from R.I. 1809–1811].

Anson G. Chandler, Me. (1818)

Hannibal Chandler, Va. (1832)

John A. Chandler, Me. (1818)

Henry W. Channing, Conn. (1809)

Moses Chapin, Mass. (1813)

Asa Chapman (1794)—Conn. Super. Ct., J. 1819–1820.

Charles Chapman, Conn. (1818)—Conn. H. of Reps. 1840, 1847–1848, 1862, 1864; U.S. Att'y for Conn. 1841–1848; U.S. H. of Reps. from Conn. (Whig) 1851–1853.

Harvey Chase, N.H. (1800)

Moses Chase, N.H. (1798)

Samuel Chase, N.Y. (1818)—Otsego County (N.Y.) Dist. Att'y 1821–1829; U.S. H. of Reps. from N.Y. (Adams Dem.) 1827–1829.

Samuel Cheever, Mass. (1812)

Henry Chester, N.Y. (1815–1816)

Stephen M. Chester, Conn. (1813)

Abiel Childs, Conn. (1821)

Timothy Childs, Jr., Mass. (1814)—B.A., Williams; Monroe County (N.Y.) Pros. Att'y 1821–1831; N.Y. Assembly 1828, 1833; U.S. H. of Reps. from N.Y. (Whig) 1829–1831, 1835–1839, 1841–1843.

Frederick Chittenden, Conn. (1824)

Aaron Church, Conn. (1800)

Leman Church, Conn. (1815)

Samuel Church, Conn. (1806)—B.A., Yale; LL.D.; Conn. Const. Conv., Del. 1818; Conn. H. of Reps. 1818–1824, Clerk, 1824; Conn. P. Ct., J. 1821–1832; Litchfield County (Conn.) State Att'y 1823–1832; Conn. Sen. 1825–1828; Conn., Super. Ct., J. 1833–1847, C.J. 1847–1854.

Gibson Clark, Ga. (1804)

James Clark, Ga. (1820)

Archibald Clarke, Ga. (1800)

Henry L. Clarke, N.Y. (1826)

Peter I. Clarke, N.J. (1811)

Robert Clarke, Ga. (1832)

John Middleton Clayton, Del. (1817)—B.A., Yale; Del. H. of Reps. 1824; Del. Sec. State 1826–1828; U.S. Sen. from Del. (Nat. Rep.) 1829–1836; Judiciary Com., Chairman; Del. Sup. Ct., C.J. 1837–1839; U.S. Sen. from Del. (Whig) 1845–1849, 1853–1856; U.S. Sec. State 1849–1850.

Stephen Cleaveland, N.Y. (1815)

William Pitt Cleaveland, Conn. (1794)—New London County (Conn.) Ct., C.J. 1830.

George W. Clinton, N.Y. (1828)—U.S. Att'y.

William C. Clifton, Ga. (1825)

William Cockburn, N.Y. (1818–1819)

Josiah H. Cogshall, Mass. (1809)

John L. Cole, N.Y. (1810)

John J. Coleman, Ala. (1827)

Samuel Coles, Conn. (1802)

John Allen Collier, Conn. (1805)—Yale; Broome County (N.Y.) Dist. Att'y 1818–1822; U.S. H. of Reps. from N.Y. (Clay Dem.) 1831–1833; Apptd. Comm'r to Revise N.Y. Statutes, 1847.

Augustus Collins, Conn. (1804)

Josiah Collins, Jr., N.C. (1826)

Jacob A. Condit, N.J. (1813)

Thomas L. Conkling, Va. (1817)

Porter Converse, Vt. (1804)

James C. Cook, Conn. (1813)

Oliver D. Cooke, Jr., Conn. (1818–1819)

Roger W. Cooke, Conn. (1817)

James Cooley, Mass. (1799)

Benjamin F. Cooper, N.Y. (1821)

Henry Booth Cowles, Conn. (1817)—B.A., Union; N.Y. Assembly 1826–1828; U.S. H. of Reps. from N.Y. 1829–1831.

Sands G. Cowles (1812)

James Crawford, Vt. (1832)

Joel Crawford, Ga. (1806)—Ga. H. of Reps. 1814–1817; U.S. H. of Reps. from Ga. (Dem.) 1817–1821; Ga. Sen. 1827–1828.

William Croghan, Ky. (1815)

Platt H. Crosby, N.Y. (1813)

Henry N. Cruger, Jr., S.C. (1821–1822)

Edward H. Cumming, N.J. (1826)

William Cumming, Ga. (1806)

Robert Cunningham, S.C. (1810)

Medad Curtis (1789)

Charles C. Cushman, Vt. (1828)

John Paine Cushman, Conn. (1808)—B.A., Yale; U.S. H. of Reps. from N.Y. 1817–1819; N.Y. Cir. Ct., J. 1838–1844.

Alfred Cuthbert, Ga. (1804)—B.A., Princeton; Ga. H. of Reps. 1810–1813; U.S. H. of Reps. from Ga. (Dem.) 1813–1816, 1821–1827; Ga. Sen. 1817–1819; U.S. Sen. from Ga. 1835–1843.

John Alfred Cuthbert, Ga. (1807)—B.A., Princeton; Ga. H. of Reps. 1811, 1813, 1817, 1822; Ga. Sen. 1814; U.S. H. of Reps. from Ga. (Dem.) 1819–1821; Ga. Sen., Sec.

1830, 1833, 1834; Mobile County (Ala.) Ct., J. 1840; Mobile County (Ala.) Cir. Ct., J. 1852.

George Y. Cutler, Conn. (1819)

Francis Brockholst Cutting, N.Y. (1823)—N.Y. Assembly 1836–1837; U.S. H. of Reps. from N.Y. (Dem.) 1853–1855.

John S. Dart, S.C. (1821)

Francis H. Davidge, Md. (1815)

Henry Davies, Md. (1809)

Israel W. Davis, Mass. (1811)

James Davis, Del. (1816)

John Davis, Va. (1811)

John B. Davis, Va. (1815)

John H. Davis, Del. (1817)

Lawrence Dawson, S.C. (1822)

William Crosby Dawson, Ga. (1817)—B.A., Univ. Ga.; Ga. H. of Reps., Clerk 1819–1831; Compiled Ga. statutes into A Compilation of the Laws of the State of Georgia, 1828–1831; Ga. H. of Reps.; U.S. H. of Reps. from Ga. 1836–1841; Ocmulgee County (Ga.) Cir. Ct., J. 1843; U.S. Sen. from Ga. 1849–1855.

Edgar B. Day, N.Y. (1826)

Thomas Day, Conn. (1797)—Hartford County (Conn.) Ct., C.J. 1830; Conn. Sup. Ct., Reporter 1814–?.

Henry Deas, S.C. (1818)

Jacob Delamotta, Ga. (1821)

Charles J. De Menou, Md. (1808)

Buel H. Deming, Conn. (1825)

Thomas Denny, Mass. (1825)

George P. Devereux, N.C. (1817)

Thomas Devereux, N.C. (1813)

Christopher C. Dexter, R.I. (1813)

Daniel Stevens Dickinson, Conn. (1827)—N.Y. Sen. 1837–1840; N.Y. Lt. Gov. 1842–1844; N.Y. Ct. Err., Pres. 1842–1844; U.S. Sen. from N.Y. (Dem.) 1844–1851; N.Y. Att'y Gen. 1861–1863; U.S. Att'y S.D.N.Y. 1865–1866.

Guy W. Doan, Conn. (1814)

Amos B. Doolittle, Conn. (1806)

Appleton Downes, Mass. (1811)

John B. Downman, Mass. (1813)

Francis Doyle, Ga. (1822)

Cornelius Dubois, Jr., N.Y. (1830)

Daniel Dunbar, Conn. (1798)

Miles Dunbar, Conn. (1809)

Henry Williams Dwight, Mass. (1809)—Williams; Mass. H. of Reps. 1818, 1834; U.S. H. of Reps. from Mass. 1821–1831.

Eliphalet Dyer, Jr., Conn. (1790) [son of Eliphalet Dyer: Conn. Super. Ct., C.J. 1789–1793; Cont. Congress 1774–1779, 1780–1783].

Thomas Dyer, Conn. (1799)

A.G. Eastman, N.Y. (1833)

Henry P. Edwards, Conn. (1828) [son of Henry Waggaman Edwards]—N.Y. Sup. Ct., J. 1848–1856.

Henry Waggaman Edwards, Conn. (1798)—B.A., Col. N.J.; U.S. H. of Reps. from Conn. (Rep.) 1819–1823; U.S. Sen. from Conn. 1823–1827; Conn. Sen. 1827–1829; Conn. H. of Reps., Speaker 1830; Conn. Gov. 1833, 1835–1838.

(John) Starke Edwards, Conn. (1798)

Johnathan Walter Edwards (1794)

Ogden Edwards, Conn. (1801)—N.Y. Cir. Ct., J. 1823–1841.

Louis Eickelberger, Md. (1810)

Hezekiah R. Elgin, Md. (1815)

Grindall R. Ellis, N.H. (1809)

Amos Stanhope Ellmaker, Pa. (1806)—B.A., Princeton; Dauphin County (Pa.) Dep. Att'y Gen. 1809–1815; Pa. H. of Reps. 1813–1814; Pa. Dis. Ct., J. 1815–1816; Pa. Att'y Gen. 1816–1819, 1828–1829.

Henry Leavitt Ellsworth, Conn. (1811) [son of Oliver Ellsworth: U.S. Sup. Ct., C.J. 1796–1799]—B.A., Yale; U.S. Comm'r of Patents 1835–1845.

William Wolcott Ellsworth, Conn. (1811) [son of Oliver Ellsworth: U.S. Sup. Ct., C.J. 1796–1799]—B.A.(Honors), Yale; LL.D.(Hon.), Univ. N.Y.; U.S. H. of Reps. from Conn. 1829–1834; Conn. Gov. 1838–1842; Conn. Sup. Ct., J. 1847–1861.

Edmund B. Elmendorf, N.Y. (1826)

William Ennis, R.I. (1820)

Isaac H. Erwin, Ala. (1828)

James Christie Esten (1792)

Sherman Everest, Conn. (1800)

Frederick Fairlie, N.Y. (1818–1819)

John Meyers Felder, S.C. (1806)—B.A., Yale; S.C. H. of Reps. 1812–1816, 1822–1824; S.C. Sen. 1816–1820, 1840–1851; U.S. H. of Reps. from S.C. (Dem.) 1831–1835.

Linus Fenn (1793)

John Fine, N.Y. (1813)—B.A., Columbia; St. Lawrence County (N.Y.) Ct. of C.P., J. 1824–1839, 1843–1847; U.S. H. of Reps. from N.Y. (Dem.) 1839–1841; N.Y. Sen. 1848.

Isaac Fisher, Jr., Md. (1811)

Samuel Fisher, Mass. (1810)

Matthew Fleming, S.C. (1815)

Timothy Follett, Vt. (1812)

Joshua Folsom, N.H. (1811) [son of Nathaniel Folsom: Cont. Congress 1774, 1775, 1777–1780].

John A. Foot, Conn. (1824)

Samuel Augustus Foote, Conn. (1797)—B.A., Yale; Conn. H. of Reps. 1817–1818, 1821–1823, 1825–1826, Speaker 1825–1826; U.S. H. of Reps. from Conn. 1819–1821, 1823–1825, (Whig) 1833–1834; U.S. Sen. from Conn. 1827–1833; Conn. Gov. 1834–1835.

Ebenezer Foote (1795)

William H. Ford, S.C. (1826)

George Foster, Mass. (1812)

James Foster, Mass. (1812)

Thomas Flourney Foster, Ga. (1816)—B.A., Franklin Col.; Ga. H. of Reps. 1822–1825; U.S. H. of Reps. from Ga. (Dem.) 1829–1835, 1841–1843.

James Fowler, Mass. (1808)

John D. Fowler, Mass. (1813)

John Brown Francis, Pa. (1813)—B.A., Brown; R.I. H. of Reps. 1821–1829; R.I. Sen. 1831, 1842, 1845–1856; R.I. Gov. 1833–1838; U.S. Sen. from R.I. 1844–1845.

Walter S. Franklin, Pa. (1818)—U.S. H. of Reps., Clerk.

Alexander G. Frazier, S.C. (1810)

Samuel Frisbie, Conn. (1809)

Henry H. Fuller, Mass. (1812)

William W. Fuller, Mass. (1814)

Alexander N. Fullerton, Vt. (1826–1827)

Thomas S. Fullerton, Vt. (1822)

Peter Gansevoort, N.Y. (1810) [son of Leonard Gansevoort: Cont. Congress 1787–1788]—N.Y. Ct. for the Correction of Errors, J.

Samuel Gantt, S.C. (1817)

Barent Gardenier, N.Y. (1796)—U.S. H. of Reps. from N.Y. (Fed.) 1807–1811; N.Y. Dist. Att'y 1813–1815.

Philip S. Gardner, R.I. (1826)

David Gibbs (1808)

Henry W. Gibbs, Conn. (1808)

William C. Gibbs, R.I. (1810)—R.I. Gen. Assembly 1816–1821; R.I. Gov. 1821–1824.

William Gibson, Ga. (1823)

Samuel Glover, N.Y. (1820)

Thomas Ruggles Gold, Conn. (1786)—B.A., Yale; N.Y. Asst. Att'y Gen. 1797–1801; N.Y. Sen. 1796–1802; N.Y. Assembly 1808; U.S. H. of Reps. from N.Y. (Fed.) 1809–1813, 1815–1817.

Thomas A. Gold, Mass. (1808)

Edward Goodwin, Conn. (1823)

Hiram Goodwin, Conn. (1829)

George Gould, Conn. (1827–1828) [son of James Gould]—B.A., Yale; N.Y. Sup. Ct., J. 1855–1868.

James Gould, Conn. (1795)—B.A., LL.D.(Hon.), Yale; Yale, Tutor 1793–1795; Conn. Super. Ct. and Ct. Err., J. 1816–1819; Author: *A Treatise on the Principles of Pleading, in Civil Actions* (Boston, MA: Lilly & Wait, 1832).

James R. Gould, Conn. (1824)

William Tracy Gould (1818) [son of James Gould]—Ga. Sup. Ct., J.; founded a proprietary law school in Augusta, Ga. in 1833.

William A. Grant, Ga. (1823)

William Grant, S.C. (1823)

Thomas C. Graves, Ky. (1808)

Thomas Gray, Conn. (1817)

Caleb Green, Jr., N.Y. (1830)

Henry Woodhull Green, N.J. (1823)—B.A., C.N.J.; N.J. Assembly 1842; N.J. Const. Conv., Del. 1844; N.J. Sup. Ct., C.J. 1846–1860; N.J. Prerogative Ct., C. & J. 1860–1866.

Albert Collins Greene, R.I. (1812)—R.I. H. of Reps. 1815–1825, 1857, Speaker 1821–1825; R.I. Att'y Gen. 1825–1843; R.I. Sen. 1843–1844, 1851–1852; U.S. Sen. from R.I (Whig) 1845–1851.

Benjamin D. Greene, Mass. (1813)

Richard W. Greene, R.I. (1812)

William Greene, R.I. (1817)

Thomas Grey, Conn. (1817)

George Griffin, Conn. (1798)—LL.D.

Shubael Griswold, Conn. (1809)

John C. Groome, Md. (1824)

Frederick Gunn, Conn. (1812)

Alpheus Gustin, N.C. (1819)

Isaac R. Gwathmey, Ky. (1813)

William B. Hadnall, Md. (1819)

Ambrose Hall, Mass. (1802)

Benjamin Hall (1796)

Gideon Hall, Conn. (1829)

Horace Hall, Vt. (1803)

Willis Hall, N.Y. (1826)—N.Y. Att'y Gen. 1839–1842.

William Halstead, Jr., N.J. (1814)—B.A., Princeton; N.J. Sup. Ct., Reporter 1821–1832; Hunterdon County (N.J.) Pros. Att'y 1824–1829, 1833–1837; U.S. H. of Reps. from N.J. (Whig) 1837–1843; U.S. Att'y for N.J. 1849–1853.

Oliver Spencer Halsted, N.J. (1813)—B.A., Princeton; N.J. H. of Reps. 1827, 1834; N.J. Const. Conv., Del. 1844; N.J. Ch. Ct., C. 1845–1852.

Robert W. Halsted, N.J. (1827)

Thomas Hamilton, Ga. (1810)

Augustus Cincinnatus Hand, Vt. (1827)—U.S. H. of Reps. from N.Y. (Dem.) 1839–1841; N.Y. Sen. 1844–1847; N.Y. Sup. Ct., J. 1847–1855.

Tipton B. Harrison, Va. (1818)

Leroy Harvey, Ga. (1821)

Abraham Bryun Hasbrouck, N.Y. (1812)—B.A., M.A., Yale; LL.D.(Hon.), Columbia; U.S. H. of Reps. from N.Y. (Nat. Rep.) 1825–1827; Rutgers, Pres. 1840–1850.

Bentley Hasell, S.C. (1825)

Moses Hatch, Conn. (1801)

Benjamin B. Hawkes, N.C. (1823)

Francis Lister Hawkes, N.C. (1818)—B.A.(1st Honours), Univ. N.C.; N.C. Sup. Ct., Reporter 1820–1826; N.C. H. of Commons 1821.

Samuel Hawkins, N.Y. (1798)

Charles Hawley, Conn. (1813)—Conn. P. Ct., J. 1830; Conn. Lt. Gov.

William Hawley (1788)

Moses Hayden, Mass. (1804)—B.A., Williams; Livingston County (N.Y.) Ct. of C.P., J. 1821–1823; U.S. H. of Reps. from N.Y. 1823–1827; N.Y. Sen. 1829–1830.

George E. Head, Mass. (1813)

Joseph L. Hepburn, Pa. (1819)

Benjamin Heyward (1795)

Guy Hiccox, Conn. (1806)

Joseph A. Hill, N.C. (1819)

William R. Hill, S.C. (1821)

Augustus L. Hillhouse, Conn. (1812)

Homer Hine, Conn. (1800)

Richard Hines, N.C. (1814)—N.C. H. of Commons 1824; U.S. H. of Reps. from N.C. (Dem.) 1825–1827.

Royal Ralph Hinman, Conn. (1806)—B.A., Yale; Conn. H. of Reps.; Conn. Sec. State 1835–1842; Committee to Revise Statutes of Conn., Chairman 1835.

Samuel Hitchcock, Ala. (1828)

William F. Hodges, Conn. (1812)

William S. Holbaird, Conn. (1815)—Conn. Lt. Gov.

Chauncey P. Holcomb, Conn. (1824)

John Milton Holley, Jr., Conn. (1823)—B.A., Yale; N.Y. Assembly 1842–1845; U.S. H. of Reps. from N.Y. (Whig) 1847–1848.

Uriel Holmes, Conn. (1785)—B.A., Yale; Conn. H. of Reps. 1803–1805; Litchfield County (Conn.) Pros. Att'y 1807–1814; Litchfield County (Conn.) Ct., J. 1814–1817; U.S. H. of Reps. from Conn. (Fed.) 1817–1818.

Hopkins Holsey, Va. (1819)—Univ. Va.; Ga. H. of Reps.; U.S. H. of Reps. from Ga. (Union Dem.) 1835–1839.

George B. Holt, Conn. (1812)—Ohio, J.

Thaddeus G. Holt, Ga. (1816)—Ga. Sup. Ct., J.

James Hooker, Conn. (1810)

Abiathar Hopkins, N.H. (1808)

Samuel Miles Hopkins, Conn. (1791)—B.A., Yale; U.S. H. of Reps. from N.Y. 1813–1815; N.Y. Assembly 1820–1821; N.Y. Sen. 1822; N.Y. Ch. Ct., Reporter 1823–1826; N.Y. Cir. Ct., J. 1832–1836.

Minor Hotchkiss, Ga. (1813)

Josiah Houghton, Me. (1817)

Patrick Houston, Ga. (1798)

Benjamin Chew Howard, Md. (1812)—B.A., M.A., Col. N.J.; Md. H. of Dels. 1824; U.S. H. of Reps. from Md. (Dem.) 1829–1833, 1835–1839; Md. Sen. 1840–1841; U.S. Sup. Ct., Reporter, 1843–1862.

John H. Howard, Ga. (1813)

Samuel Howe, Mass. (1805)—B.A., Williams; Mass. Ct. of C.P., J. 1821; Conducted a proprietary law school in Northampton, Mass. 1823–1830.

Henry S. Hoyt, N.Y. (1829)

Elijah Hubbard, Conn. (1798)

Elizur Hubbard, Vt. (1799)

James Hubbel, Vt. (1802)

Jonathon Trumbull Hudson, Conn. (1826)

William Huffington, Del. (1823)

Hezekiah B. Hull, Conn. (1813)

Joseph Humphrey, Conn. (1812)

Hiram Paine Hunt, N.Y. (1817)—B.A., Union; U.S. H. of Reps. from N.Y. (Whig) 1835–1837, 1839–1843.

Jonathan Hunt, Vt. (1808)—B.A., Dartmouth; Vt. H. of Reps. 1811, 1816, 1817, 1824; U.S. H. of Reps. from Vt. (Nat. Rep.) 1827–1832.

Nathaniel Hunt (1797)

Ward E. Hunt, N.Y. (1830)—B.A.(Hon.), LL.D.(Hon.), Union; LL.D.(Hon.), Rutgers; N.Y. Assembly 1838; N.Y. Ct. App., J. 1865–1868, C.J. 1868–1869; Comm'r 1869–1873; U.S. Sup. Ct., J. 1873–1886.

Jabez Williams Huntington, Conn. (1808)—B.A., Yale; Conn. H. of Reps. 1829; U.S. H. of Reps. from Conn. 1829–1834; Conn. Sup. Ct. Err., J. 1834–1840; U.S. Sen. from Conn. (Whig) 1840–1847.

John J. Hyde, Conn. (1829)

Charles M. Ingersoll, N.H. (1812)

David Bryan Ingersoll (1792)

Alpheus Ingham, Pa. (1825)

Henry C. Ives, N.Y. (1831)

Moses B. Ives, R.I. (1812)

Thomas Ives (1778)

Ebenezer Jackson, Jr., Ga. (1814)—B.A., St. Mary's Col. (Md.); Conn. H. of Reps. 1829–1832, 1849; U.S. H. of Reps. from Pa. (Whig) 1834–1835.

John P. Jackson (1824)—N.J. H. of Reps., Speaker.

Joseph Webber Jackson, Ga. (1817)—Ga. H. of Reps.; Ga. Sen.; U.S. H. of Reps. from Ga. (Dem.) 1850–1853; Ga. Super. Ct., J.

Oliver P. Jackson, N.Y. (1823)

Thomas L. Jackson, Ga. (1823)

George W. Jacobs, Pa. (1819)

William C. Jacobs, Pa. (1820)

Edward N. James, N.Y. (1805)

Thomas Janvier, Jr., Del. (1828)

Russel Jarvis, Mass. (1813)

Charles M. Jenkins, N.Y. (1831)

Ebenezur Jesup, Jr., Conn. (1825)

Ezra Jewell, Conn. (1809)

Kensey Johns, Jr., Del. (1812) [son of Kensey Johns: Del. Sup. Ct., C.J. 1799]—B.A., Princeton; LL.D.(Hon.), Jefferson Col. (Pa.); U.S. H. of Reps. from Del. (Fed.) 1827–1831; Del. Ch. Ct., C. 1832–1857.

Charles F. Johnson, Conn. (1824)

Edwards Johnson, Conn. (1826)

James Johnson, S.C. (1816)

William Samuel Johnson, Jr., Conn. (1816) [son of William Samuel Johnson: Cont. Congress 1784–1787; U.S. Const. Conv., Del. 1787; U.S. Sen. from Conn. (Fed.) 1789–1791; Columbia Col., Pres. 1787–1800].

James T. Johnstone, Ga. (1816)

John E. Joline (1796)

Henry Jones, Calcutta, India (1810)

Joel Jones, Conn. (1819)—B.A., Yale; LL.D.; Lafayette Col., Founder; Comm'r to revise civil code of Pa. 1830; Philadelphia (Pa.) Dist. Ct., J. 1835–1845, Presiding

J. 1845–1847; Girard Col. (Pa.), Pres. 1847–1849; Author: *Report of the Commissioners to Revise the Civil Code of Pennsylvania* . . . (Harrisburg, PA: H. Welsh, 1831–1836); *A Syllabus of the Law of Land and Titles in Pennsylvania* (Philadelphia: H. Perkins, 1850).

John Q. Jones, N.Y. (1817)

Rice Jones, La. (1807)

Robert Jones (1813)

Noah Judson, Mass. (1799)

William M. Kaleb, Md. (1827)

Edward Kellogg, Mass. (1823)

Charles W. Kelso, Pa. (1828)

Joseph C. Kerr, N.C. (1817)

Philip Barton Key, Jr., Md. (1829) [son of Philip Barton Key: U.S. 4th C.C., C.J. 1800–1802].

Eleazer W. Keyes (1795)

Austin Kilbourn, Conn. (1821)

Edward King, N.Y. (1813)—founder of the Cincinnati (Ohio) Law School 1833; Ohio H. of Reps., Speaker.

George Gordon King, R.I. (1820)—B.A., Brown; R.I. H. of Reps., Speaker 1845–1846; U.S. H. of Reps. from R.I. (Whig) 1849–1853.

James Gore King, N.Y. (1810)—B.A., Harvard; N.Y. Sup. Ct., J.; U.S. H. of Reps. from N.J. (Whig) 1849–1851.

John Kingsbury, Conn. (1788)—Conn. P. Ct., J. 1830.

Sanford Kingsbury, N.H. (1801)

Thomas Kinnecutt, Mass. (1823)—Lt. Gov.

Reynold M. Kirby, Conn. (1809)

Charles P. Kirkland, N.Y. (1818)

Frederick Knight, Mass. (1812)

Joseph Lake, Ohio (1820)

Lucius Quintis Cincinnatus Lamar, Ga. (1817)—Ga. Sup. Ct., J. 1830–1834; Revisor: *Clayton's Georgia Justice* (Milledgeville, GA: S. Grantland, 1824).

Benjamin F. Langdon, Vt. (1821)

Chauncey Langdon, Conn. (1787)—B.A., Yale; Vt. P. Ct., J. 1798–1799; Vt. H. of Reps. 1813–1814, 1817, 1819–1820, 1822; U.S. H. of Reps. from Vt. (Fed.) 1815–1817.

Leviness S. Lansing, N.Y. (1830)

John Lashell, Pa. (1810)

Allen Latham, Mass. (1814)

Lyman Law, Conn. (1791)—B.A., Yale; Conn. H. of Reps. 1801–1802, 1806, 1809–

1810, 1819, 1826, Speaker 1806, 1809–1810; U.S. H. of Reps. from Conn. (Fed.) 1811–1817.

Samuel Andrew Law (1793)

Augustus A. Lawrence, N.Y. (1813)

Philip K. Lawrence, N.Y. (1814)—U.S. D. for La., J. 1837–1841.

William Beach Lawrence, N.Y. (1819)—B.A.(High Honors), Columbia; Sorbonne; Ecole de Droit; DCL(Hon.), Univ. N.Y.; LL.D.(Hon.), Brown; R.I. Lt. Gov. 1851; R.I. Gov. 1852; R.I. Const. Conv., Del. 1853; Social Science Congress in Bristol, England, named member of a Commission to compile a code of International law; Columbian Univ. (D.C.), Lecturer on Int'l Law 1872–1873.

Elias Warner Leavenworth, N.Y. (1825–1827)—B.A., Yale; N.Y. Assembly 1850, 1857; N.Y. Sec. State 1854–1855; N.Y. Const. Comm'r 1872; U.S. H. of Reps. from N.Y. (Rep.) 1875–1877.

Nathan Leavenworth, N.Y. (1813)

William Leavenworth, Conn. (1822)

Harvey F. Leavitt, N.H. (1816)

Henry Ledyard, N.Y. (1830)

Cornelius Leonard, N.Y. (1810)

Daniel Wadsworth Lewis (1791)

John L. Lewis, La. (1825)

Robert H. Lewis, Va. (1821)

Henry W. Livingston, N.Y. (1820)

James K. Livingston, N.Y. (1818–1819)

John R. Livingston, N.Y. (1823)

Robert Livingston, N.Y. (1829)

Walter Livingston, N.Y. (1820)

Joseph R. Lloyd, N.C. (1818)

Ephraim Lockwood, Conn. (1798)

Augustus Baldwin Longstreet, Ga. (1813)—B.A., Yale; LL.D.; Ga. Legislature 1821; Ga. Super. Ct., J. 1822–1825; Univ. Miss., Pres. 1849–1856; Univ. S.C., Pres. 1857.

Daniel Lord, Jr., Conn. (1814)—B.A., Yale; prominent corporate lawyer; Author: *The Effect of Secession upon the Commercial Relations between the North and South* . . . (London: H. Stevens, 1861; New York: New York Times, 1861).

Charles G. Loring, Mass. (1813)

Edward G. Loring, Mass. (1822)—Suffolk County (Mass.) P. Ct., J.; U.S. Ct. Cl. for Mass., J. 1858–1877.

Cyrus H. Lathrop, Mass. (1810)

Adrian Lott, N.Y. (1831)

Cornelius F. Low, N.Y. (1812–1814)

Benjamin Lowdnes, Va. (1825)

Alfred Ludlow, N.Y. (1822)

Ethelred Lundy, Va. (1818)

Darius Lyman, Conn. (1811)

Samuel F. Lyman, Mass. (1819)

Theodore Lyman, Mass. (1811)

Robert M'Cawley, Va. (1819)

James G. M'Clean, Md. (1822)

James M'Elhenny, S.C. (1822)

William H. M'Farland, Va. (1818)

J. A. McKaleb, Md. (1829)

John Maberry, Md. (1813)

Elisha Mack, Mass. (1805)

Peter Mackie, N.Y. (1813)

Enoch Magruder, Md. (1816)

Garrick Mallery, Pa. (1810)—B.A., Yale; LL.D., Pa. Legislature 1827–1831 (largely aided in establishing Pa. penitentiary system); Pa. Dis. Ct., J. 1831–1836.

Horace Mann, Mass. (1822)—B.A., Brown; Theron Metcalf's Law School, Dedham, Mass.; Mass. H. of Reps. 1827–1833; Mass. Sen. 1833–1837, Pres. 1835–1837; Comm'r for Revision of Mass. Statutes 1835; U.S. H. of Reps. from Mass. (Whig) 1848–1853; Antioch Col. (Ohio), Pres. 1852–1859.

Edward Deering Mansfield, N.Y. (1823–1825)—B.A., West Point; B.A., Princeton; Cincinnati Col. (Ohio), Prof. of Constitutional Law & History 1858–1868; Author: *The Legal Rights, Liabilities and Duties of Women* (Cincinnati, OH: W. H. Moore, 1845).

Benjamin A. Markley, S.C. (1806)

Charles Marsh, Conn. (1787)—B.A., Dartmouth; U.S. Att'y D. Vt. 1797–1801; U.S. H. of Reps. from Vt. (Fed.) 1815–1817.

Charles Marsh, Jr., Vt. (1813) [son of Charles Marsh: U.S. Att'y D. Vt. 1797–1801; U.S. H. of Reps. from Vt. (Fed.) 1815–1817].

Samuel Marsh (1787)

Joseph F. Martin, R.I. (1818)

William Dickinson Martin, S.C. (1810)—S.C. H. of Reps. 1816–1818; S.C. Sen., Clerk 1818–1826; U.S. H. of Reps. from S.C. (Dem.) 1827–1831; S.C. Cir. Ct., J. 1831–1833.

Ebenezer Marvin, Vt. (1799)

John Young Mason, Va. (1817)—B.A., Univ. N.C.; Va. H. of Reps. 1823–1827; Va. Sen. 1827–1831; Va. Const. Conv., Del. 1829–1830; U.S. H. of Reps. from Va. (Dem.) 1831–1837; U.S. D.Va., J. 1837; U.S. Sec. Navy 1844–1845, 1846–1849; U.S. Att'y Gen. 1845–1846; Va. Const. Conv., Presiding Officer 1850–1851.

William J. Mason, Va. (1821)

Nathaniel Mather, Conn. (1811)

Virgil Maxcy, Mass. (1805)—B.A., M.A., Brown; Md. H. of Reps.; Md. Sen. 1815–1830; U.S. Sollicitor of the Treasury 1830–1837.

Robert Maxwell, Md. (1817)

Abraham Mayer, Pa. (1817)

John B. Mayer, Pa. (1823)

Harman B. Mayo, N.Y. (1821)

Charles C. Mayson, S.C. (1814)

Elijah B. Merwin, Vt. (1801)

Theron Metcalf, Mass. (1806)—B.A., LL.D., Brown; Dedham County (Mass.) Att'y 1817–1829; Mass. H. of Reps. 1831, 1833–1834; Judiciary Comm., Chairman 1831, 1833–1834; Mass. Sen. 1835, Judiciary Comm., Chairman 1835; Mass. Sup. Jud. Ct., Reporter 1840–1847, J. 1848–1865; Author: *Digest of the Cases Decided in the Supreme Judicial Court of the Commonwealth of Massachussetts* (Boston, MA: Richardson & Lord, 1825); *Principles of the Law of Contracts, as applied by Courts of Law* (New York: Hurd & Houghton, 1867).

Henry Middleton, S.C. (1817)

Henry A. Middleton, S.C. (1815)

Bowyar Millar (Boyer F. Miller), Va. (1817)

Charles Miller, Conn. (1818)

Joseph Miller, Conn. (1801)

Morris Smith Miller, N.Y. (1798)—B.A., Union; Oneida County (N.Y.) Ct. of C.P., J. 1810–1824; U.S. H. of Reps. from N.Y. (Fed.) 1813–1815.

Rutger Bleeker Miller, N.Y. (1824) [son of Morris Smith Miller: Oneida County (N.Y.) Ct. of C.P., J. 1810–1824; U.S. H. of Reps. from N.Y. (Fed.) 1813–1815]—Catholic Col. (Can.); Yale; N.Y. Assembly 1832; U.S. D., Clerk 1833–1834; U.S. H. of Reps. from N.Y. (Dem.) 1836–1837.

Solomon S. Miller, Vt. (1811)

Michael F. Mills, Conn. (1801)—Conn. P. Ct., J. 1830.

Roger Mills, Conn. (1798)

Phineas Miner, Conn. (1796)—Conn. H. of Reps. 1809, 1811, 1813, 1814, 1816, 1823, 1827, 1829, 1835; Conn. Sen. 1830–1831; U.S. H. of Reps. from Conn. (Whig) 1834–1835; Conn. P. Ct., J. 1838–1839.

Alexander Minor (1797)

Thomas R. Minturn, N.Y. (1826)

Charles Mitchell, Conn. (1804)

Donald Grant Mitchell (1792)

Henry A. Mitchell, Conn. (1826)

Lewis C. Mitchell, Conn. (1807)

Louis Mitchell, Conn. (1813)

Stephen Mix Mitchell, Jr., Conn. (1800) [son of Stephen Mix Mitchell: Cont. Congress 1783–1788; U.S. Sen. from Conn. (Fed.) 1793–1795; Conn. Sup. Ct. Err., J. 1795–1807, C.J. 1807–1814].

Walter Mitchell (1796)

Thomas Moffit, Ga. (1816)

Robert Moore, Ga. (1822)

Henry Morris, N.Y. (1826)

James E. Morris (1803)

James Morrison, N.H. (1809)

Sidney E. Morse, Mass. (1814)—B.A., Yale.

Arthur A. Morson, Va. (1823)

Marcus Morton, Mass. (1806)—B.A., Brown; Mass. Sen., Clerk 1811; U.S. H. of Reps. from Mass. (Dem.) 1817–1821, 1824–1825; Mass. Lt. Gov. 1823; Mass. Sup. Ct., J. 1825–1840; Mass. Gov. 1840–1841, 1843–1844; Mass. Const. Conv., Del. 1853; Mass. H. of Reps. 1858.

Charles Moseley, Conn. (1806)

William W. Mumford, N.Y. (1815)

Warren Munger, Conn. (1811)

Losson Nash, Mass. (1803)

George P. Neill, Pa. (1829)

Armistead Nelson, Md. (1814)

Isaac M. Newcomb, N.Y. (1828)

Edward Nichol, Conn. (1813)

Joseph H. Nichols, N.Y. (1827)

John C. Nicoll, Ga. (1814)—U.S. D. D. Ga., J. 1839–1848; U.S. D. N. & S. Ga., J. 1848–1861.

Eugenius Aristides Nisbet, Ga. (1823)—B.A., LL.D.(Hon.), Univ. Ga.; Ga. H. of Reps. 1827–1830; Ga. Sen. 1830–1837; U.S. H. of Reps. from Ga. (Whig) 1838–1842; Ga. Sup. Ct., J. 1845–1853; Secession Convention, Committee which drafted Ordinance of Secession, Chairman 1861; Confederate Congress 1861 (served on Committee to draft Confederate Constitution).

Henry G. Nixon, S.C. (1820)

Theodore North, Conn. (1808)

James C. Norton, N.Y. (1819)

William B. Nutall, N.C. (1823)

Jesse Oakley, N.Y. (1814)

Matthias B. Ogden, N.J. (1813)

Arthur H. O'Hara, S.C. (1814)

Theophilos Olcott, N.H. (1801)

Henry Oliver, Md. (1821)

Samuel W. Oliver, Ga. (1820)—Ala. H. of Reps., Speaker.

Charles G. Olmstead, Conn. (1810)

Edgar S. Ormsbee, Vt. (1824)

Henry Orne, Mass. (1811)

Thomas B. Overton, Pa. (1813)

Benjamin Page, R.I. (1805)

Henry Page, R.I. (1816)

Elijah J. Paine, Jr., Vt. (1815) [son of Elijah J. Paine: Vt. Sup. Ct., J. 1791–1795; U.S. D. for Vt., J. 1801–1842; U.S. Sen. from Vt. (Fed.) 1795–1801].

Alexis Painter, Conn. (1817)

Amasa J. Parker, Conn. (1809)—N.Y. Sup. Ct., J.; founded the Albany (N.Y.) Law School 1851.

Aurelius D. Parker, Mass. (1826)

Charles T. Parker, Mass. (1828)

William M. Parker (1820)

Abner B. Parrott, Ga. (1821)

Anson V. Parsons, Mass. (1825)—Pa. Sup. Ct., J.

Edward G. Pasteur, N.C. (1823)

Robert Patten (1814)

Christopher S. Patterson, Pa. (1821)

Amos Pearce (1786)

William V. Peck, Conn. (1824)—Ohio, J.

Duncan C. Pell, N.Y. (1826)

Samuel Penny, N.Y. (1828)

Charles Perkins, Conn. (1813)

Thomas S. Perkins, Conn. (1812)

Joel T. Petit, Conn. (1800)

William W. Petit, Ohio (1815)

Augustus Pettibone, Conn. (1788)—Litchfield County (Conn.) Ct., J. 1820, C.J. 1830.

Serono Pettibone, Conn. (1802)

Charles B. Phelps, Vt. (1806)—Conn. P. Ct., J. 1830.

Edward A. Phelps, Conn. (1828)

Elisha Phelps, Conn. (1801)—B.A., Yale; Conn. H. of Reps. 1807, 1812, 1814–1818, 1821, 1829, 1835, Speaker 1821, 1829; U.S. H. of Reps. from Conn. (Dem.) 1819–1821, 1825–1829; Conn. Sen. 1822–1824; Comm'r to revise and codify Conn. laws 1835.

Jedediah Phelps, Mass. (1810)

Oliver Leicester Phelps (1794)

Samuel Shethar Phelps, Conn. (1811)—B.A., Yale; Vt. H. of Reps. 1821–1832; Vt. Sup. Ct., J. 1832–1838; Vt. Sen. 1838–1839; U.S. Sen. from Vt. (Whig) 1839–1851, 1853–1854.

Reuben Picket, N.C. (1825)

William D. Pickett, N.C. (1826)

James Pierce, Conn. (1798)

Levi Pierce, Md. (1815)

William L. Pierce, Jr., Ga. (1809) [son of William Leigh Pierce: U.S. Const. Conv., Del. 1787; Cont. Congress 1787].

John Pierpont, Conn. (1809)—B.A., Yale.

John Pierpont, Conn. (1825)—Vt., C.J.

George Pierson, N.Y. (1830)

William Pilsbury, Mass. (1813)

John Pitcher, N.Y. (1815)

Philip E. Pitcher, N.Y. (1828)

John R. Pitt, Md. (1816)

David Plant, Conn. (1804)—B.A., Yale; Conn. P. Ct., J.; Conn. H. of Reps. 1817–1820, Speaker; Conn. Sen. 1821–1822; Conn. Lt. Gov. 1823–1827; U.S. H. of Reps. from Conn. (Nat. Rep.) 1827–1829.

Thompson T. Player, S.C. (1826)

Washington Poe, Ga. (1823)—U.S. H. of Reps.

Thomas G. Polk, N.C. (1811)

John Porteous, S.C. (1800)

George Bryan Porter, Pa. (1812)—Pa. Att'y Gen.; Pa. H. of Reps.; Mich. Territory Gov. 1831–1834.

Peter Buell Porter, Conn. (1791)—B.A., Yale; N.Y. Assembly 1802, 1828; U.S. H. of Reps. from N.Y. (Dem.) 1809–1813, 1815–1816; N.Y. Sec. State 1815–1816; U.S. Sec. War 1828–1829.

Timothy Hopkins Porter, N.H. (1807)—N.Y. Assembly 1816–1817, 1838, 1840; N.Y. County Ct., J. 1817–1819; N.Y. Ct. of C.P., J. 1819; N.Y. Dis. Att'y 1819–1820, 1824; N.Y. Sen. 1823, 1828–1831; U.S. H. of Reps. from N.Y. 1825–1827.

Alfred L. Post (1832)

Ansel Potter, Conn. (1805)

Asa Potter, R.I. (1826)

Henry E. Prentice (1832)

Isaac T. Preston, Va. (1812)—La. Sup. Ct., J.

Benjamin Price, Md. (1820)

George J. Pumpelly, N.Y. (1826)

Austin Putnam, N.Y. (1828)

Charles Putnam, Mass. (1814)

Robert G. Rankin, N.Y. (1827)

Daniel Raymond, Conn. (1810)—Author: *The Elements of Constitutional Law* (Baltimore, MD: Cushing & Brother, 1840).

David H. Raymond, Conn. (1810)

James Raymond, Conn. (1820)

Benjamin L. Rayner, Conn. (1824)

George Read, Del. (1808)

John D. Read, Del. (1823)

John H. Read, S.C. (1809)

William T. Read, Del. (1812)

William Rees (before 1801)

Aaron Burr Reeve, Conn. (1802)—B.A., Yale.

Walter Reynolds, N.Y. (1822)

George H. Richards, Conn. (1809)

Henry S. Richards, N.Y. (1826)

Robert K. Richards, N.Y. (1829)

Benjamin Ridgate, Md. (1814)

Greensburg Ridgely, Ky. (1816)

Addison Ridout, Md. (1813)

Samuel H. Robbins, Conn. (1817)

Silas Robbins, Conn. (1808)—Ky., J.

Archibald G. Rogers, N.Y. (1823)

Artemas Rogers, Mass. (1811)

Charles W. Rogers, Ga. (1829)

Edward Rogers, Conn. (1810)—B.A., Williams; B.A., Yale; N.Y. Const. Conv., Del. 1822; N.Y. Ct. of C.P., J.; U.S. H. of Reps. from N.Y. (Dem.) 1839–1841.

Henry Rogers, Pa. (1823)

Henry A. Rogers, R.I. (1821)

Henry B. Rogers, Mass. (1823)

Henry W. Rogers, Conn. (1810)

John Rogers, Del. (1813)

Moulton Cropper Rogers, Del. (1807)—B.A., M.A., Princeton; Pa. Sen. 1819–1823; Pa. Sec. State 1823–1826; Pa. Sup. Ct., J. 1826–1851.

William M. Rogers, Ga. (1829)

Thomas Ross, Pa. (1827)—B.A., Princeton; Pa. Deputy Att'y Gen. 1829; U.S. H. of Reps. from Pa. (Dem.) 1849–1853.

Heman Ruggles, Conn. (1803)

Henry J. Ruggles, N.Y. (1832)

Philo Ruggles (1790)

John Rutherford, Ga. (1829)

Robert Rutherford, Ga. (1806)

Benjamin H. Rutledge, S.C. (1817)

Dudley Saltonstall (1791)

John P. C. Samson, N.Y. (1817)

Beverley Samuel, S.C. (1819)

Nathan Sanford, N.Y. (1798)—Yale; U.S. Comm'r in Bankruptcy 1802; U.S. Att'y for N.Y. 1803–1816; N.Y. Assembly 1810–1811, Speaker 1811; N.Y. Sen. 1812–1815; U.S. Sen. from N.Y. (Dem.) 1815–1821, 1826–1831 (urged the creation of the Dep't of Justice); N.Y. Const. Conv., Del. 1821 (introduced & promoted resolution abolishing property qualifications for suffrage); N.Y. Ch. Ct., C. 1823–1826.

Rollin Sanford, Conn. (1831)

Joseph S. Sankey, Ga. (1826)

Willim F. W. Sargent, Miss. (1817)

Curtius H. Saunders, Tenn. (1833)

Thomas Savage (1792)

Augustus Schell, Conn. (1830–1831)—B.A., Union; corporate lawyer for Cornelius Vanderbilt & Jay Gould; Tammany Hall, Grand Sachem 1872–1884; Nat. Dem. Comm., Chairman 1872–1876.

John T. Schley, Md. (1828)

Robert Schuyler, N.Y. (1818–1819)

Jessup W. Scott, Conn. (1822)

John Ray Scott, Va. (1807)—B.A., Princeton; U.S. H. of Reps. from Mo. Territory 1816–1817, 1817–1821; U.S. H. of Reps. from Mo. 1821–1827.

Philip J. Scudder, N.J. (1813)

Henry Dwight Sedgwick, Mass. (1807)—B.A., Williams; Author: *The English Practice* . . . (New York: J. Seymour, 1822).

Philo C. Sedgwick, Conn. (1831)

Ulysses Seldon, Conn. (1802)

William H. Sewall, Md. (1816)

Horatio Seymour, Conn. (1798)—B.A., Yale; LL.D.; Addison County (Vt.) State Att'y 1810–1813; 1815–1819; U.S. Sen. from Vt. (Clay Dem.) 1821–1833; Vt. P. Ct., J. 1847–1856.

Isaac G. Seymour, Ga. (1825)

Origen Storrs Seymour, Conn. (1824)—B.A., Yale; Conn. H. of Reps. 1842, 1849–1850, 1880, Speaker 1850; U.S. H. of Reps. from Conn. (Dem.) 1851–1855; Conn. Super. Ct., J. 1855–1863; Conn. Sup. Ct., J. 1870–1873, C.J. 1873–1874.

Ozias Seymour, Vt. (1821)

Thomas Hart Seymour, Conn. (1829)—Conn. P. Ct., J. 1836–1838; U.S. H. of Reps. from Conn. (Dem.) 1843–1845; Conn. Gov. 1850–1853.

Joseph L. Shaffer, Ga. (1825)

Charles W. Shamburgh, La. (1827)

Henry Shaw, Vt. (1810)—U.S. H. of Reps. from Mass. (Fed.) 1817–1821; Mass. H. of Reps. 1824–1830, 1833; Mass. Sen. 1835; N.Y. Assembly 1853.

Daniel Sheldon, Jr., Conn. (1798)

Isaac Sheldon, Conn. (1810)

William Sheldon, Conn. (1822)

Stephen Shelton, Conn. (1809)

Samuel Shepherd, Vt. (1799)

Elkanah C. Sherman, N.Y. (1825)

Roger Sherman, Jr., Conn. (1792) [son of Roger Sherman: signer of Declaration of Independence, Articles of Confederation, U.S. Constitution].

Roger Minott Sherman (1794)

Joseph Sherrill, Mass. (1815)

Theodore Sill, Conn. (1798)

Eldred Simkins, S.C. (1803–1805)—B.A., S.C. Col.; S.C. Sen. 1810–1812; S.C. Lt. Gov. 1812–1814; U.S. H. of Reps. from S.C. (Dem.) 1818–1821; S.C. H. of Reps. 1824.

Edward P. Simmons, S.C. (1815)

Moses Simons, S.C. (1810)

John G. Sims, Pa. (1812)

John B. Skinner, Conn. (1819–1820)

Oliver Skinner, Conn. (1800)

Richard Skinner, Conn. (1798)—Bennington County (Vt.) State Att'y 1801–1813, 1819; U.S. H. of Reps. from Vt. (Dem.) 1813–1815; Vt. Sup. Ct., J. 1815–1816; Vt. H. of Reps. 1815, 1818, Speaker 18; Vt. Gov. 1820–1823; Vt. Sup. Ct., C.J. 1823–1828.

Roger S. Skinner, Conn. (1815)

Douglas W. Sloan, Mass. (1804)

Barzillai Slosson, N.Y. (1830)

William A. Smallwood, D.C. (1824)

Aaron Smith (1791)

Archibald Smith, N.Y. (1814)

Charles Smith, Mass. (1810)

Henry B. Smith, Mass. (1809)

Ira Smith, Conn. (1809)

James H. Smith, N.C. (1818)

John Cotton Smith, Conn. (1787)—B.A., Yale; Conn. H. of Reps. 1793, 1796, 1800, Clerk 1799, Speaker 1800; U.S. H. of Reps. from Conn. (Fed.) 1800–1806; Conn. H. of Reps. 1808–1809; Conn. Sup. Ct., J. 1809; Conn. Lt. Gov. 1810; Conn. Gov. 1813–1818.

Joseph L. Smith, Conn. (1800)—Florida Territory Super. Ct., J. 1838–1845.

Junius Smith, Conn. (1802–1804)—B.A., LL.D.(Hon.), Yale.

Lemuel Smith, Mass. (1817–1818)

Levi B. Smith, Pa. (1825)

Nathan Smith, Conn. (1790)—M.A.(Hon.), Yale; New Haven County (Conn.) State Att'y 1817–1835; Conn. Const. Conv., Del. 1818; an author of Conn. Const. of 1818; U.S. Att'y for Conn. 1829; Conn. H. of Reps. 1833–1835; U.S. Sen. from Conn. (Whig) 1833–1835.

Nathaniel Smith, Conn. (1786)—M.A.(Hon.), Yale; Conn. H. of Reps. 1789–1795; U.S. H. of Reps. from Conn. (Fed.) 1795–1799; Conn. Sen. 1800–1805; Conn. Sup. Ct., J. 1806–1819.

Nathaniel B. Smith, Conn. (1817)

Perry Smith, Conn. (1807)—Conn. H. of Reps. 1822–1823, 1835–1836; Conn. P. Ct., J. 1833–1835; U.S. Sen. from Conn. (Dem.) 1837–1843.

Truman Smith, Conn. (1817)—B.A., Yale; Conn. H. of Reps. 1831–1832, 1834; U.S. H. of Reps. from Conn. (Whig) 1839–1843, 1845–1849; U.S. Sen. from Conn. 1849–1854; Ct. of Arbitration for Trial of British and American Vessels Suspected of Engaging in Slave Trade, J. 1862–1870; Ct. Cl. under 1862 Treaty with Great Britain, J. 1862.

Samuel W. Southmayd (1793)

Charles G. Spaight, Ga. (1822)

William Henry Sparks, Ga. (1820)—Ga. Legislature 1829.

Richard B. Spaulding, Ga. (1809)

Robert H. Speed, Va. (1827)

Alexander O. Spencer, N.Y. (1818–1819)

Oliver M. Spencer, Ohio (1829)

Bracney T. Spires (1832)

William Spooner, Mass. (1813)

Peleg Sprague, Jr., Mass. (1813) [son of Peleg Sprague: U.S. H. of Reps. from N.H. (Fed.) 1797–1799]—B.A., LL.D.(Hon.) Harvard; Me. H. of Reps. 1821–1822; U.S. H. of Reps. from Me. 1825–1829; U.S. Sen. from Me. 1829–1835; U.S. D. for Mass., J. 1841–1865.

Peter Stagg, N.Y. (1823)

Henry Stanley, N.Y. (1801)

G. A. Stansbury, N.Y. (1827)

Seth Perkins Staples (17 ?)—No record survives that lists Staples as having attended Litchfield, but lecture notes from Litchfield in the handwriting of Staples are in the possession of the Yale Law School Library. However, the brevity of the notes may indicate that they were copied from another student's notebook, which would suggest that Staples was never a student at Litchfield.

Caleb Stark, Jr., Vt. (1823)

Wyatt W. Starke, S.C. (1811)

Ephraim Starr, Jr., Conn. (1803)

Henry Starr, Conn. (1809)

William F. Steele, Md. (1814)

John Lloyd Stephens, N.J. (1823)—B.A., Columbia; N.Y. Const. Conv., Del. 1846.

Elisha Sterling, Conn. (1789)—Litchfield County (Conn.) State Att'y 1820.

Micah Sterling, Conn. (1804)—B.A., Yale; U.S. H. of Reps. from N.Y. (Fed.) 1821–1823; N.Y. Sen. 1836–1839.

William P. Sterett, Ga. (1821)

John Sterett, Pa. (1822)

Henry W. Stevens, Conn. (1811)

James Stevens, Conn. (1796)—Conn. H. of Reps. 1804–1805, 1808–1810, 1814–1815, 1817–1818; Conn. P. Ct., J. 1819; U.S. H. of Reps. from Conn. (Dem.) 1819–1821; Fairfield County (Conn.) Ct., J. 1823.

Thomas Stevens, Ga. (1823)

Charles S. Stewart, N.Y. (1817)

Joseph C. Stiles, Ga. (1817 & 1819)

Richard Stites, Ga. (1822)

John Truman Stoddert, Md. (1813)—B.A., Princeton; Md. H. of Dels. 1820; U.S. H. of Reps. from Md. (Jackson Dem.) 1833–1835.

Gregory D. Stone, N.H. (1823)

Juba Storrs, Conn. (1806)

Martin Strobel, S.C. (1806)

Elisha B. Strong, Conn. (1810)

Martin Strong, Conn. (1801)

Moses McCure Strong, Vt. (1830–1833)—Middlebury; B.A., Dartmouth; U.S. Att'y Territory Wis. 1838–1841; Wis. Const. Conv., Del. 1846; Wis. Assembly 1850–1857.

Theron Rudd Strong, Conn. (1822)—Wayne County (N.Y.) Dis. Att'y 1835–1839; U.S. H. of Reps. from N.Y. (Dem.) 1839–1841; N.Y. Assembly 1842; N.Y. Sup. Ct., J. 1851–1859; N.Y. Ct. App., J. 1859.

Francis Stuart, S.C. (1809)

Josephus B. Stuart, Mass. (1812)

James Sullivan, Mass. (1822)

Josiah Sutherland, Jr., N.Y. (1825)—Columbia County (N.Y.) Dis. Att'y 1832–1843; U.S. H. of Reps. from N.Y. (Dem.) 1851–1853; N.Y. Sup. Ct., J. 1857–1871; N.Y. Ct. of Gen. Sessions, J. 1872–1878.

Cyrus Swan (1796)

Thomas Sweezy, Mass. (1811)

Benjamin Swift, N.Y. (1801)—Vt. H. of Reps. 1813, 1825–1826; U.S. H. of Reps. from Vt. (Fed.) 1827–1831; U.S. Sen. from Vt. 1833–1839.

William Swift, Vt. (1817)

William J. Tabor, Conn. (1813)

William F. Taliaferro, Va. (1813)

Frederick Augustus Tallmadge, Conn. (1811) [son of Benjamin Tallmadge: U.S. H. of Reps. from Conn. (Fed.) 1801–1817]—B.A., Yale; N.Y. Sen. 1837–1840, Pres. Pro Temp., 1840; U.S. H. of Reps. from N.Y. (Whig) 1847–1849; N.Y. Ct. App., Clerk 1862–1865.

Edward Fenwick Tatnall, Ga. (1810)—educated in England; Ga. Solicitor Gen. 1816–1817; Ga. H. of Reps. 1818–1819; U.S. H. of Reps. from Ga. 1821–1827.

Edwin M. Taylor, N.Y. (1832)

Hubbard Taylor, Ky. (1810)

James S. Taylor, S.C. (1818)

John Gilman Taylor, Mass. (1803)

William Taylor, S.C. (1828)

James D. Teakle, Md. (1817)

Josiah Telfair, Ga. (1804)

Thomas Telfair, Ga. (1806)—B.A., Princeton; U.S. H. of Reps. from Ga. (Dem.) 1813–1817.

William Tenney, N.H. (1809)

Alfred Terry, Conn. (1823)

James Thayer, Mass. (1815)

Alexander Thomas, Ga. (1810)

Charles Thomas, Jr., Del. (1812)

Henry Thompson, Mass. (1814)

James Thompson (1790)

Larkin Thorndike, Mass. (1809)

Uriah Thweatt, Ga. (1802)

George Tod, Conn. (1796)—B.A., Yale; Trumball County (Ohio) Pros. Att'y 1800; Ohio Sen. 1804–1806; Ohio Sup. Ct., J. 1807–1810; Ohio Sen. 1810–1812; Ohio Cir. Ct. App., J. 1816–1829.

Charles S. Todd, Ky. (1810)—William & Mary; Ky. Sec. State 1816; Ky. Legislature 1817–1818.

Thomas Tolman, Ky. (1813)

Charles Torrey, Mass. (1814)

George H. Tracy, N.Y. (1830)

Uriah Tracy, Conn. (1778)—B.A., Yale; Conn. H. of Reps. 1788–1793, Speaker 1793; Litchfield County (Conn.) State Att'y 1794–1799; U.S. H. of Reps. from Conn. (Fed.) 1793–1796; U.S. Sen. from Conn. (Fed.) 1796–1807, Pres. Pro Temp. 1800; Author: *Scipio's Reflections on Monroe's View of the Conduct of the Executive* (Boston, MA: Caleb P. Wayne, 1798).

Selah B. Treat, Conn. (1825)

James G. Trotter, Ky. (1809)

Robert R. Troup, N.Y. (1809) [son of Robert Troup: U.S. D. N.Y., J. 1796].

George J. Tucker (1824)

Bates Turner (1790)

Cornelius Tuthill, N.Y. (1815)

Stephen Twining (1796)

Thomas Twining, Jr., Mass. (1814)

Nathan Tyler, Conn. (1825)

Samuel Vanderheyden, N.Y. (1820)

William Vandeusen, Conn. (1803)

Kensey J. Vandyke, N.J. (1818)

John Inskeep Vanmeter, Va. (1821)—William & Mary; B.A., Princeton; Va. H. of Dels. 1824; Ohio H. of Reps. 1836; Ohio Sen. 1838; U.S. H. of Reps. from Ohio (Whig) 1843–1845.

Garrit G. Vanwagenen, N.Y. (1823)

James D. Verplanck, N.Y. (1827)

Noah S. Wadhams (1791)

John Wager, Va. (1823)

Johnathon Wakeman, Conn. (1807)

George M. Walburg, Ga. (1815)

William B. Waldo, N.Y. (1828)

Charles Walker, Mass. (1822)

George J. S. Walker, Ga. (1826)

James W. Wallace, Pa. (1829)

Isaac Ward, N.J. (1813)

Richard R. Ward, N.Y. (1817)

Solomon Ward, Mass. (1802)

Nicholas Ware, Va. (1792)—Ga. H. of Reps. 1808–1811, 1814–1815; U.S. Sen. from Ga. 1821–1824.

Nathaniel F. Waring, N.Y. (1827)

Eli Warner, Conn. (1808)—Middlesex County (Conn.) Ct., C.J. 1830.

Thomas Warner, Mass. (1809)

Andrew O. Waterhouse, Mass. (1811)

George Claibourne Watkins, Ky. (1833)—Ark. Att'y Gen. 1843; Ark. Sup. Ct., C.J. 1852–1854.

John B. Watson III, Conn. (1815)

Samuel Watson, Mass. (1826)

William Watson, Conn. (1831)

Sumner A. Webber, Mass. (1823)

Alfred A. Weeks, N.Y. (1823)

James J. Weems, D.C. (1820)

Ralph Wells, Conn. (1812)

Thomas L. Wells, N.Y. (1823)

William C. Wetmore, Conn. (1815)

Justus P. Wheeler, Mass. (1804)

John P. White, Conn. (1799)

Thomas White, Ga. (1816)

William White, N.H. (1818)

John C. Whiting, Mass. (1823)

John Whitman, Del. (1808)

Lemuel Whitman, Conn. (1805)—B.A., Yale; Conn. Super. Ct., J. 1818; Hartford County (Conn.) Ct., J. 1819–1821, C.J. 1821–1823; one of a Committee of three to revise the statutes of Conn. in 1821; Conn. Sen. 1822; U.S. H. of Reps. from Conn. (Dem.) 1823–1825; Conn. H. of Reps. 1831, 1832.

Elisha D. Whittlesey, Conn. (1813)—Ohio H. of Reps. 1820–1821; U.S. H. of Reps. from Ohio 1823–1838.

Frederick Whittlesey, Conn. (1819)—B.A., Yale; U.S. H. of Reps. from N.Y. (Whig) 1831–1835; N.Y. Ch. Ct., Vice C. 1839–1847; N.Y. Sup. Ct., J. 1847–1848; Genesee Col. (N.Y.), Prof. of Law 1850–1851.

Roger Whittlesey (1788)

Thomas Tucker Whittlsey, Conn. (1818)—B.A., Yale; Conn. P. Ct., J.; U.S. H. of Reps. from Conn. (Dem.) 1836–1839; Wis. Sen. 1853–1854.

John L. Wight, Va. (1824)

Edmond Wilkins, N.C. (1817)

John L. Wilkins, N.C. (1820)

William Wyche Wilkins (1793)

David Williams, La. (1816)

Elisha Williams, Conn. (1792)—N.Y. Assembly 1800, 1812–1815; N.Y. Const. Conv., Del. 1821; leader of N.Y. Fed. Party.

Jared Warner Williams, Conn. (1819–1820)—B.A., Brown; N.H. H. of Reps. 1830–1831, 1835, 1836; N.H. Sen. 1832–1834; U.S. H. of Reps. from N.H. (Dem.) 1837–1841; N.H. Gov. 1847–1849; U.S. Sen. from N.H. 1853–1854.

Lemuel Williams, Jr., Mass. (1806) [son of Lemuel Williams: U.S. H. of Reps. 1799–1805].

Thomas Scott Williams, Conn. (1796)—B.A., Yale; Zepheniah Swift's Law School; Conn. H. of Reps. 1813, 1815–1816, Clerk 1815–1816; U.S. H. of Reps. from Conn. 1817–1819; Conn. H. of Reps. 1819, 1825, 1827–1829; Conn. Super. Ct., J. 1829–1833, C.J. 1834–1847, Reporter 1847–1848.

William G. Williams, Mass. (1799)—Litchfield County (Conn.) J.P. Ct., J. 1820–1830.

Andrew P. Wilson, Pa. (1825)

John C. M. Winship, Mass. (1810)

Edward D. Winslow, N.C. (1831)

Lucius L. Wittich, Ga. (1824)

Frederick Wolcott, Conn. (1787)—Litchfield County (Conn.) Ct., Clerk 1820–1830; Conn. Super. Ct., Clerk 1820–1830; Conn. P. Ct., J. 1820–1830.

Oliver Wolcott, Jr., Conn. (1778)—son of Oliver Wolcott (Cont. Congress 1775–1778, 1780–1784; signer of the Declaration of Independence; Conn. Gov. 1796–1797); B.A., LL.D.(Hon.), Yale; LL.D.(Hon.), Princeton; LL.D.(Hon.), Brown; U.S. Sec. Treasury 1795–1800; U.S. C.C., J. 1801–1802; Conn. Gov. 1817–1827; Conn. Const. Conv., Pres. 1818.

Oliver S. Wolcott, Conn. (1818)

Bradford Ripley Wood, Conn. (1825)—B.A., Union; N.Y. Ch. Ct., Sollicitor 1827–1830, C. 1830; U.S. H. of Reps. from N.Y. (Dem.) 1845–1847; member of U.S. Sup. Ct. Bar 1845–1889.

James Wood (1798)

William Woodbridge, Ohio (1802)—Ohio H. of Reps. 1807; Ohio Sen. 1808–1814; New London County (Ohio) Pros. Att'y 1808–1814; Mich. Territory, Secretary 1814–1828; U.S. H. of Reps. from Mich. Territory 1819–1820; Mich. Territory Sup. Ct., J. 1828–1832; Mich. Const. Conv., Del. 1835; Mich. Sen. 1837; Mich. Gov. 1840–1841; U.S. Sen. from Mich. (Whig & Dem.) 1841–1847.

Levi Woodbury, N.H. (1809)—B.A., LL.D.(Hon.), Dartmouth; LL.D.(Hon.), Wesleyan; N.H. Super. Ct., J. 1817–1823; N.H. Gov. 1823–1824; N.H. H. of Reps., Speaker 1825; U.S. Sen. from N.H. (Dem.) 1825–1831, 1841–1845; U.S. Sec. Navy 1831–1834; U.S. Sec. Treasury 1834–1841; U.S. Sup. Ct., J. 1845–1851.

George Catlin Woodruff, Conn. (1825)—B.A., Yale; Conn. H. of Reps. 1851, 1866, 1874; U.S. H. of Reps. from Conn. (Dem.) 1861–1863.

Lewis Bartholemew Woodruff, Conn. (1830)—B.A., Yale; LL.D.(Hon.), Columbia; N.Y. City Ct. C.P., J. 1850–1855; N.Y. Sup. Ct., J. 1855–1869; N.Y. Ct. App., J. 1868–1870; U.S. Cir. (2nd), J. 1869–1875.

Thomas Wooldridge, S.C. (1815)

Perry Worthington, Md. (1831)

Augustus Romaldus Wright, Ga. (1833)—Franklin Col.; Univ. Ga.; Ga. Super. Ct., J. 1842–1849; U.S. H. of Reps. from Ga. (Dem.) 1857–1859; Ga. Const. Conv., Del. 1877.

John Crafts Wright, Conn. (1808)—U.S. Att'y Ohio 1817; U.S. H. of Reps. from Ohio (Dem.) 1823–1829; Ohio Sup. Ct., J. 1831–1835.

Metcalf Yates, N.Y. (1821)

William Yates, N.Y. (1824)

Charles C. Young, N.Y. (1827)

Ebenezer Young, Conn. (1809)—Conn. H. of Reps. 1810–1811, 1811, 1816, 1826–1828, Speaker 1827–1828; Conn. Sen. 1823–1825; U.S. H. of Reps. from Conn. (Fed.) 1829–1835, Conn. P. Ct., J. 1830.

Sources: Reeve Family Papers, 1766–1813, Yale University Library, New Haven, Connecticut; Correspondence, 1771–1885, Fairfield Historical Society, Fairfield, Connecticut; "The Litchfield Law School—Catalogue" (1900), Yale University Library, New Haven, Connecticut; *Dictionary of American Biography*, s.v.

2. Van Schaak's Law School, Kinderhook, New York 1786–1830

Proprietor:

Peter Van Schaak—B.A., Kings Col.; LL.D.(Hon.), Columbia; Revisor of the laws of the Colony of N.Y. 1773–1774; Author: *Laws of New York, from the year 1691, to 1773 inclusive*, 2 vols. (N.Y.: Hugh Gaine, 1774).

Number of students = 100+

Students:

Frederic De Peyster, Jr. (1818–1819)

Charles Augustus Foote, N.Y. (1807)—B.A., Union; U.S. H. of Reps. from N.Y. (Dem.) 1823–1825.

Henry I. Frey

William Kent, N.Y. (1820–1821) [son of James Kent: N.Y. Sup. Ct., C.J.; N.Y. Ch. Ct., C.; Columbia, Prof. of Law]—N.Y. Cir. Ct., J. 1841–1845.

James Alsop King [son of Rufus King: Cont. Congress 1784–1787; U.S. Const. Conv. , Del. 1787; U.S. Sen. from N.Y. (Fed.) 1789–1796, 1813–1825]—Harrow School (Eng.); N.Y. Assembly 1819–1821, 1832, 1838, 1840; N.Y. Sen. 1823–1825; U.S. H. of Reps. from N.Y. (Whig) 1849–1851; N.Y. Gov. 1857–1858.

Joseph D. Monell

James I. Roosevelt, N.Y.—B.A., Columbia; N.Y. Assembly 1835, 1840; U.S. H. of Reps. from N.Y. (Dem.) 1841–1843; N.Y. Sup. Ct., J. 1851–1859; N.Y. Ct. App., Ex Officio J. 1859; U.S. Att'y for S.D.N.Y. 1860–1861.

Theodore Sedgwick, Jr. [son of Theodore Sedgwick: Cont. Congress 1785–1788; U.S.

H. of Reps. from Mass. (Fed.) 1789–1796; U.S. Sen. from Mass. (Fed.) 1796–1799, Pres. Pro Temp. 1799; U.S. H. of Reps. from Mass. (Fed.), Speaker 1799–1801; Mass. Sup. Jud. Ct., J. 1802–1813]—B.A., Yale; Mass. Legislature 1824–1825, 1827.

Theodore Spencer, N.Y. (1819–1820) [son of Ambrose Spencer: N.Y. Att'y Gen. 1802–1804; N.Y. Sup. Ct., J. 1804–1819, C.J. 1819–1823.

John Sudam—N.Y. Ct. of Correction of Err., J.

William C. Van Ness, N.Y. (1818—?) [son of William W. Van Ness: N.Y. Sup. Ct., J. 1807–1822].

David Van Schaack, N.Y. (1811–1816)

Henry C. Van Schaack, N.Y. (1819–?)

Peter Van Schaack, Jr., N.Y. (1816–1817)

Abraham P. Vosburgh, N.Y. (1811–1813)

Henry Walton

Sources: Henry C. Van Schaack, *The Life of Peter Van Schaack, LL.D.* (New York: D. Appleton & Co., 1842), pp. 428–446; Edward A. Collier, *A History of Old Kinderhook* (New York: G.P. Putnam & Sons, 1914), p. 404; Collection of Cases and Opinions, Van Schaack Family Papers, Columbia County Historical Society, Kinderhook, New York; New York Certificates of Clerkships, Admission of Attorneys, New York State Archives, Albany, New York; *Dictionary of American Biography*, s.v.

3. Staples Law School, New Haven, Connecticut 1800–1849

Proprietors:

Seth P. Staples (1800–1824)—Staples was one of the nation's leading patent attorneys. He is particularly known for having represented Charles Goodyear in cases over his patent for vulcanized rubber and Eli Whitney in cases over his patent for the cotton gin and his system of interchangeable parts.

Samuel Johnson Hitchcock (1820–1845)—B.A., Yale; founder and first Dean of the Yale Univ. Law School.

David Daggett (1824–1846)—B.A., LL.D., Yale; Conn. H. of Reps. 1791–1796, 1805, Speaker 1794–1796; Conn. Council 1797, 1809–1813; Conn. Ct. Err., J. 1797, 1809–1813, 1826–1832, C.J. 1832–1834; U.S. Sen. from Conn. (Fed.) 1813–1819; New Haven (Conn.) State Att'y 1811–1813; Conn. Super. Ct., J. 1826–1828; Yale, Kent Prof. of Law 1826–1848.

Isaac Thownsend (1845–1849)

Tutors:

John Hiram Lathrop, Sherburne, N.Y. (1823)—B.A., Yale; Hamilton, Maynard Prof. of Law 1835; Univ. of Mo., Pres. 1841–1849; Univ. of Wis., C. 1849–1859; Ind. Univ., Pres. 1859–1860.

Solomon Stoddard (1823)

Number of students = 47

Students:

Sherlock James Andrews, Conn. (1824)—B.A., Union; U.S. H. of Reps. from Ohio (Whig) 1841–1842; Ohio Super. Ct., J. 1848–1850; Ohio Const. Conv., Del. 1850, 1873; Cleveland (Ohio) Bar Assoc., Pres. 1873.

Charles Atwood (1823)

William Barnes, Conn. (1822–1823)

Apollo D. Bates (1818–1820)

John Huggins Boyd, Conn. (1823)—N.Y. Assembly 1840; U.S. H. of Reps. from N.Y. (Whig) 1851–1853.

John Hall Brockway, Conn. (1821)—B.A., Yale; Conn. H. of Reps. 1832–1838; Conn. Sen. 1834; U.S. H. of Reps. from Conn. (Whig) 1829–1843; Tolland County (Conn.) Pros. Att'y 1849–1867.

Asa Butts, Conn. (1822), died 1823

Edward Chapin (1819)

Asa Child, Conn. (1821)

Linus Child, Conn. (1824)

Sherman Crosswell, Conn. (1823)

Simeon F. Dixon, Conn. (1823)

Walter Edwards, Conn. (1821)

Henry Collins Flagg, S.C. (1811–1812)—B.A., Yale; New Haven (Conn.) Mayor 1820.

Horace Foot (1820)

Eleazor Foster (1804–1805)

Samuel Hayes, Conn. (1823)

Joel Hinman, Conn. (1822)—Conn. P. Ct., J. 1830–1840; Conn. Sen. 1836; Conn. Super. Ct., J. 1842–1851; Conn. Super. Ct., J. 1851–1860, C.J. 1860–1870.

Theodore Hinsdale, Conn. (1821)

Sam C. Jackson, Vt. (1822)

Charles F. Johnson (1823)

Samuel Johnson Hitchcock (1812–1814)—B.A., Yale; founder and first Dean of the Yale Univ. Law School 1826.

Samuel Dickinson Hubbard (1819)—B.A., Yale; U.S. H. of Reps. from Conn. (Whig) 1845–1849; U.S. Postmaster Gen. 1852–1853.

James S. Huggins (1820)

Hector Humphrey (1819)

Ralph Isaacs Ingersoll (1808)—B.A., Yale; Conn. H. of Reps. 1820–1825, Speaker 1824–1825; U.S. H. of Reps. from Conn. (Dem.) 1825–1833; New Haven County (Conn.) State Att'y 1833.

Pollard McCormick (1820)

Timothy Merwin (1828)

Horatio Miller (1820)

Thomas Burr Osborne (1818–1820)—B.A., Yale; Conn. County & Super. Cts., Clerk 1826–1839; Conn. H. of Reps. 1836, 1850; U.S. H. of Reps. from Conn. (Whig) 1839–1843; Conn. Sen. 1844; Fairfield County (Conn.) Ct., J. 1844; Conn. P. Ct., J. 1851; Yale, Prof. of Law 1855–1865.

Henry E. Peck (1823)

Thomas Clapp Perkins (1818)—B.A., Yale.

Amasa G. Porter (1823)

William Read, Ga. (1824–1825)

George B. Ripley, Conn. (1824)

Edward Rockwell (1823)

William Rockwell, Conn. (1823)

Oliver A. Shaw, Va. (1822)

Aaron N. Skinner, Conn. (1823)

William P. Skinner, Ohio (1824)

John Thompson, N.Y. (1812–1814)—B.A., Union; Yale; U.S. H. of Reps. from N.Y. (Rep.) 1857–1859.

Isaac Henry Townsend (1822)

Ira L. Ufford, Conn. (1822)

Isaac Webb (1824)

G. Fitch Wheeler, Conn. (1822)

Daniel Whiting (1823)

Frederick R. Whittelsey, Conn. (1823)

Rufus Woodward (1819)

Source: Frederick C. Hicks, "Yale Law School: The Founders and the Founders' Collection," in *Tercentenary Commission of the State of Connecticut, Committee on Historical Publications* (New Haven, CT: Yale University Press, 1935), Vol. 39; Admission to the Bar, 1700–1755, County Court, New Haven County, Connecticut State Archives, Hartford, Connecticut; *Dictionary of American Biography*, s.v.

4. Gilbert's Law School, Hebron, Connecticut 1810–1818

Proprietor:

Sylvester Gilbert—B.A., Dartmouth; Conn. H. of Reps. 1780–1812, 1826; Tolland County (Conn.) State Att'y 1786–1807; Tolland County (Conn.) Ct., C.J. 1807–1818; Conn. P. Ct., J. 1807–1818; Conn. Sen. 1815–1816; U.S. H. of Reps. from Conn. 1818–1819; Tolland County (Conn.) Ct., J. 1820–1825.

Number of students = 56

Students:

Samuel Ingham, Conn. (1815)—Middlesex County (Conn.) State Att'y 1827–1835, 1843, 1844; Conn. H. of Reps. 1828, 1834, 1851, 1852, Speaker 1851, 1852; Conn. P. Ct., J. 1829–1833; Middlesex County (Conn.) Ct., J. 1849–1853; U.S. H. of Reps. from Conn. (Dem.) 1835–1839; Conn. Sen. 1843–1850; U.S. Comm'r Customs 1857–1861.

Abiel A. Loomis (1814)—Middlesex County (Conn.) J.P. Ct., J. 1830.

Charles Olcott (1817–1819)—also attended Swift's law school.

Isaac Toucey, Conn. (1818)—Hartford County (Conn.) State Att'y 1822–1835, 1842–1844; U.S. H. of Reps. from Conn. (Dem.) 1835–1839; Conn. Gov. 1846; U.S. Att'y Gen. 1848–1849; Conn. Sen. 1850; Conn. H. of Reps. 1852; U.S. Sen. from Conn. 1852–1857; U.S. Sec. Navy 1857–1861.

Azel Utley (1818)—also attended Swift's law school; Middlesex County (Conn.) J.P. Ct., J. 1830.

William G. Williams—Litchfield County (Conn.) J.P. Ct., J. 1820–1830.

Sources: Journal or Chronicle of Sylvester Gilbert of Hebron, Connecticut, Connecticut State Library, Hartford, Connecticut; Applications for Admission to the Bar, Windham County Superior Court, Connecticut State Archives, Hartford, Connecticut; *Dictionary of American Biography*, s.v.

5. Swift's Law School, Windham, Connecticut 1805–1823

Proprietor:

Zephania Swift, Mass.—B.A., M.A., Yale; Conn. H. of Reps., 1787–1793, 1820–1822, Clerk 1787–1791, Speaker 1792; U.S. H. of Reps. from Conn. (Fed.) 1793–1797; Conn. Super. Ct., J. 1801–1810; Conn. Sup. Ct. Err., C.J. 1806–1819; Conn. H. of Reps. 1820–1822. Author: *A System of the Laws of the State of Connecticut* (Windham, CT: John Byrne, 1795); *A Digest of the Law of Evidence, in Civil and Criminal Cases* (Hartford, CT: Oliver D. Cooke, 1810).

Number of students = 12+

Students:

Cyrus Beardsley (1820)

Joseph L. Coit (1818–1819)

Samuel H. Devotion (1806–1808)

Jonathon Edwards (1820–1822)

Uriel Fuller (1818–1819)

Josiah Gallup (1823)

James Howard (1807–1809)

Francis B. Johnson (1823)

Charles Olcott (1819)—also attended Gilbert's law school.

John M. Sterling (1822)

Arel Utley (1819–1820)—also attended Gilbert's law school.

Thomas D. Webb (1805–1807)

Sources: Applications for Admission to the Bar, Windham County Superior Court, Connecticut State Archives, Hartford, Connecticut; *Dictionary of American Biography*, s.v.

6a. Taylor's Law School, Richmond, Virginia 1810–1811?

Proprietor:

Creed Taylor—Va. H. of Del. 1788; Va. Sen. 1798–1805; Va. Sen., Speaker 1804–1805; Va. Gen. Ct. 1805–1806; Va. High Ct. of Ch., C. 1806–1831. Author: *Journal of the Law School and of the Moot Court Attached to It* (Richmond, VA: Cochran, 1822).

Number of students = 14+

Students:

Gordon H. Bacchus, Va. (1810–1811)

John Dickinson

Francis Sargent Gibbon (1810–1811)

Francis Walker Gilmer, Va.—B.A., W & M; Univ. Va., Prof. of Law 1825.

John Grantland, Va.

William Lambert, Va. (1810–1811)

T. Mason (1810–1811)

S.A. Myers (1810–1811)

William Garland Pendleton, Va. (1810–1811)

Anderson Scott, Va. (1810–1811)

William Selden, Va. (1810–1811)

Linnaeus Smith (1810–1811)

Abel Parker Upshur, Va. (1810–1811)—Princeton; Yale; Va. H. of Del. 1812–1813, 1825–1827; Va. Const. Conv., Del.; Va. Sup. Ct., J. 1826–1841; U.S. Sec. Navy 1843; U.S. Sec. State 1843.

Thomas Robertson Yeatman, Va.

Sources: E. Lee Shepard, "The Known Alumni of the Proprietary Law Schools," in W. Hamilton Bryson, *Legal Education in Virginia 1779–1979* (Charlottesville: University Press of Virginia, 1982), p. 762; *Dictionary of American Biography*, s.v.

6b. Taylor's Law School, Needham, Virginia 1821—1827?

Proprietor:

Creed Taylor—Va. H. of Del. 1788; Va. Sen. 1798–1805; Va. Sen., Speaker 1804–1805; Va. Gen. Ct. 1805–1806; Va. High Ct. of Ch., C. 1806–1831. Author: *Journal of the Law School and of the Moot Court Attached to It* (Richmond, VA: Cochran, 1822).

Number of students = 29

Students:

William L. Booker, Va.

John Minor Botts, Va. (1821–1822)—Va. H. of Dels. 1833–1839; U.S. H. of Reps. from Va. (Henry Clay Whig) 1839–1843, 1847–1849.

John Bushrod Bramham, Va. (1821–1822)

Philip Alexander Bramham, Va. (1821–1822)

John Thompson Brown, Va.

Peter Guerrant Camden, Va. (1821–1822)

Joseph William Chinn, Va. (1821–1822)—B.A., Union; Va. H. of Dels. 1826–1828; Va. Sen. 1829–1831; U.S. H. of Reps. from Va. (Dem.) 1831–1835.

William Sidney Crawford, Va. (1821–1822) [son of William Crawford: U.S. D. D. Ala., J. 1826–1849].

William Cunliffe, Va. (1821–1822)

William Dudley

Edward J. Elliott

James Fontaine, Va. (1821–1822)

John Hall Fulton, Va. (1822–1823)—B.A., Hampden–Sydney; Va. H. of Dels. 1823–1824; Va. Sen. 1829–1831; U.S. H. of Reps. from Va. (Whig) 1833–1835.

William Yates Gholson, Va. (1825–1826)—B.A., Col. N.J.; Cincinnati (Ohio) Super. Ct., J. 1854–1859; Ohio Sup. Ct., J. 1859–1863.

Peter Guerrant, Va. (1821–1822)

Addison Hall, Va. (1822–1823)

Robert R. Headley, Va. (1821–1822)

Edward Johnston, Va. (1826–1827)

John D. Leland, Va. (1821–1822)

Harvey Mitchell, Va. (1821–1822)

James Turner Morehead, N.C. (1821–1822)—Univ. N.C.; N.C. Sen. 1835–1836, 1838, 1840, 1842; U.S. H. of Reps. from N.C. (Whig) 1851–1853.

Samuel Hays Myers, Va. (1821–1822)

Richard Gregory Pegram, Va. (1821–1822)

Sterling Price, Va.—Hampden–Sydney; Mo. H. of Reps. 1836–1838, 1840–1845, Speaker 1840–1844; U.S. H. of Reps. from Mo. (Dem.) 1845–1846; Mo. Gov. 1853–1857.

Holden Rhodes, Va. (1821–1822)

William Henry Roy, Va. (1821–1822)

James Taylor, Va. (1821–1822)

Samuel Taylor, Va.

William H. Terrill, Va. (1821–1822)

Sources: E. Lee Shepard, "The Known Alumni of the Proprietary Law Schools," in W. Hamilton Bryson, *Legal Education in Virginia 1779–1979* (Charlottesville: University Press of Virginia, 1982), p. 762; *Dictionary of American Biography*, s.v.

7. Winchester Law School, Winchester, Virginia 1824–1831

Proprietor:

Henry St. George Tucker, Va.—B.A., LL.D., William & Mary; Va. H. of Dels. 1807–1808; U.S. H. of Reps. from Va. 1815–1819; Va. Sen. 1819–1823; Va. Super. Ct. of Ch., C. 1824–1831; Va. Sup. Ct. App., Pres. 1831–1841; Univ. Va., Prof. of Law 1841–1845, Faculty Chairman 1842; Author: *Notes on Blackstone's Commentaries for the Use of Students* (Winchester, VA: Davis, 1826); *Commentaries on the Laws of Virginia* (Winchester, VA: Tucker, 1831).

Number of students = 83+

Students:

William Dandridge Alexander, Va. (1827–1828)

J. Y. Armstrong (1830–1831)

Thomas Atkinson, Va.—Yale; B.A., Hampden–Sidney; D.D.(Hon), Trinity; LL.D. (Hon), Univ. N.C.; Cambridge; Univ. of the South, Founder.

Mason Barnes, Md. (1828–1829)

Samuel Wootton Beall, Md. (1827–1829)—B.A., Union; Wis. Const. Conv., Del. 1846–1847 (drafted Wis. Const.); Wis. Lt. Gov. 1851–1853.

Mr. Bower, Va. (1828–1829)

Flavius Braden, Va. (1828–1829)

John Brewer, Md. (1827–1828)

John White Brockenbrough, Va. (1827–1828)—B.A., William & Mary; Univ. Va.; Hanover County (Va.) Commonwealth Att'y late 1820s; founded proprietary law school, Lexington, Va. 1849–1861; U.S. D. for Western Va., J. 1846–1861; Confederate Congress (Judiciary Committee); Confederate Ct. for Western Va., J. 1861–1865; Washington & Lee Univ., Prof. of Law 1866–1873.

Mr. Bronaugh, Romney, Va. (1828–1829)

Mr. Cabell (1824–1825)

Charles Campbell, Va. (1826–1827)

William Bowen Campbell, Tenn. (1828–1829)—Tenn. Legislature 1835; U.S. H. of Reps. from Tenn. (Whig) 1837–1843, 1866–1867; Tenn. Gov. 1851–1853; Tenn. Cir. Ct., J. 1857.

John Armistead Carter, Va. (1827–1829)

Robert Hill Carter, Va. (1827–1828)

Wilson Miles Cary, Va. (1827–1828)

John Randolph Chambliss, Va. (1828–1829)—Greensville County (Va.) Commonwealth Att'y 1849; Confederate Congress 1862–1864.

Mr. Chandler, Ga. (1827–1828)

Mr. Claiborne, Va. (1828–1829)

Giles Cook, Va. (1830–1831)

William Henry Daingerfield, Va. (1830–1831)

William S. Daniel, Va. (1827–1828)

Mr. Davidson, D.C. (1827–1828)

Mr. Davis, Md. (1828–1829)

Lewis F. Douglass, Va. (1827–1828)

Alexander Parker Eskridge, Va.

Charles James Faulkner, Va. (1829–1830)—B.A., Georgetown; Va. H. of Dels. 1829, 1831–1834; Va. Sen. 1838–1842; Va. Const. Conv., Del. 1850; W. Va. Const. Conv., Pres. 1872.

Mr. Field, Va. (1827–1828)

Mr. Fry, Va. (1827–1828)

Mr. Gibbs, S.C. (1828–1829)

Mr. Glover, Mass. (1828–1829)

William Leftwich Goggin, Va. (1827–1828)

T.S. Hall (1830–1831)

Mr. Henderson, W. Va. (1828–1829)

John Zachary Holladay, Va. (1829–1830)

Edmund P. Hunter, Va. (1828–1829)

Robert Mercer Taliaferro Hunter, Va. (1829–1830)—B.A., Univ. Va.; Va. H. of Dels. 1833; Va. Sen. 1835–1837; U.S. H. of Reps. from Va. (Dem.) 1838–1843, Speaker 1839–1841; U.S. Sen. from Va. 1847–1861; Confederate States of Amer., Sec. State 1861–1862; Confederate Sen. from Va. 1862–1865.

Mr. Huston, Va. (1827–1828)

James Madison Jeffries, Va. (1830–1831)

Henry W. Johnson, Va. (1830–1831)

William Coit Johnson, Md. (1827–1829)—Md. H. of Reps. 1831–1832; U.S. H.

of Reps. from Md. (Whig) 1833–1835, 1837–1843; Md. Const. Conv., Del. 1835.

William A. Jones, La., (1828–1829)

Philip P. Kennedy, Va. (1827–1828)

George Hay Lee, Va.

Robert Eden Lee, Va. (1830–1831)

Zaccheus Collins Lee, D.C. (1827–1828)

Mr. Lewis, W. Va. (1828–1829)

James D. Ligon, Va. (1828–1829)

William Lucas, Va.—Va. H. of Dels. 1838–1839; U.S. H. of Reps. from Va. (Whig) 1839–1841, 1843–1845; Va. Const. Conv., Del. 1850–1851.

Mr. McDonald, Va. (1827–1828)

Benjamin Henry Magruder, Va. (1828–1829)

Wiley Roy Mason, Va. (1827–1828)

Josiah Matthews, Ga.

Samuel A. Maverick, S.C. (1828–1829)

Mr. Nesbit, Ga. (1827–1828)

Levi Orme Conner Nicklin, Va. (1828–1829)

Uriah Parke, Va. (1827–1828)

Robert Jacob Paulson, Va.

Isaac Samuel Pennybacker, Va. (1826–1827)—U.S. H. of Reps. from Va. (Dem.) 1837–1839; U.S. D. W. Va., J. 1839–1845; declined appt. as U.S. Att'y Gen.; U.S. Sen. from Va. 1845–1847.

John Pierce, Va. (1827–1828)

George N.N. Porter, Va. (1828–1829)

Charles L. Powell, Va. (1824–1825)

Green Berry Samuels, Va.—U.S. H. of Reps. from Va. (Dem.) 1839–1841; Va. Const. Conv., Del. 1850–1851; Va. Cir. Ct., J. 1850–1852; Va. Ct. App., J. 1852.

Mr. Selden, Va. (1828–1829)

Mr. Servis, D.C. (1827–1828)

Washington George Singleton, Va. (1827–1829)

Thomas Skinker, Va. (1825–1826)

Francis Lee Smith, Va. (1827–1829)

George Washington Southall, Va. (1827–1829)

Alexander M. Sterrett, Md. (1827–1828)

Henry Street, Va. (1828–1829)

S. F. Strother (1830–1831)

William H. Syme, Va. (1828–1829)

Tazwell Taylor, Va. (1828–1829)

Mr. Thompson, S.C. (1828–1829)

William B. Tinsley, Va. (1827–1828)

Mr. Van Ness, Vt. (1826–1827)

Gerard Bond Wager, Va. (1827–1828)

George R. Warner, Md. (1827–1828)

Mr. Watkins, Va. (1827–1828)

John Wilson, Va. (1827–1829)

Henry Alexander Wise, Va. (1827–1828)—B.A. (1st in class), Washington Col. (Pa.); U.S. H. of Reps. from Va. (Jackson Dem.) 1833–1834; Va. Const. Conv., Del. 1850–1851; Va. Gov. 1856–1860.

Uriel Wright, Va.

Sources: E. Lee Shepard, "The Known Alumni of the Proprietary Law Schools," in W. Hamilton Bryson, *Legal Education in Virginia 1779–1979* (Charlottesville: University Press of Virginia, 1982), p. 762; *Dictionary of American Biography*, s.v.

8. Metcalf's Law School, Dedham, Massachusetts 1828–1829

Proprietor:

Theron Metcalf—B.A., LL.D., Brown; Litchfield; Dedham County (Mass.) Att'y 1817–1829; Mass. H. of Reps. 1831, 1833–1834, Judiciary Comm., Chairman 1831, 1833–1834; Mass. Sen. 1835, Judiciary Comm., Chairman 1835; Mass. Sup. Jud. Ct., Reporter 1840–1847, J. 1848–1865; Author: *Digest of the Cases Decided in the Supreme Judicial Court of the Commonwealth of Massachussetts* (Boston, MA: Richardson & Lord, 1825); *Principles of the Law of Contracts, as Applied by Courts of Law* (New York: Hurd & Houghton, 1868).

Number of students = 9+

Students:

Seth Ames [son of Fisher Ames: Mass. Sup. Ct. J.].

Ira Cleveland

John Henry Clifford—B.A., LL.D(Hon.), Brown; LL.D(Hon.) Harvard; LL.D(Hon.), Amherst; Mass. Gen. Ct. 1835; Mass. Dist. Att'y 1839–1849; Mass. Att'y Gen. 1849, 1854–1858; Mass. Gov. 1853; Mass. Sen. 1862; U.S. Comm'n on Fisheries under Arbitration Treaty with Great Britain 1875.

John Doggett

Samuel F. Haven

Horace Mann, Mass.—B.A., Brown; Litchfield; Mass. H. of Reps. 1827–1832; Mass. Sen. 1835–1837, Pres. 1836–1837; Comm'r for Revision of Mass. Statutes 1835; U.S. H. of Reps. from Mass. 1848–1853; Antioch, Pres. 1852–1859.

Virgin D. Paris

Mr. Tuxbery, Me.

Ezra Wilkinson

Sources: Conrad Reno, *Memoirs of the Judiciary and the Bar* (Boston, MA: Century Memorial Publishing Co., 1901), 2:681; Frank Smith, *A History of Dedham, Massachusetts* (Dedham, MA: The Transcript Press, Inc., 1936), p. 136; *Dictionary of American Biography*, s.v.

9. Dorsey's Law School, Baltimore, Maryland ?–1823

Proprietor:

Walter Dorsey—Md. Ct. App., J.

Number of students = 2+; "a large and successful law school"[1]

Students:

John J. Llyod

George R. Richardson

Source: "Tribute of Respect," in *American & Commercial Daily Advertiser* (Baltimore), 4 August 1828, 48:3.

10. Howe's Law School, Northampton, Massachusetts 1823–1830

Proprietors:

Samuel Howe—B.A., Williams; attended Litchfield; Mass. Ct. of C.P., J.

Elijah Hunt Mills—B.A., Williams; Mass. Sen. 1811–1814, 1819–1820, Speaker 1820; U.S. H. of Reps. from Mass. 1815–1819; U.S. Sen. from Mass. 1820–1827.

Instructors:

John Hooker Ashmun—B.A., Williams and Harvard (Ashmun vacated his position to become the first Royall Prof. of Law in the Dane Law School of Harvard Univ.)

Charles Augustus Dewey—B.A., Williams (Dewey vacated his position to become a justice on the Mass. Sup. Jud. Ct.)

Number of students = 100+

Students:

Philip H. Amidon

Osmyn Baker, Mass.—B.A., Yale; Mass. H. of Reps. 1833, 1834, 1836, 1837; U.S. H. of Reps. from Mass. (Whig) 1840–1845.

Edward Blake, Mass.

Jacob Crowninshield, Jr., Mass.

Charles P. Huntington, Mass.

Andrew A. Locke

George A. Meredith, Mass.

Franklin Pierce, N.H.—B.A., Bowdoin; N.H. H. of Reps. 1829–1833, Speaker 1832–1833; U.S. H. of Reps. from N.H. (Dem.) 1833–1837; U.S. Sen. from N.H. 1837–1842; N.H. Const. Conv., Pres. 1850; U.S. Pres. 1853–1857.

Epaphroditus H. Ransom, Vt. (1823)—Vt. H. of Reps.; Mich. Sup. Ct., J. 1836–1843, C.J. 1843–1847; Mich. Gov. 1847–1850; Mich. H. of Reps. 1853–1854.

Nathaniel A. Sturgis, N.Y.

Timothy Walker—B.A., Post–grad. in law, Harvard; Teacher and Organiser with Judge John C. Wright of a Proprietary Law School in Cincinnati (Ohio) 1833 [later became Univ. of Cincinnati (Ohio) Law School]; Hamilton County (Ohio) Ct. of C.P., J. 1842–1843; Western Law Journal, Founder and Editor, 1843.

Sources: Charles J. Dean, "Northampton Was Location for 19th Century Law School," *Daily Hampshire Gazette* (Northampton, Mass.), 19 May 1961; "The Law School," *Centenial Gazette* (Northampton, Mass.), 6 September 1886; *Address of Chief Justice Parker to the Bar of the County of Suffolk Re: Hon. Samuel Howe* (Boston, MA: Nathan Hale Press, 1828); *Dictionary of American Biography*, s.v.

11. Turner's Law School, Fairfield, Vermont 1806–1812

Proprietor:

Bates Turner—Litchfield; Vt. Sup. Ct., J.

Number of students = 175

Sources: *Fairfield, Vermont Reminiscences, 1763–1977* (Fairfield: Fairfield Bicentennial Committee, 1977), p. 24; Lewis C. Aldrich, *History of Franklin and Grand Isle Counties, Vermont* (Syracuse, NY: D. Mason & Co., 1891), pp. 225–226; Hamilton Child, *Gazetteer and Business Directory of Franklin and Grand Isle Counties 1882–1883* (Syracuse, NY: Journal Office, 1883), p. 190; Abby Hemenway, *Vermont Historical Gazetter* (Burlington, VT: A. Hemenway, 1871), 2:312–313.

12. Haywood's Law School, Nashville, Tennessee 1807–1826?

Proprietor:

John C. Haywood, N.C.—Solicitor-Gen. 1790–1791; N.C. Att'y Gen. 1791–1793; N.C. Super. Ct., J. 1793–1800; Tenn. Sup. Ct., J. 1818–1826; Author: *The Christian Advocate* (Nashville, TN: Thomas G. Bradford, 1819); *The Civil and Political History of the State of Tennessee* (Knoxville, TN: Heiskell & Brown,

1823); *The Statute Laws of the State of Tennessee* (Knoxville, TN: T.F.S. Heiskell, 1831).

Number of students = ?

Source: Dictionary of American Biography, s.v.

NOTE

1. "Tribute of Respect," in *American & Commercial Daily Advertiser* (Baltimore), 4 August 1828, 48:3.

APPENDIX **III**

Statistical Data and Graphs Indicating the Impact of Proprietary Law Schools on the American Bar and Judiciary

TABLE 1. Proportion of Proprietary Law School Affiliates Registered with the Connecticut Bar in the Years 1800, 1820 and 1830, Illustrating Their Disproportionately High Representation in the Judiciary

	Year		
Positions	1800	1820	1830
Attorneys			
PLS Affiliates*	51	80	127
Total	652	971	1,084
% PLS Affiliates	**8**	**8**	**12**
Judges			
PLS Affiliates	4	7	20
Total	59	38	39
% PLS Affiliates	**7**	**18**	**51**
Other Judicial Positions**			
PLS Affiliates	4	12	6
Total	25	62	18
% PLS Affiliates	**16**	**19**	**33**

*PLS Affiliates = Proprietary Law School Affiliates, including graduates, instructors and proprietors.

**Other Judicial Positions include Court Clerks, State Attorneys, Court Treasurers and U.S. Attorneys.

FIGURE 1. Known Graduates of Proprietary Law Schools: Connecticut

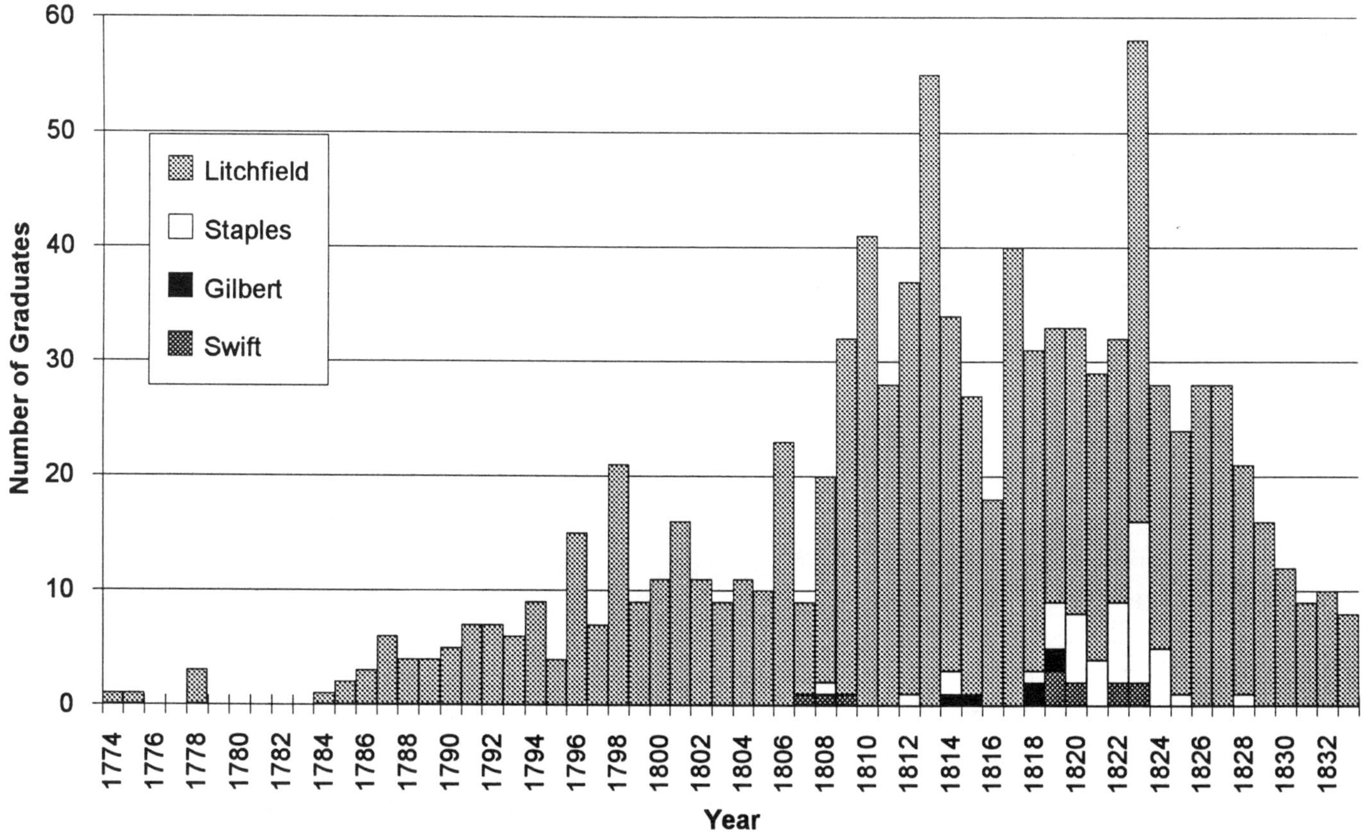

FIGURE 2. Known Graduates of Proprietary Law Schools: Total, All Schools

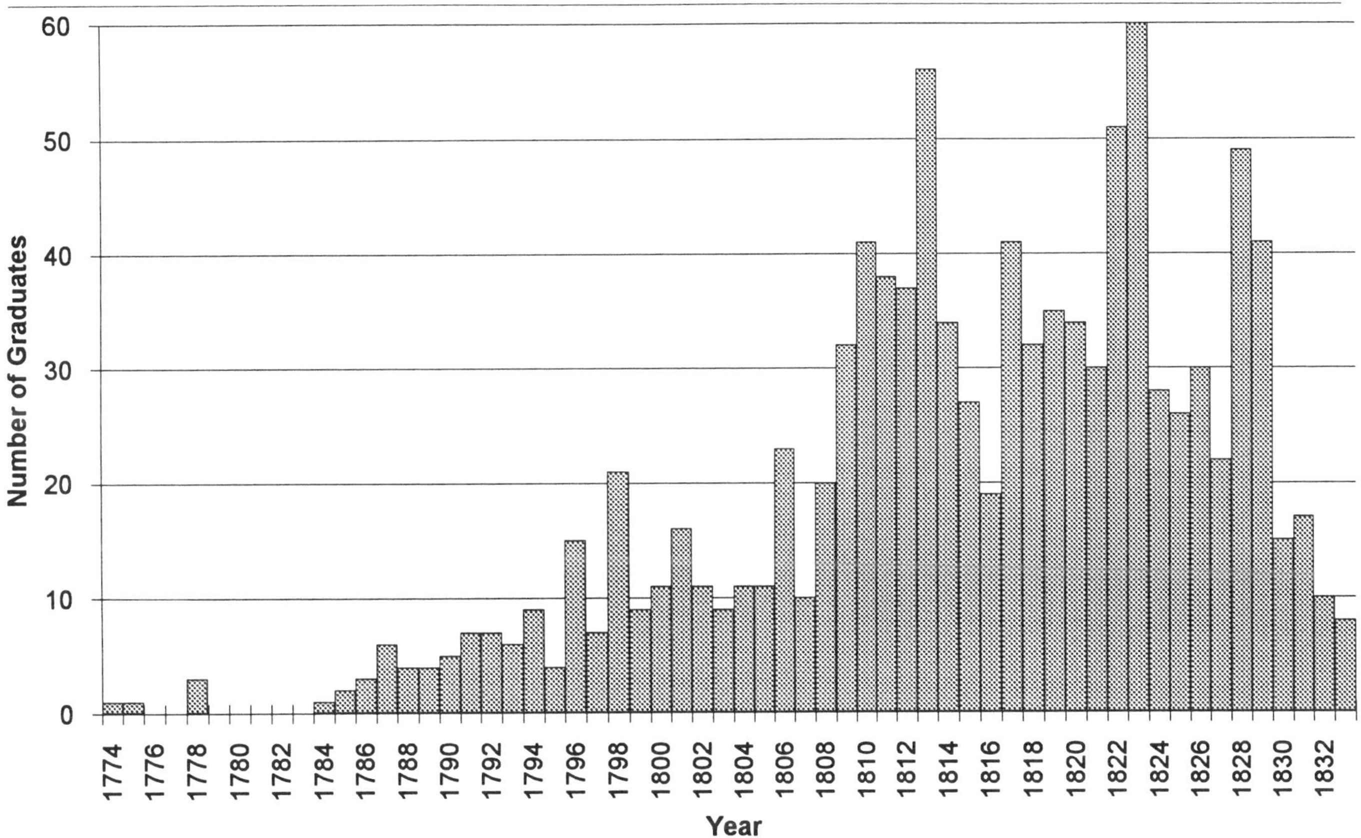

APPENDIX **IV**

List of American Analytical Law Treatises Published Between 1794 and 1826

Anthon, John. *The Law of Nisi Prius*. . . . New York: Gould and Banks, 1820.

Blake, Dominick T. *An Historical Treatise on the Practice of the Court of Chancery of the State of New-York*. . . . New York: J. T. Murden, 1818.

Brackenridge, Hugh Henry. *Law Miscellanies*. . . . Philadelphia: P. Byrne, 1814.

Chipman, Daniel. *An Essay on the Law of Contracts*. Middlebury, VT: Daniel Chipman, 1822.

Chipman, Nathaniel. *Reports and Dissertations*. . . . Rutland, VT: Anthony Haswell, 1793.

Cooper, Thomas. *Tracts on Medical Jurisprudence*. . . . Philadelphia: James Webster, 1819.

Cooper, Thomas. *The Bankrupt Law of America, Compared with the Bankrupt Law of England*. Philadelphia: John Thompson, 1801.

Dunlap, John A. *A Treatise on the Practice of the Supreme Court of the State of New-York in Civil Actions, together with the proceedings in error*. 2 vols. Albany, NY: E.F. Backus, 1821.

Du Ponceau, Peter S. *A Dissertation on the Nature and Extent of the Jurisdiction of the Courts of the United States*. . . . Philadelphia: Abraham Small, 1824.

Fessenden, Thomas Green. *An Essay on the Law of Patents for New Inventions*. Boston, MA: D. Mallory & Co.; Portland, ME: Lyman, Hall & Co.; Middlebury, VT: Swift & Chipman; New York: S. Gould; Albany, NY: D. W. Farrand & Green; Philadelphia: Farrand & Nicholas; Baltimore, MD: P. H. Nicklin & Co., 1810 (2nd edition, Boston, MA: Charles Ewer, 1822).

Goodenow, John M. *Historical Sketches of the Principles and Maxims of American Jurisprudence, in Contrast with the Doctrines of the English Common Law on the Subject of Crimes and Punishments*. Stubenville, OH: James Wilson, 1819.

Hall, John Elihu. *The Practice and Jurisdiction of the Court of Admiralty*. Baltimore, MD: Dobbin & Murphey, 1809.

Hay, George. *A Treatise on Expatriation*. Washington, DC: A. & G. Way, 1814.

Hoffman, David. *A Course of Legal Study*. Baltimore, MD: Coale and Maxwell, 1817 (2nd edition, Baltimore, MD: J. Neal; London: J. Miller, 1836).

Hoffman, David. *A Lecture Being the Second of a Series of Lectures. . . .* Baltimore, MD: John D. Toy, 1825.

Hoffman, David. *A Lecture Being the Third of a Series of Lectures. . . .* Baltimore, MD: J. D. Toy, 1826.

Ingraham, Edward D. *A View of the Insolvent Laws of Pennsylvania*. Philadelphia: P. H. Nicklin, 1822 (2nd edition, 1827).

Laussat, Jr., Anthony. *An Essay on Equity in Pennsylvania*. Philadelphia: Robert Desilver, 1826.

Livermore, Samuel. *A Treatise on the Law Relative to Principals, Agents, Factors, Auctioneers, and Brokers*. Boston, MA: Thomas B. Waite, 1811 (2nd edition, Baltimore, MD: Joseph Robinson, 1818).

Maltby, Isaac. *A Treatise on Court Martial and Military Law. . . .* Boston, MA: Thomas B. Waite, 1813.

Reeve, Tapping. *Law of Baron and Femme, of Parent and Child, of Guardian and Ward, of Master and Servant. . . .* New-Haven, CT: Oliver Steele, 1816 (2nd edition, 1846; 3rd edition, 1862; 4th edition, 1867; 5th edition, 1888).

Reeve, Tapping. *A Treatise on the Law of Descents. . . .* New York: Collins & Hannay, 1825.

Swift, Zephania. *A System of the Laws of the State of Connecticut*. Windham, CT: John Byrne, 1795.

Swift, Zephania. *A Digest of the Law of Evidence, in Civil and Criminal Cases. . . .* Hartford, CT: Oliver D. Cooke, 1810.

Tucker, Henry St. George. *Notes on Blackstone's Commentaries for the Use of Students*. Winchester, VA: S. H. Davis, 1826.

Tucker, St. George. *Blackstone's Commentaries. . . .* Philadelphia: Birch and Small, 1803.

Verplanck, Gulian C. *An Essay on the Doctrine of Contracts. . . .* New York: G. & C. Carvill, 1825.

Wilson, James. *The Works of the Honourable James Wilson, LL.D.*, ed. Bird Wilson. Philadelphia: Lorenzo Press, 1804 (2nd edition, 1896).

Wyche, William. *A Treatise on the Practice of the Supreme Court of Judicature of the State of New-York in Civil Actions*. New York: T. & J. Swords, 1794.

Wyche, William. *An Essay on the Theory and Practice of Fines; With Precedents*. New York: T. & J. Swords, 1794.

Bibliography

STATUTES

Acts and Laws of Connecticut in America. Hartford, CT: Hudson and Goodwin, 1796.

American Law Institute. *Uniform Commercial Code*, 9th ed. Minneapolis, MN: West Publishing Co., 1978.

An Act directing the Course of Descents, 1785 Va. Acts c. 60.

An Act for the Union of the Transylvania Seminary and Kentucky Academy, 1798 Ky. Acts 234, ch. 166.

"Code Napoleon." 20 *North American Review* 400 (1825).

The Commercial Code of France. . . . Translated by John Rodman. New York: C. Wiley, 1814.

"Constitution and Penal Code of France." 1 U.S.L.J. 405 (1823).

"Penal Code of the French Empire." Reprinted in *American Review of History and Politics*. Philadelphia: Ferrand & Nicholas, 1811.

The Revised Statutes of the State of New York, Passed in the Years, 1827–1828. Albany, NY: Banks & Gould, 1830.

MANUSCRIPT SOURCES

Columbia University, New York, NY. Rare Book and Manuscript Library, Van Schaack Family Papers.

Connecticut State Library, Hartford, CT. 920 G375 Vault, "Journal or Chronicle of Sylvester Gilbert."

Connecticut State Library, Hartford, CT. 974.62 L719Ln Vault 3, "Litchfield Law School Lecture Notes," 1808.

Connecticut State Library, Hartford, CT. Abiel A. Loomis, "Hebron Law Lectures," 1814.

Earl Gregg Swem Library, College of William and Mary, Williamsburg, VA. Tucker-Coleman Collection.
Hall of Records, New York, NY, *Minutes of the Supreme Court of Judicature of the State of New York, 1775–1781.*
Library of Congress, Washington, DC. Kent Papers.
Litchfield Historical Society, Litchfield, Connecticut. Reeve Collection.
Litchfield Historical Society, Litchfield, CT. Woodruff Collection.
New York Public Library, New York, NY. Robert Troup Papers.
Transylvania University, Lexington, KY. Department of Special Collections, Board of Trustees Minutes. 16 April 1799 to 22 March 1816.
United States Library of Congress Law Library, Washington, D.C. KF272.H6, David Hoffman, *Introductory Lectures.*
University of Virginia Library, Charlottesville, VA. Cabell Deposits: "A System of Readings on the Subjects of Politics & Law Recommended by Mr. Tucker, Professor of Law & Politics in the College of William and Mary."
Virginia Historical Society, Richmond, VA. Box 47, Charles James Faulkner Papers.
William & Mary Quarterly, Series 1 (1904), 13:109. Reprint of letter from William T. Barry to his brother, 30 January 1804.
William & Mary Quarterly, Series 1 (1900–1901), 9:80. Reprint of letter from John Brown to William Preston, 6 July 1780.
Yale University Law Library, New Haven, CT. "'The Founders' Collection being the library of Staple's Law School."

PRINTED SOURCES

Primary Sources

Books

Anthon, John. *The Law of Nisi Prius. . . .* New York: Gould and Banks, 1820.
Bacon, Matthew B. *A New Abridgement of the Law.* 8 vols. London: E. and R. Nutt, 1736.
Beccaria, Cesare. *An Essay on Crimes and Punishments.* Charlestown, NC: David Bruce, 1777; Philadelphia: Robert Bell, 1778; Philadelphia: William Young, 1793.
Blackstone, William. *An Analysis of the Laws of England.* 6th rev. ed. Oxford: Clarendon Press, 1771.
Blackstone, William. *Commentaries on the Laws of England.* 4 vols. Oxford: The Clarendon Press, 1765.
Blackstone, Sir William. *Commentaries on the Laws of England.* 4 vols. Philadelphia: Robert Bell, 1771–1772.
Blackstone, William. *Commentaries on the Laws of England.* 4 vols. 1765. Reprint. Chicago: The University of Chicago Press, 1979.
Blackstone, William. *Considerations on the question, whether tenants . . . are free-holders qualified to vote in elections for knights of the shire.* London: Printed for R. Baldwin, 1763.
Blackstone, William. *Law Tracts.* 2 vols. Oxford: The Clarendon Press, 1762.
Brackenridge, Hugh Henry. *Law Miscellanies. . . .* Philadelphia: P. Byrne, 1814.

Burlamaqui, Jean Jacques. *The Principes of Natural and Politic Law*. Translated by Thomas Nugent. Boston, MA: Joseph Bumstead, 1792; Cambridge: Harvard University Press, 1807.

Butler, William A. *The Revision of the Statutes of the State of New York and the Revisers*. New York: Banks and Bros., 1889.

The Case of Elizabeth Rutgers verses Joshua Waddington . . . August 7, 1786. New York: Bradstreet Press, 1866.

A Catalogue of the Officers and Students of Transylvania University. Lexington, KY: T. Smith, 1821.

Chastellux, Francois Jean de. *Voyages de M. le Marquis de Chastellux dans l'Amerique septentrionale dans les annees 1780, 1781, & 1782*. 2 vols. Paris: Prault, 1786.

Chipman, Daniel. *An Essay on the Law of Contracts, for the Payment of Specifick Articles*. Middlebury, VT: J.W. Copeland, 1822.

Chipman, Nathaniel. *Reports and Dissertations*. Rutland, VT: Anthony Haswell, 1793.

Colton, Calvin. *The Works of Henry Clay*. New York: Henry Clay Publications, 1896.

Domat, Jean. *The Civil Law in its Natural Order. . . .* London: J. Bettenham, 1722.

Gilbert, Baron Jeffrey. *A Treatise on Rents*. London: Henry Lintot, 1758.

Goodenow, John Milton. *Historical Sketches of the Principles and Maxims of American Jurisprudence*. Steubenville, OH: James Wilson, 1819.

Griffith, William. *Annual Law Register of the United States*. Burlington, NJ: David Allinson, 1822.

Grotius, Hugo. *The Right of War and Peace*. London: W. Innys, 1738.

Hale, Sir Matthew. *The History of the Common Law of England*. 1739. Reprint. Edited by Charles M. Gray. Chicago: The University of Chicago Press, 1971.

Hay, George. *A Treatise on Expatriation*. Washington, DC: A. & G. Way, 1814.

Hoffman, David. *A Course of Legal Study*. Baltimore, MD: Coale and Maxwell, 1817.

Hoffman, David. *A Lecture Being the Second of a Series of Lectures. . . .* Baltimore, MD: John D. Toy, 1825.

Hoffman, David. *A Lecture Being the Third of a Series of Lectures. . . .* Baltimore, MD: J.D. Toy, 1826.

Hoffman, David. *To the Trustees of the University of Maryland in Relation to the Law Chair*. Baltimore, MD: J. D. Toy, 1826.

Home, Henry, Lord Kames. *Principles of Equity*. 2 vols. 2nd ed. rev. Edinburgh: Kincaid & J. Bell; London: A. Millar, 1767.

Hume, David. *A Treatise of Human Nature*. 1739. Reprint. Edited by L. A. Selby-Bigge. Oxford: Oxford University Press, 1975.

Jefferson, Thomas. *The Papers of Thomas Jefferson*. Edited by Julian P. Boyd et al. 23 vols. to date. Princeton, NJ: Princeton University Press, 1950–.

Jefferson, Thomas. *The Writings of Thomas Jefferson*. Edited by H. A. Washington. 9 vols. Washington, DC: Taylor and Maury, 1853–1854.

Johnson, William. *Reports of Cases Adjudged in the Supreme Court of Judicature of the State of New York. . . .* 3 vols. 2nd ed. rev. New York: Banks, Gould & Co., 1846.

Kent, James. *Commentaries on American Law*. 4 vols. 1826. Reprint. New York: Da Capo Press, 1971.

Kent, William. *Memoirs and Letters of James Kent, LL.D.* Boston, MA: Little, Brown & Co., 1898.

Laussat, Anthony Jr. *An Essay on Equity in Pennsylvania*. Philadelphia: Robert Desilva, 1826.

Livermore,Samuel. *A Treatise on the Law of Principal and Agent; and of Sales by Auction*. 2 vols. Baltimore, MA: Joseph Robinson, 1818.

Maine, H.J.S. "Roman Law and Legal Education," in *Cambridge Essays*. London: John W. Parker and Son, 1856.

Martens, Georg Friederich von. *Summary of the Law of Nations. . . .* Translated by William Cobbett. Philadelphia: Thomas Bradford, 1795.

Montesquieu, Charles Louis de Secondat, Baron de la Brède et de. *De L'Esprit des Lois*. Geneva: Barillot, 1748.

Montesquieu, Charles Louis de Secondat, Baron de la Brède et de. *The Spirit of Laws*. Translated by Thomas Nugent. London: Nourse, 1750.

Montesquieu, Charles Louis de Secondat, Baron de la Brède et de. *The Spirit of Laws*. Translated by Thomas Nugent. 5th ed. London: Nourse, 1773. Reprint. Worcester, MA: Isaiah Thomas, Jr., 1802.

Ponceau, Peter S. Du. *A Dissertation on the Nature and Extent of the Jurisdiction of the Courts of the United States. . . .* Philadelphia: Abraham Small, 1824.

Proposed Revision of the Statute Laws of the State of New-York. Albany, NY: Croswell & Van Benthuysen, 1827–1828.

Pufendorf, Samuel Freiherr von. *The Law of Nature and Nations. . . .* London: J. & J. Bonwicke, 1749.

Reeve, Tapping. *The Law of Baron and Femme. . . .* New Haven, CT: Oliver Steele, 1816.

Reeve, Tapping. *A Treatise on the Law of Descents in the several United States of America*. New York: Collins & Hannay, 1825.

Reid, Thomas. *An Inquiry into the Human Mind, on the Principles of Common Sense*. Edinburgh: Kincaid & Bell, 1764.

Report of the Commissioners Appointed to Revise the Statute Laws of the State of New-York. . . . Albany, NY: Croswell, Barnum & Van Benthuysen, 1826.

Report of the Commissioners Appointed to Revise the Statute Laws of this State. . . . Albany, NY: Croswell and Van Benthuysen, 1827.

Rodman, John. *Commercial Code of the French Empire Translated for the American Review, With Explanatory Notes of Commerce in General*. Philadelphia: C. Wiley, 1811.

The Secretary of the State of Connecticut, *The Connecticut Annual Register*. New London, CT: Samuel Green, 1830.

The Secretary of State of Connecticut, *The Connecticut Register*. New London, CT: Samuel Green, 1820.

Stokes, Anthony. *A View of the Constitution of the British Colonies in North America and the West Indies at the time the Civil War broke out on the Continent of America. . . .* London: Anthony Stokes, 1783.

Swift, Zephaniah. *A System of the Laws of the State of Connecticut*. 2 vols. Windham, CT: John Byrne, 1795.

Taylor, Creed. *Journal of the Law School, and of the Moot-Court attached to it; at Needham, in Virginia. . . .* Richmond, VA: J. & G. Cochran, 1822.

Tucker, Henry St. George. *Commentaries on the Laws of Virginia, comprising the substance of a course of lectures delivered to the Winchester law school*. Winchester, VA: Tucker, 1831.

Tucker, St. George. *Blackstone's Commentaries: with Notes of Reference, to the Constitution and Laws, of the Federal Government of the United States; and of the Commonwealth of Virginia.* 5 vols. Philadelphia: William Young Birch and Abraham Small, 1803.

Tyler, Lyon Gardiner. *The Letters and Times of the Tylers.* Richmond, VA: Whittet & Shepperson, c1884–1896.

Van Schaack, Henry C. *The Life of Peter Van Schaack, LL.D.* New York: D. Appelton & Co., 1842.

Varnum, James M. *The Case, Trevett against Weeden . . . Superior Court in the County of Newport, September Term, 1786. . . .* Providence, RI: John Carter, 1787.

Vattel, Emmerich de. *The Law of Nations. . . .* New York: Samuel Campbell, 1796. Northampton, MA: S. Butler, 1820.

Verplanck, Gulian C. *An Essay on the Doctrine of Contracts. . . .* New York: G. & C. Carvill, 1825.

Wilson, James. *The Works of the Honourable James Wilson, LL.D.* Edited by Bird Wilson, 3 vols. Philadelphia: Bronson and Chauncey, 1804.

Wilson, James. *The Works of the Honourable James Wilson, LL.D.* Edited by Bird Wilson. 2 vols. Philadelphia: Lorenzo Press, 1804.

Wilson, James. *The Works of the Honourable James Wilson, LL.D.* 1804. Reprint. Edited by Robert Green McCloskey. 2 vols. Cambridge: The Belknap Press of Harvard University Press, 1967.

Wyche, William. *Treatise on the Practice of the Supreme Court of Judicature of the State of New-York in Civil Actions.* New York: T. & J. Swords, 1794.

Periodicals

"Tribute of Respect," in *American & Commercial Daily Advertiser* (Baltimore), 4 August 1828, 48:3.

Aurora General Advertiser (Philadelphia), 14 August to 6 November 1797.

Boston Gazette, 23 September to 7 October 1771 & 29 March to 9 August 1784.

General Advertiser (Philadelphia), 28 June to 1 September 1791 & 8 May to 18 May 1793.

Livingston, William. "Sic vos, non vobis, Mellificatis opis." *The New-York Weekly Post-Boy*, 19 August 1745.

Maryland Gazette, 26 August 1762.

New York American, 8 October 1824.

"On the Study of the Civil Law." Anonymous. 11 *North American Review* 407. Boston, MA: Cummings and Hillard, 1820.

Sedgewick, Henry David. "The Common Law." 19 *North American Review* 424. Boston, MA: Cummings and Hillard, 1824.

Secondary Sources

Books

An Address by Charles Kerr On the Occasion of the Sesqui-Centennial of the Signing of the Constitution. 6 October 1937, Under the Auspices of Transylvania College. Transylvania University Library, Lexington, Kentucky.

Bailyn, Bernard. *The Ideological Origins of the American Revolution*. Cambridge: Harvard University Press, 1977.

Bauer, Elizabeth. *Commentaries on the Constitution, 1790–1860*. Studies in History, Economics and Public Law, No. 575. New York: Columbia University Press, 1952.

Biographical Directory of the United States Congress 1774–1989. Washington, DC: United States Government Printing Office, 1989.

Bloomfield, Maxwell. *American Lawyers in a Changing Society, 1776–1876*. Cambridge: Harvard University Press, 1976.

Boorstin, Daniel J. *The Americans: The Colonial Experience*. New York: Vintage Books, 1958.

Boorstin, Daniel J. *The Americans: The National Experience*. New York: Vintage Books, 1965.

Boorstin, Daniel J. *The Lost World of Thomas Jefferson*. Chicago: The University of Chicago Press, 1981.

Boorstin, Daniel J. *The Mysterious Science of Law*. Cambridge: Harvard University Press, 1941.

Breuer, Ernest Henry. *The New York Revised Statutes—1829*. Albany, NY: New York State Library, 1961.

Brewer, John. *Party Ideology and Popular Politics at the Accession of George III*. Cambridge: Cambridge University Press, 1981.

Brock, Robert Kincaid. *Needham Law School, 1821–1842, Cumberland County, Virginia, Founded and Conducted by Chancellor Creed Taylor*. Farmville, VA: The Farmville Herald, 1935.

Brock, William R. *Scotus Americanus*. Edinburgh: Edinburgh University Press, 1982.

Brown, Elizabeth G. *British Statutes in American Law, 1776–1836*. Ann Arbor: University of Michigan Law School, 1964.

Brown, Imogene E. *American Aristides: A Biography of George Wythe*. Rutherford, NJ: Fairleigh Dickinson University Press, 1981.

Brown, Wallace. *The King's Friends*. Providence, RI: Brown University Press, 1965.

Bryson, W. Hamilton. *Legal Education in Virginia, 1779–1979*. Charlottesville: University Press of Virginia, 1982.

Chinard, Gilbert. *The Commonplace Book of Thomas Jefferson*. Baltimore, MD: The Johns Hopkins Press, 1926.

Chroust, Anton-Hermann. *The Rise of the Legal Profession in America*. 2 vols. Norman: University of Oklahoma Press, 1965.

Commanger, Henry Steele. *The Empire of Reason*. London: Weidenfeld and Nicolson, 1978.

Cook, Charles M. *The American Codification Movement*. Westport, CT: Greenwood Press, 1981.

Cullen, Charles T. *St. George Tucker and Law in Virginia 1772–1804*. New York: Garland Publishing, 1987.

Dargo, George. *Law in the New Republic*. New York: Alfred A. Knopf, 1983.

Dickinson, H.T. *Liberty and Property: Political Ideology in Eighteenth-Century Britain*. London: Methuen & Co., 1977.

Dictionary of American Biography.

Ellis, Richard E. *The Jeffersonian Crisis: Courts and Politics in the Young Republic.* New York: W.W. Norton & Co., 1974.

Ferguson, Robert A. *Law and Letters in American Culture.* Cambridge: Harvard University Press, 1984.

Freund, Paul A., ed. *History of the Supreme Court of the United States.* 11 vols. New York: The MacMillan Co., 1971.

Friedman, Lawrence M. *A History of American Law.* New York: Simon and Schuster, 1973.

Gay, Peter. *The Enlightenment: The Science of Freedom.* New York: W.W. Norton & Co., 1977.

Goebel, Julius, Jr. et al. *A History of the School of Law, Columbia University.* New York: Columbia University Press, 1955.

Goebel, Julius, Jr., ed *The Law Practice of Alexander Hamilton.* 5 vols. New York: Columbia University Press, 1964.

Goldstein, Laurence, ed. *Precedent in Law.* Oxford: Clarendon Press, 1987.

Greene, Jack P., ed. *The Reinterpretation of the American Revolution 1763–1789.* New York: Harper & Row, 1968.

Hall, Kermit. *A Comprehensive Bibliography of American Constitutional and Legal History, 1896–1979.* 5 vols. Millwood, NY: Kraus International Publications, 1984.

Kall, Kermit. *The Magic Mirror.* New York: Oxford University Press, 1989.

Hamlin, Paul M. *Legal Education in Colonial New York.* New York: New York University Law Quarterly Review, 1939.

Harno, Albert J. *Legal Education in the United States.* San Francisco: Bancroft-Whitney Co., 1953.

Harno, Albert J. *Legal Education in the United States.* 1953. Reprint. Westport, CT: Greenwood Press, 1980.

Hicks, Frederick C. *Yale Law School: The Founders and the Founders' Collection.* New Haven, CT: Yale University Press, 1935.

Hoffer, Peter Charles. *Law and People in Colonial America.* Baltimore: The Johns Hopkins University Press, 1992.

Hont, Istvan and Ignatieff, Michael, eds. *Wealth & Virtue: The Shaping of Political Economy in the Scottish Enlightenment.* Cambridge: Cambridge University Press, 1983.

Horton, John T. *James Kent, A Study in Conservatism: 1763–1847.* New York: D. Appleton-Century Co., 1939.

Horwitz, Morton J. *The Transformation of American Law 1780–1860.* Cambridge: Harvard University Press, 1977.

Hurst, James Willard. *Law and the Conditions of Freedom.* Madison: The University of Wisconsin Press, 1956.

Hurst, James Willard. *Law and Social Order in the United States.* Ithaca: Cornell University Press, 1977.

Hurst, James Willard. *Law and Social Process in United States History.* Ann Arbor: University of Michigan Press, 1960.

Hurst, James Willard. *The Growth of American Law.* Boston: Little, Brown & Co., 1950.

Jensen, Merrill. *The New Nation.* New York: Vintage Books, 1950.

Jones, E. Alfred. *American Members of the Inns of Court.* London: The Saint Catherine Press, 1924.

Katz, Stanley N., ed. *James Alexander's Brief Narrative of the Case and Trial of John Peter Zenger, Printer of the New York Weekly Journal.* Cambridge: Harvard University Press, 1963.

Kirk, Harry. *Portrait of a Profession.* London: Oyez Publishing, 1976.

Konesfsky, Alfred S. and King, Andrew J., eds. *The Papers of Daniel Webster.* 2 vols. Hanover, NH: University Press of New England, 1982.

Kerber, Linda. *Women of the Republic.* Chapel Hill: University of North Carolina Press, 1980.

Levi, Edward H. *An Introduction to Legal Reasoning.* Chicago: The University of Chicago Press, 1949.

Lieberman, David. *The Province of Legislation Determined.* Cambridge: Cambridge University Press, 1989.

Llewellyn, Karl N. *The Bramble Bush.* New York: Oceana Press, 1951.

Main, Jackson Turner. *The Sovereign States, 1775–1783.* New York: Franklin Watts, 1973.

Malone, Dumas. *Jefferson the Virginian.* Boston, MA: Little, Brown and Company, 1948.

May, Henry F. *The Enlightenment in America.* New York: Oxford University Press, 1976.

McKenna, Marian C. *Tapping Reeve and the Litchfield Law School.* New York: Oceana Publications, 1986.

Miller, Perry, ed. *The Legal Mind in America.* Ithaca, NY: Cornell University Press, 1969.

Nelson, William E. *Americanization of the Common Law.* Cambridge: Harvard University Press, 1975.

Nowak, John E.; Rotunda, Ronald D.; and Young, J. Nelson. *Handbook on Constitutional Law.* St. Paul, MN: West Publishing Company, 1978.

Pound, Roscoe. *The Formative Era of American Law.* Boston, MA: Little, Brown and Company, 1938.

Pound, Roscoe. *The Lawyer from Antiquity to Modern Times.* St. Paul, MN: West Publishing, 1953.

Rabkin, Peggy A. *Fathers to Daughters: The Legal Foundations of Female Emancipation.* Westport, CT: Greenwood Press, 1980.

Radin, Max. *The Rivalry of Common-law and Civil Law Ideas in the American Colonies.* New York: New York University Press, 1937.

Reed, Alfred Z. *Training for the Public Profession of the Law.* New York: The Carnegie Foundation, 1921.

Reed, Alfred Z. *Training for the Public Profession of the Law.* 1921. Reprint. New York: Arno Press, 1976.

Robson, R. J. *The Oxfordshire Election of 1754: A Study in the Interplay of City, County and University Politics.* Oxford: Oxford University Press, 1949.

Robson, Robert. *The Attorney in Eighteenth-Century England.* Cambridge: Cambridge University Press, 1959.

Seed, Geoffrey. *James Wilson.* Millwood, NY: KTO Press, 1978.

Shepard, E. Lee. "George Wythe." In W. Hamilton Bryson, *Legal Education in Virginia, 1779–1979.* Charlottesville: University Press of Virginia, 1982.

Snowiss, Sylvia. *Judicial Review and the Law of the Constitution*. New Haven, CT: Yale University Press, 1990.

Sonne, Niels. *Liberal Kentucky, 1780–1828*. New York: Columbia University Press, 1939.

Spurlin, Paul Merrill. *The French Enlightenment in America*. Athens: The University of Georgia Press, 1984.

Spurlin, Paul Merrill. *Montesquieu in America, 1760–1801*. New York: Octagon Books, 1969.

Stevens, Robert. *Law School: Legal Education in America from the 1850's to the 1980's*. Chapel Hill: The University of North Carolina Press, 1983.

Stein, Peter and Shand, John. *Legal Values in Western Society*. Edinburgh: Edinburgh University Press, 1974.

Stimson, Shanon C. *The American Revolution in the Law*. London: MacMillan, 1990.

Tribe, Laurence H. *American Constitutional Law*. New York: The Foundation Press, 1978.

Van Tyne, Claude Halstead. *The Loyalists in the American Revolution*. Gloucester, MA: Peter Smith, 1959.

Warden, Lewis C. *The Life of Blackstone*. Charlottesville, VA: The Michie Co., 1938.

Warren, Charles. *History of the Harvard Law School and of Early Legal Conditions in America*. 3 vols. NY: Lewis Publishing Co., 1908.

Wettach, Robert H., ed. *A Century of Legal Education*. Chapel Hill: University of North Carolina Press, 1947.

Who Was Who in America, Historical Volume 1607–1896. Chicago: A.N. Marquis Co., 1967.

Wood, Gordon S. *The Creation of the American Republic, 1776–1787*. New York: W.W. Norton & Co., 1972.

Wood, Gordon S. *The Radicalism of the American Revolution*. New York: Alfred A. Knopf, 1992.

Wright, John D. Jr. *Transylvania: Tutor to the West*. Lexington: The University Press of Kentucky, 1975.

Zweiben, Beverly. *How Blackstone Lost the Colonies*. New York: Garland Publishing, 1990.

Unpublished Materials

Basch, Norma. "From the Bonds of Empire to the Bonds of Matrimony: The Emerging Right of Divorce in the Context of American Independence." Paper Delivered at the 1990 meeting of the Organization of American Historians.

Consalus, Charles E. "The History of Legal Education in New Jersey." Ph.D. dissertation, Columbia University Teachers College, 1979.

Cullen, Charles T. "St. George Tucker and Law in Virginia, 1772–1804." Ph.D. dissertation, University of Virginia, 1971.

Hamlin, Paul M. "Legal Education in Colonial New York." Ph.D. dissertation, Columbia University, 1942.

Hemphill, W. Edwin. "George Wythe, America's First Law Professor and the Teacher of Jefferson, Marshall and Clay." M.A. thesis, Emory University, 1933.

Laska, Lewis L. "A History of Legal Education in Tennessee, 1770–1970." Ph.D. dissertation, Peabody College for Teachers, 1978.

Mann, Bruce H. "Parishes, Law and Community in Connecticut, 1700–1760." Ph.D. dissertation, Yale University, 1977.

Masur, Louis P. "The Culture of Executions and the Conflict Over Capital Punishment in America, 1776–1860." Ph.D. dissertation, Princeton University, 1985.

Senese, Donald J. "The Development of Legal Thought in South Carolina, 1800–1860." Ph.D. dissertation, University of South Carolina, 1970.

Smith, Alan M. "Virginia Lawyers, 1680–1776: The Birth of an American Profession." Ph.D. dissertation, The Johns Hopkins University, 1967.

Periodicals

Baldwin, Simon E. *The Study of Elementary Law, The Proper Beginning of a Legal Education.* 13 YALE L. J. No. 1 (1903).

Bloomfield, Maxwell. *David Hoffman and the Shaping of a Republican Legal Culture.* 38 MD. L. REV. 673 (1979).

Brisbin, Richard A., Jr. *John Milton Goodenow and Early Ohio Jurisprudence: Political Liberalism and the Transformation of American Law.* 6 OHIO N.U.L. REV. 509 (1979).

Consalus, Charles E. *Legal Education During the Colonial Period, 1663–1776.* 29 J. LEGAL ED. 295, 308 (1978).

Gawalt, Gerald W. *Massachusetts Legal Education in Transition, 1766–1840.* 17 AM. J. LEGAL HIST. 27 (1973).

Finnis, John M. *Blackstone's Theoretical Intentions.* 12 NAT. L. F. 163 (1967).

Friedlander, Robert A. *Social Utility and the American Transformation of the English Common Law.* 26 CHITTY'S L.J. 279 (1978).

Fullman, David. *The European Background of Early American Ideas Concerning Property.* 14 TEMP. L.Q. 497 (1940).

Hemenway, Abby. "Bates Turner." *Vermont Historical Magazine.* 2 (1871).

Hoffer, Peter Charles. *Honor and the Roots of American Litigiousness.* 33 AM. J. LEG. HIST. 295 (1989).

Hogan, John C. *Blackstone and Joseph Story—Their Influence on the Development of Criminal Law in America.* 40 MINN. L. REV. 107 (1956).

Holdsworth, W. S. *The Disappearance of the Educational System of the Inns of Court.* 69 U. PA. L. REV. 201 (1921).

Howe, William Wirt. *Roman and Civil Law in America.* 16 HARV. L. REV. 342 (1903).

Johnson, John W. *Creativity and Adoption: A Reassessment of American Jurisprudence, 1801–1857 and 1908–1940.* 7 RUT.-CAM. L.J. 625 (1976).

Katz, Stanley N. "The Problem of Colonial Legal History." In Jack P. Greene and J.R. Pole, eds., *Colonial British America.* Baltimore, MD: The Johns Hopkins University Press, 1984.

Lucas, Paul. *Ex parte Sir William Blackstone, "Plagiarist" : A Note on Blackstone and the Natural Law.* 7 AM. J. LEGAL HIST. 142 (1963).

McCaughey, Elizabeth "*Marbury v. Madison*: Have We Missed the Real Meaning?" *Presidential Studies Quarterly*, Vol. XIX, No. 3 (Summer 1989).

McKirdy, Charles R. *The Lawyer as Apprentice: Legal Education in Eighteenth Century Massachusetts.* 28 J. LEGAL ED. 124, 125–126 (1976).

McManis, Charles R. *The History of First Century American Legal Education: A Revisionist Perspective.* 59 (part 2) WASH. U. L. Q. 597, 603 (1981).

Morrow, Clarence J. *Louisiana Blueprint: Civilian Codification and Legal Method for State and Nation.* 17 TUL. L. REV. 351, 388 (1943).

Nolan, Dennis R. *Sir William Blackstone and the New American Republic: A Study of Intellectual Impact.* 51 N.Y.U. L. REV. 731 (1976).

Obering, William F. "The Philosophy of Law of James Wilson: A Study in Comparative Jurisprudence." *Philosophical Studies of the American Catholic Philosoph-ical Association.* 1 (1938): 9.

O'Connor, John E. *Legal Reform in the Early Republic: The New Jersey Experience.* 22 AM. J. LEG. HIST. 95 (1978).

Orth, John V. *After the Revolution: "Reform" of the Law of Inheritance.* 10 LAW & HIST. REV. 33 (1992)

Pound, Roscoe. *The Influence of the Civil Law in America.* 1 LA. L. REV. 1 (1939).

Rogers III, C. Paul. *Scots Law in Post-Revolutionary and Nineteenth-Century America: The Neglected Jurisprudence.* 8 LAW & HIST. REV. 205 (1990)

Ross, William E. *History of Virginia Codification.* 11 VA. L. REG. 79, 90 (June, 1905).

Shaffer, Thomas L. *David Hoffman's Law School Lectures, 1822–1833.* 32 J. LEGAL ED. 127, 129 (1982).

Stein, Peter. *The Attraction of the Civil Law in Post-Revolutionary America.* 52 VA. L. REV. 403–434 (1966).

Swindler, William. *John Marshall's Preparation for the Bar—Some Observations on His Law Notes.* 2 AM. J. LEGAL HIST. 207–13 (1967).

Thayer, James Bradley. *The Teaching of English Law at Universities.* 9 HARV. L. REV. 169 (1895).

Waterman, Julian S. *Thomas Jefferson and Blackstone's Commentaries.* 27 ILL. L. REV. 629 (1932–33).

Table of Cases

Index

ABOUT THE AUTHOR

CRAIG EVAN KLAFTER is Research Fellow in the Department of History at the University of Southampton, England. He received his education at the University of Chicago and Oxford University and has held lectureships at the Universities of Manchester and Southampton. He has contributed articles to the *American Journal of Legal History* and the *Journal of the Early Republic*, and his essay, "The Americanization of Blackstone's *Commentaries*," was co-winner of the 1992 Webb-Smith Essay Prize.